Praise for *Russia Reconsidered*

"The book is a powerful argument against many oversimplified, black-and-white, one-sided interpretations of the current crisis between Russia and the West. The collection of essays offers a remarkable diversity of views, narratives, and perceptions—a valuable source for those trying to get beyond usual stereotypes and conventional wisdom."

—**Andrey Kortunov**
Director General of the
Russian International Affairs Council

"*Russia Reconsidered: Putin, Power and Pragmatism* casts doubt on the myths and stereotypes about Russia prevalent in the West and in the United States."

—**Sergey Fedorchenko, PhD**
Department of Political Science and Law,
Moscow State Regional University

"Crosston's newest text, *Russia Reconsidered: Putin, Power, and Pragmatism*, is well written, comprehensive, extremely timely, and engaging. Crosston's insights on the political and security implications of modern Russia under Putin are based on solid scholarship and a keen amalgam of history and current events. Crosston's observations about how Russia is engaging in the 'new' Cold War are poignant, pragmatic, and spot on—and the implications for a safe and secure United States are clear. I find this text to be essential reading for diplomats, policy makers, security experts, and academics."

—**Jim Ramsay, PhD, MA, CSP**

Chair, Department of Business, Politics and Security Studies; Coordinator, Homeland Security Program, University of New Hampshire; President, International Society for Preparedness, Resilience, and Security (INSPRS.org)

"Dr. Matthew Crosston's book *Russia Reconsidered: Putin, Power and Pragmatism* is one of the most relevant, timely, and thought-provoking texts recently published. Crosston's analyses of Russia, Russian foreign policy, US-Russia relations, the conflict in Ukraine, American perspectives on Russia, and more are informative and systematic, building on the strengths of his previous works to provide detailed accounts of the complex relations between the two states, their actions, and consequences. This challenging and wide-ranging text introduces the reader to the multiplicity of nuanced narratives on the interactions, signals, and interpretations used by both states. The portrayal of actors and contexts is direct, honest, and revealing. Because of this approach, the book is able to not only offer insights into a wide variety of questions of interest to many scholars of different disciplines but also invite new types of questions, fresh understandings, and stimulating debates to the study of contemporary Russia unlike what is usually offered in the discipline of Russian Studies."

—**Lada V. Kochtcheeva, PhD**

Associate Professor of Political Science, School of Public and International Affairs, North Carolina State University

"Dr. Crosston's work in *Russia Reconsidered* is second to none when it comes to the most important issues of global security and international affairs in the twenty-first century. Dr. Crosston's overall scope of engagement here is well above most of the globally recognized scholars within Russian and Eurasian Studies. In Crosston I see someone who is finally talented enough to surpass Mintz's methodology panic and ambitious enough to embrace Singer's call for real-world impact and relevance, putting the study of Russia back on a more ethically important and empirically genuine track where our research is not just a critical esoteric examination of current reality but is rigorously constructed, carefully oriented, and skillfully written so as to produce solutions and product that make our world truly a better place. This is an important new endeavor that should make people see Russian-American relations in an innovative new light."

—**Maorong Jiang, PhD**

Director, Asian World Center; Associate Professor of Political Science & International Relations, Creighton University

"In this time when Russian-American relations is stuck in one of the worst conditions since the Cold War, this attempt by Professor Matthew Crosston to bring new conclusions and perspectives to light earns a particularly important level of attention from scholars of Russian Studies. Because Crosston has a deft capability with the Russian language, a unique professional history across the post-Soviet space, and maintains important and serious contacts within Russia, he was able to gain access to relevant information and process powerful arguments that stand as a counterargument to many of the myths plaguing Russian-American relations today. His systemic and rigorous analysis allows Western readers to form an objective perspective on so-called 'Russian aggression.' Especially important is his original conception of 'the New Fake Cold War' and how it powers so much between the countries today. In my opinion, this book is an important new contribution in the contemporary world's war against fake news."

—**Vladimir Kolotov, PhD**

Head of the Far East Department, Faculty of Asian and African Studies, St. Petersburg State University; Member, Russian National Committee of the Council of Security Cooperation in the Asia-Pacific

"We need multiple courageous, directed efforts from all sides to defeat the repressive intellectual orthodoxy currently plaguing Russian-American relations and, therefore, hindering Russia's relations with many other states. This does not mean everyone will get along perfectly and all sides will always agree. But it does mean relations will finally take on a less shrill, less melodramatic timbre, and that will only be good for all concerned. I fully agree and strongly support Crosston's timely, wise, and forward-looking wisdom and insight. *Russia Reconsidered* is critically needed today, both in Russia and the United States."

—**Jumber Asatiani, PhD**

Faculty of Foreign Languages and Area Studies, Lomonosov Moscow State University

RUSSIA RECONSIDERED

RUSSIA RECONSIDERED

PUTIN, POWER, AND PRAGMATISM

MATTHEW CROSSTON, PhD

BROWN BOOKS
PUBLISHING GROUP

Russia Reconsidered
Putin, Power, and Pragmatism

Brown Books Publishing Group
16250 Knoll Trail Drive, Suite 205
Dallas, Texas 75248
www.BrownBooks.com
(972) 381-0009

A New Era in Publishing®

Publisher's Cataloging-In-Publication Data

Names: Crosston, Matthew, author, editor. | Adriance, Bruce, contributor.
Title: Russia reconsidered : Putin, power, and pragmatism / Matthew Crosston, PhD ; contributors, Bruce Adriance [and 29 others].
Description: Dallas, Texas : Brown Books Publishing Group, [2018] | All essays in English, with two interviews in English and Russian. | Includes bibliographical references.
Identifiers: ISBN 9781612549842
Subjects: LCSH: Russia (Federation)--Foreign relations--United States. | United States--Foreign relations--Russia (Federation) | Russia (Federation)--Politics and government--21st century. | Putin, Vladimir Vladimirovich, 1952- | Cold War.
Classification: LCC E183.8.R9 C76 2018 | DDC 327.73047--dc23

ISBN 978-1-61254-984-2
LCCN 2017958298

Printed in the United States
10 9 8 7 6 5 4 3 2 1

For more information or to contact the author,
please go to www.RussiaReconsidered.com.

To Karen, who understands, tolerates, and supports more than any other, who has been on this journey from the very beginning and still dares to ride the waves!

Rough work, iconoclasm, but
the only way to get at truth.

—Oliver Wendell Holmes

Most people guard against going
into the fire, and so end up in it.

—Jalal-Uddin Rumi

To today's iconoclasts, never dulled by
orthodoxy. Go into the fire that does not
burn. It was never very hot to begin with.

—MDC

CONTENTS

xix Foreword

xxii Acknowledgments

1 Introduction: Fighting the Orthodoxy

9 **PART I: COLD WAR RESIDUES**

11 The Bully Brothers: Why the World Should Be Happy about a Fake Cold War

18 Syria, Russia, and the United States: Cold War Residue Redux

23 Putin-Mongering

29 America's National Security Schizophrenia: Damning Russia with "Partnership"

33 US-Russia Redux: The Problem of Intellectual Insincerity

39 Obama v. Putin: A Tale of the Posturing President

43 The Ass and the Elephant: Russia and the American Presidency

55 Resisting Globalistan: Why Putin Is Winning the New Cold War
Rakesh K. Simha

61 The Real Estate Cold War: Russia and America Fighting over "Parity"

65 **PART II: THE UKRAINE CONFLICT**

67 *Viva la Revolutsione*! Now, Don't Mess It Up Like Everyone Else, Ukraine!

70 The Dilemma of Duplicity: The Three Maestros of the Crimea

75 What Is to Be Done, or, What Happens Now beyond Crimea?

80 Beware the Sheep with Fangs

84 The Unintended Precedent of Maidan

89 To Live and Die in Donetsk

93 Saving Lives or Saving Face? Sanctions, Russia, and the West

98 This Little Piggy Won't Be Missed

102 Putin: Cleaning up an American Mess

107 Hypocrisy, Crisis, Catharsis
Igor Ivanov

113 **PART III: DIPLOMACY, ECONOMICS, AND FOREIGN POLICY**

115 The United States and the Problem of Being a Geopolitical Prom Queen

119 Putin and the West: To Dance or Not to Dance?

123 The American Failure behind "Grand Strategic Cultures" and Modern Conflict

128 Bears and Byzantium: How America Misreads Russian Grand Strategy

132 America v. Russia: Bringing a Knife to a Foreign Policy Gunfight

137 Blowback Diplomacy: How the United States Was Locked Out of the Caspian
Laura Garrido

141 Chessboard Strategy: Russia and UN Resolution 2117
ZR

145 Playing Chess, Not Checkers: Russian Responses to US Hegemony in Kind
Logan Wilde

150 Russia and Africa: More Than Economics
Kester Klenn Klomegah

155 Russia and the United States: An Alliance in the Making
Luis Durani

159 **PART IV: SYRIA, SANCTIONS, AND EXTREMISM**

161 Old American Punishment, New Russian Strength: The Strange World of Unintended Consequences

165 An Anti-Theory of Sanctions: Why an Iranian New Deal Was Necessary
Dianne Valdez

170 Spilt Milk: The Unintended Consequences of Russian Sanctions
Vladislav Lermontov

175 An Entanglement of Enemies: What Russia's Presence in Syria Really Means

180 The Russia-OPEC-America Nexus: Reimagining the Great Oil Game
Brian Hughes

185 Russia Wants to Use the CSTO in Syria
Uran Botobekov

190 False Promise: How the Turkish-Russian Dilemma Unmasks NATO
Evan Thomsen

194 More Bear Than Eagle: Russia Taking Advantage of an American Vacuum
Nenad Drca

198 Russia Self-Trapped in Abkhazia and South Ossetia
Rahim Rahimov

202 World War Z: Why Russia Fights DAESH Zealots

209 **PART V: EDUCATION, MEDIA, AND ANALYSIS**

211 Cold War Triumphalism and Chicken-and-Egg Dilemmas

215 Keeping Russia the Enemy: Congressional Attitudes and Biased Expertise

218 Unbiased Media, Biased Agendas: How to Make a Russian Demon

225 Russia's Right to Revive
Hasan Ehtisham

228 Censorship or Saving Grace? Academic Scholarship and Intelligence Vetting

234 Rethinking Russia Expert Interview with Dr. Matthew Crosston

248 America's Lost Generation: Russian Expertise within Generation X

253 **PART VI: REGIONAL POLITICS AND GEOSTRATEGY**

255 Sons of Orthodoxy: EU Austerity and a Russian-Greek Orthodox Alliance
Brian Hughes

260 Russian Victim? Repositioning Strategies and Regional Dreams of Dominance
Jeanette Harper

265 For Members Only: The Consequences of the Caspian Summit's Foreign Military Ban
Megan Munoz

270 Dethroning the Dollar Dictatorship
with Andy Deahn

274 Why the Bear Is Back in Vietnam
Rakesh K. Simha

280 Challenging Russia's Arctic: America's Uneven Policy
Gregory Roudybush

284 New Grounds for War: How the Power of Siberia Pipeline Impacts the Arctic
Alexander S. Martin

289 The Mighty Have Fallen: American Space Dependency on Russia
Nenad Drca

294 Walk the Line: Russia as Chair of the United Nations Security Council

305 Russian Arctic Development Hampered by Moscow's Strategic Engagements
Elena Pavlova and Victor Chauvet

308 Mongolia and the New Russian Oil Diplomacy
Samantha Brletich

312 "Pivot to the East" and Russia's Southeast Asia Gambit
Tony Rinna

316 Russia and Nigeria Deepen Cooperation
Kester Kenn Klomegah

321 Neopopulism and the Gray Cardinal: Volodin to Head the CSTO Parliamentary Assembly

325 **PART VII: CYBER, SPIES, AND INTELLIGENCE**

327 The Industrial Spy Game: FSB as Russian Economic Developer
Jared S. Easton

331 All Eyes on Me: The Emergence of a Russian Surveillance State
Jonathan Hartner

335 China and Russia: Cyber Cousins but not Cyber Brothers

342 A Perfect Cyber Storm: Russia and China Teaming Together
Laura Garrido

346 The FSB and SIGINT: Absolute Power at Home and Abroad
Bruce Adriance

351 Brothers-in-Unethical-Arms: The American and Russian Intelligence Services
Amy Hanlon

356 Cyber-Prepping the Battlefield: Does Russia Have a New Way to Wage War?
Laura Garrido

360 FSB's Snowden War: Using the American NSA Against Itself
Alexander S. Martin

365 The Grand Cyber Spy Game: Russia, America, and China Stealing the World One Byte at a Time
with Anonymous

372 No Victory for Putin: The Dossier Scandal

379 Conclusion: Standing for Iconoclasm

385 Suggested Readings

401 Contributors

409 About the Author

FOREWORD

Russia's relations with the West—and especially with the United States—have become increasingly conflictual in the last decade. With Russia taking a more assertive stance and challenging American hegemony globally and regionally, some observers have referred to the development of tensions between Russia and the West as a new Cold War. What can be done, they discuss, to avoid the escalation of conflict or escape the dead end?

Other observers claim that the political instability of the decades following the Cold War was due to heavy world imbalances, such as the expansion of global governance and its security system, which makes states adapt to a highly uneven paying field. This produced a competition of ideas, values, and avenues for development—largely a competition between liberal globalist and nationalist principles of regulating socioeconomic and political systems. Still others reflect on the global power shift and volatile character of the contemporary international system, which is gradually fashioning new expectations and directions for state and system behavior. While the United States continues to underscore its place and identity in the world, Russia and other non-Western states are believed to be in quest of sculpting a new place and position for themselves in the evolving world order. Essentially, the international system remains the highly resilient sphere of American dominance because of this country's unmatched advantages in political, economic, and technological aspects. Other countries, including Russia, have no interest and are in no position to overthrow the world order due to a large gap in capacities.

The world, however, is shifting from this US-centric viewpoint. Russia and other countries are developing a vision of global politics and nurturing a pragmatic strategy, based on national interest, that fits with this vision: aligning with the West where necessary, reproving it where conflict is inevitable.

In this very well researched volume, Matthew Crosston provides a fascinating and novel approach to the study of international relations, Russian politics, power, and foreign policy through the lens of national security and intelligence studies. He challenges much of the standard perception and commentary and instead questions assumptions about Russia's international behavior and foreign policy that are too often deemed axiomatic, offering a very important invitation to traditional Russian studies scholars to be willing to consider more alternative viewpoints that are less US centric. His engaging, brave, and interesting contrarian views are not polemical or vitriolic; they are based on extensive analysis of empirical facts that have often been underemphasized—or wholly ignored—by many in Western media, diplomatic, and academic communities. *Russia Reconsidered* offers a balanced and thought-provoking exploration of Russia-US relations by highlighting some of the more controversial and important arguments. Crosston also brings together an interesting mix of contributing authors, allowing readers to see far more subtleties and nuances in this relationship.

Ultimately, the author's desire is that this book will operate as a platform to initiate and facilitate new, open dialogue about the international system, the emerging challenges within the system, and challenges between the actors in the system—which is a welcome and needed change. By effectively underlining opportunities to overcome misperceptions in our understanding of Russian-American relations, Crosston shows us how those relations might somehow improve so that these two major powers can concentrate on issues of common concern and engage one another in a nonconfrontational way.

—**Lada Kochtcheeva, PhD**
North Carolina State University

ACKNOWLEDGMENTS

My deepest appreciation and acknowledgment goes to the entire amazing team and crew at Brown Books Publishing Group, who proved themselves critical and impressive at every step of development. A very special nod of gratitude and wonder for their great leader, Ms. Milli Brown, who believed in the importance of this work above and beyond the call of duty.

INTRODUCTION

Fighting the Orthodoxy

DR. MATTHEW CROSSTON 2017

In the early autumn of 2016 I was invited by Dr. Richard Mahoney, director of the School of Public and International Affairs (SPIA) at North Carolina State University, to come to campus and give a talk on problematic Russian-American relations. The title of that talk was "Putin-Mongering." In it I laid out a contrarian argument to the standard orthodoxy still running rampant in today's academic and diplomatic world: that the conflictual relations between Russia and the United States today are a complex diplomatic geometry that is the result of many multilayered interactions from *both* sides. The idea that one side is entirely to blame while the other is an innocent rube trying to valiantly persevere through unjust behavior is not only inaccurate but dangerously reckless for anyone wishing to see this relationship become improved. Even more disconcerting is the fact that the West has largely bought into this closed-off orthodox thinking and has labeled itself the innocent rube and Russia the black-hatted villain. Keep in mind I gave this talk *before* Donald Trump was elected president of the United States, and the Russian hacking scandal was only in its infancy. As this present work will show, there is ample evidence to contradict this silly posturing: at the moment, the situation between Russia and the United States seems to only be getting worse, not better, and it will require more works like this one to get new ideas, new thinkers, and bold new proposals to the table so as to create a better relationship atmosphere between the two.

It was in the aftermath of that successful and popular talk with SPIA at North Carolina State that I realized I had already chronicled much of the evidence for this contrarian argument through my extensive commentaries, commissioned articles, and requested op-eds over the previous three years. The problem was that they were all disparate, disconnected pieces showcased in diverse venues that no reader would be able to piece together as one solid whole. This is what has been done for you here. It has not only taken all of my pieces written from 2014 to the present day but also includes an impressive number of truly fine mentored/edited pieces I brought to publication (first with my students as a professor and then with rising Global South scholars as the vice chairman of ModernDiplomacy.eu).

The newly edited and refined pieces you will read here have been published in previous forms with such prestigious venues as the Atlantic Council, Rethinking Russia, *New Eastern Outlook,* Modern Diplomacy, *The Greater Caspian Project,* the Russian International Affairs Council, *Journal of Rising Powers,* and IntelNews. I willingly and gladly give all of them my initial thanks and encourage all readers to make their sites a regular stopping point for global analysis and hard-hitting, unbiased reporting and commentary. Perhaps most importantly to me, these groups of collected works represent a fundamental part of the solution to the problem that is Russian-American interaction: on the American side, we need more professors and institutions willing to mentor and push university students to research the Russian-American dynamic from a perspective that does not predetermine the Cold War ethos or presume hero/villain roles automatically. This is why I have highlighted exemplar pieces from the program I developed at Bellevue University, which was a member of the Great Plains National Security Education Consortium and made an Intelligence Community Center of Academic Excellence. The works presented in this compilation show that the reality of the situation between Russia and the United States is far more complex, fluctuating, and ambiguous than is generally recognized. On the international side, we need to give voice to and a platform for more Global South scholars who bring unique approaches, opinions, and worldviews to this discussion. We are undeniably enriched and rewarded when a spotlight is shone on such new talents. Hopefully, this work properly represents and respects these two groups, for they truly can be the opening of a new door in an analytical world in desperate need of one.

Before you dive into the extensive offerings in this work, please allow me a moment to give you a synopsis of why I am the one best positioned to take this risk and challenge the current orthodoxy. My personal love of the post-Soviet world began twenty-five years ago, when I majored in Russian Studies at Colgate University under the tutelage of Dr. Alice Nakhimovsky, Dr. Richard Sylvester, Dr. Anthony Olcott, and Dr. Martha Brill Olcott, all of them shining lights in the study of the Soviet Union and post-Soviet space. I spent my junior year abroad and alone, opening what had been a previously closed city in the southern agricultural region of Russia called Tambov. It also happened to be *the* year, in that the day after my arrival, the August coup transpired. When you acquire fluency in a foreign language while persevering through the dissolution of an empire, it tends to be a transformative moment that never weakens.

This is what made me then pursue my master's degree at University College of London's School of Slavonic and East

European Studies (SSEES) in 1993–94 under the mentorship of Professors Peter Duncan, Geoffrey Hosking, and Martin McCauley, all major figures in Russian studies to this day. This passion, which only grew and deepened under their tutelage, was maintained from 1995 to 1997, when I served as executive director of the East-West Fund for International Education, a private foundation where I acted as liaison between Middlebury College and the top Russian and post-Soviet universities to create exchanges for professionals wishing to study in the United States.

My doctoral dissertation research (where I was mentored by the amazing Dr. Linda Cook, yet another major figure in Russian studies, and befriended by none other than Sergei Khrushchev, the son of Nikita, who was lecturing at the time for Brown University) involved spending nearly three years in Southern Russia, the Republic of Tatarstan, and the Urals (2000–02), writing what would become my first book, *Shadow Separatism*. While an assistant professor at Clemson University, I created the Russian Provincial Politics Summer Study Abroad Program, which was a unique immersion opportunity from 2005 to 2008 for students to experience life in rural Russia far outside the standard study abroad meccas of Moscow and Saint Petersburg. This is also when I published my second book, *Fostering Fundamentalism*, which required extensive research in and on the Ferghana Valley, working on radical groups in Uzbekistan, Kyrgyzstan, and Tajikistan. In 2014, I successfully concluded a bilateral exchange agreement between Tambov State University and Bellevue University. While there, I pushed new intellectual content from the program to the policy magazine I created with Modern Diplomacy, *The Greater Caspian Project*, which is already followed widely across Europe, Asia, and the Middle East and is commendably known as a “Caspian STRATFOR.” It became a go-to policy analysis source to understand the expansive and diverse political economy and foreign-policy issues native to the post-Soviet space.

Fully fluent in Russian, I was invited as the first American analytical blogger for the Russian International Affairs Council, regularly contribute to Rethinking Russia, and have collaborative relationships with the Moscow State Institute of International Relations, Moscow State University in the name of Lomonosov, and the Alexander Gorchakov Public Diplomacy Fund. This unique combination of academic and professional experience has allowed me to present at such fine venues as the US Department of State, the Defense Intelligence Agency, the Washington Institute for Near East Policy, the Woodrow Wilson International Center for Scholars, Creighton University, and Rhodes College. In the fall of 2016 I was invited to run a two-day seminar for the Russian desk at the Ninety-Seventh Intelligence Squadron, and I will also be doing another Russian seminar for the generals and executive leaders of USSTRATCOM in March.

I have, over a decade and a half, taught the challenges to and future trajectories of political economy, security, intelligence, and development as impacted by competing paradoxes within democratic consolidation (a foundation first established for me at SSEES a quarter century ago). This has resulted in one of the most prolific and diverse publishing portfolios on the post-Soviet space that can be found today: leadership and elite politics, politics and law, gender politics, the politics of Russia’s regions, energy politics, Russia’s information politics, counterterrorism, intelligence, foreign policy, migration issues, and “soft-power” policy have all figured prominently in my teaching and research and are the spokes giving solidity to a lifetime spent trying to understand the "enigma" that is the Russian political mind. This work honors that diversity and depth, providing readers with over seventy-five analytical commentaries divided into seven sections: Cold War residues; the Ukraine conflict; diplomacy, economics, and foreign policy; Syria, sanctions, and extremism; education, media, and analysis; regional politics and geostrategy; and cyber, spies, and intelligence. You will find not only the common themes you see discussed on the nightly news about Russia; here you will find every aspect of Russian power, strategy, and politics analyzed in an easily accessible but still probing writing style.

Taking my professional and academic life in sum, I do not believe there are many people who can surpass the obvious intellectual commitment I have shown for this area of the world. It gives me a unique personal knowledge and network that I gladly now share with all of you. I hope you find it as thought provoking, intriguing, and debate inducing as I intended it to be. Indeed, that is what I hope for most of all: that *Russia Reconsidered* launches a thousand debates around the world in the finest academic institutions. I have for several years offered an open invitation to come to any university, think tank, or agency and debate the resident experts on how much we are getting the Russian-American dynamic wrong. So far, there have been no real takers. May this work in your hands be a spur to finally get that atmosphere of inspired, heated, profound civil discourse blossoming. Because if one thing is certain, it is that the same old, same old when it comes to Russian analysis is getting us nowhere. We must find a new generation of thinkers or a new school of thought that is not so determined to interpret every maneuver from the Russian side as an homage to 1985. Or 1972. Or 1963. This is not to say Russia must be supported or its initiatives deemed superior. This is not an attempt to replace one tired orthodoxy with a new one that commits the same false assumptions in the opposite direction. Above all else, this work is an attempt to let Russian analysis finally be based solely on the fact that we are in the twenty-first century, not the twentieth. The orthodoxy must fall, and iconoclasm must reign. If we succeed, then a new day of engagement will dawn in Russian-American relations.

I would like to thank all of the following for their support and unique contributions to the field over the years. May they continue to fight the good fight.

- The Atlantic Council
- intelNews.org
- Modern Diplomacy
- New Eastern Outlook
- Rethinking Russia
- The Russian International Affairs Council

PART I

COLD WAR RESIDUES

The Bully Brothers

Why the World Should Be Happy about a Fake Cold War

FEBRUARY 17, 2017

As America slowly immolates under the creeping self-implosion of chaos and possibly dangerous, extreme partisan politics, it is time to take a step back and realize something the world should be thankful for. While most media outlets all over the world sit enraptured with and concerned over each new episode of Cold War 2.0, the majority of countries do not seem to realize that this rebirth of old animosity and tension is a boon for them.

This neo–Cold War is, in reality, much ado about nothing. It is an awful lot of posturing for the cameras and a blowing of mighty wind that signifies little. How could I say such a thing? Am I ignorant? Am I naively optimistic? Am I a Putin plant in the West trying to distract audiences from the very real and impending danger of a coming WWIII? Nothing of the sort. I believe this is a fake Cold War based on the ample evidence being provided by both sides. Allow me to count the ways.

ACTIONS BY AMERICA:

- The Magnitsky Act.
- Comprehensive sanctions after the Ukrainian affair.
- Intervening in Libya and Yemen.
- Lobbying against the JCPOA by relevant political leaders, threatening to repeal it.

- Deployment of THAAD in South Korea.
- Freedom of Navigation patrols in the South China Sea.
- Open hostility from prominent members of Congress.
- Various expulsions of Russian diplomatic corps members from Washington.
- Boots on the ground and more in Syria against Assad.

ACTIONS BY RUSSIA:

- Intervening in the Maidan revolution.
- Enforcing the secession vote in Crimea.
- Exiting specific nuclear proliferation treaties.
- Reforming and modernizing its military arsenal.
- Hacking scandals.
- Possibly compromising the US presidential election.
- Strategic moves against NATO relevance.
- Various expulsions of American diplomatic corps members from Moscow.
- Boots on the ground and more in Syria against Assad opposition.

This is not even a full list, but most of the events listed above form the core evidence used to justify the declaration that a new Cold War has begun. But I believe it is quite the opposite: several individual items on the above lists alone would be reason enough for countries in other locales and contexts to go to war with each other. Not only do we presently live in a moment where many in the United States have their perceptions reinforced that Russia apparently tried to undermine the presidential election of 2016 (though, at this point in time, the credible evidence showing that a foreign nation had a truly impactful and decisive influence on election results is quite scant) and that the current president sitting in the Oval Office is Putin's puppet, but Russia for its part believes the United States has de facto tried to kill Russian citizens through the soft-power manipulation of sanctions, purposely trying to force a revolution from within against Putin by making regular people suffer. It is not important whether these two belief systems are factually true. What matters are the disturbing percentages within both populations that believe they are. Name me other situations where two powerful countries can think such things about the other and not end up going to war or escalating their animosity beyond competing press conferences and media blasts (which, in real time, is all this so-called new Cold War has amounted to so far).

Even more incredulously, both the United States and Russia are presently intervening inside of a foreign country that has disintegrated into near anarchy, but they are intervening on opposite sides of the conflict. Russia has openly questioned the wisdom of removing the Assad regime from power. They are at least semijustifiably suspicious of the membership of many opposition groups in terms of their allegiance to democratic institutions or radical Islamist ones. America has steadfastly accused Russia of not only supporting a man who committed war crimes by using biological weapons against his own people but using the Russian air force to indiscriminately bomb areas of Syria that were purely civilian, thereby violating the Geneva Convention. I am hard pressed to think of worse accusations for opposing sides to lob at one another during a conflict. But then remember that these two sides have both personnel and materiel in the battle arena, pursuing contradictory objectives, and that neither side has engaged the other in any manner within Syria, not even once, and the lack of escalation becomes simply incomprehensible. Incomprehensible, that is, if this truly was a real Cold War. This implausible level of good luck and/or coincidence can only come about from a deliberate strategy of restraint. And that is my point: it *is* a deliberate strategy of restraint manifested on both sides toward each other. Yes, Russia and America have different interests on a number of issues and have pursued those interests with an impressive projection of power in various arenas around the world. But despite this, neither has fallen victim to misperception, misdirection, manipulation, what have you, to the degree that either wanted to incite a real war between them.

I can believe in coincidence in foreign affairs. I can even believe in coincidence a couple of times. But at this point in the so-called New Cold War, these two opponents are benefiting from nearly a dozen coincidences in order to not be in an all-out, full-scale war. That is too much for even my bleeding, optimistic heart. This consistent ability to antagonize but pull back, to accuse but go no further, to reprimand but not retaliate in force, is why Cold War 2.0 is empty. And thank goodness for that: not only does it mean the world is not truly under the threat of nuclear annihilation, but as long as America and Russia continue to play enemy footsie with each other, they are suitably distracted from noticing areas where they in fact have common interests and might even benefit from uniting into a team. If most of the international community thinks the world is not in a safe place when America and Russia are not getting along, just imagine how much consternation there might be in certain places if they actually became real strategic and foreign-policy allies? The meddling under that context would make the current complaints of meddling seem infantile.

So cheer up, world. Sit back, and watch the Bully Brothers do their thing with each other. In the end, it's not going to amount to very much, and it prevents them from ganging up on you. Because if there is one thing both Russia and America have had in common for generations, it is a sense of global importance and messianism that is breathtaking to behold, if not also mind-blowingly uncontrolled. It just might be better to have those tendencies obsessed with each other rather than focused on someone else.

CONCLUSION—STANDING FOR ICONOCLASM

What this work has aimed to provide is a foundation for all aspiring iconoclasts in the field of Russian studies. For a full generation and beyond, since the dissolution of the Soviet Union, the study of Russia has slowly disintegrated into a cynical morass of doubt, suspicion, and presumptive academic constraint. This has not only vexed those on the Russian side looking to establish relations with the United States that are not path dependent and mimics of history; it has drained an entire generation of young minds in America out of the field and left Russian studies still leaning heavily on those who were raised and baptized in the fire of the original and authentic Cold War. This work hopefully gives reason for all those who want to believe that not only is the Cold War 2.0 not nearly as authentic or as menacing as they are being driven to believe but that there is a place intellectually, diplomatically, and academically for those who do not wish to mindlessly follow an orthodox line of thinking that is hindering new ideas and new thinkers from gaining the stage. This latter fact is the true crime of modern scholarship on Russia today and something I hope this work starts to overcome.

This is, of course, not to say Russia is blameless for the state of affairs between the two countries. That accusation is also part and parcel of this damning orthodoxy: if you do not toe the line against Russia, you are labeled a sycophant or shill for Russia. We must stop this rigid binary categorization, because it completely shuts down the more accurate third line of analysis: one devoid of partisanship, nationalism, and patriotism that seeks to effectively shed light on opportunities to overcome misunderstanding and misperception so that two major powers can finally engage one another without the result predetermined in the negative. More often than not, it is the orthodoxy of assumed animosity that keeps Russia and the United States from finding negotiated common ground on a host of issues. The dozens of works you will read in this volume show just how expansive that list of issues is and will continue to be. But they also show how frustratingly misleading the standard analyses seem to be, time and time again. This is the orthodoxy that must be ameliorated if not outright defeated.

Where are the thinkers willing to step up and challenge preordained results? Who is willing to smash down the walls of academic and diplomatic orthodoxy so that the false binary we are currently being fed will disappear? This work is a clarion call for that new generation of thinkers, whether it is the millennial generation, just now entering advanced graduate study, or members of my own lost generation X, wanting to return to this field of study but wanting to do so on their own terms and with their own ambitions and projects unhindered by the scholarly legacies and assumptions of the past. To do this does not mean that everything turns upside down: that now America is the black-hatted villain, and Russia is the valiant squire trying to survive. This dichotomy has always been humorously childish and dangerously misleading. In the field of Russian studies, when it tackles the complex layers of global engagement and foreign affairs, in particular with the United States, it is time to produce an entire army of thinkers, diplomats, and scholars who understand that there is no single universal Truth with a capital *T* and that most of the issues to be analyzed and discussed will never be resolved by having a single victor and definitive vanquished. That language and those thought processes no longer bear any tasty fruit. Rather, they bring bitterness and resentment. So may this new cadre of iconoclastic scholars follow this humble first step: reject the presumed resentment, and follow a path that actually allows us all something other than a single dull conclusion.

This is your challenge.

This is our duty.

Perhaps the fate of the world really does depend on it.

Syria, Russia, and the United States

Cold War Residue Redux

APRIL 15, 2014

Though Syria has somewhat fallen off the media radar in the West because of a Malaysian plane crashing into the Indian Ocean and Crimean referendum consequences booming across Europe, an ongoing conflict and crisis continues in a critically important region of the world. The problems in Syria remain poorly understood in the West across the board, but especially so when it comes to understanding Russian strategy on Syria vis-à-vis the United States. The common US position has simply dismissed Russian initiatives as knee-jerk anti-Americanism: getting in the way for the sake of being a nuisance to American power. This is, in fact, incorrect: it is the somewhat myopic Western tendency to view the agendas of other states strictly through their relative positioning with the United States that blinds Western analysis to real motivations and prevents better analyses from being produced.

For example, the West on the whole wanted to see the Arab Spring more with optimism and hope, as a confirmation of its own principles and political ideals and a reflection that its engagement with the region paid off. Most Western politicians, therefore, have been reluctant to consider more cautious or even skeptical viewpoints about the long-term trajectories to come in its aftermath. Russia, however, with its unique perspective on radical Islamism because of the long and bloody conflict with Chechnya, has always been rightfully disturbed about what can emerge in the vacuum of authoritarian regime change where radical Islam already exists. While the West has been comfortable viewing the Arab Spring as a groundswell of grassroots democratic ideals and sought to actively encourage and support its development, Russia has warily seen it as a potential "Great Islamist Revolution." Keeping in mind the new regimes in Egypt, Tunisia, Yemen, and Libya are not exactly blossoming with democratic institutions and stability, the Russian skepticism about Arab Spring futures seems somewhat affirmed. The issue, therefore, when it comes to Syria is not that Russia finds Assad superior and essential but simply that the status quo seems less chaotic and destabilizing to the region's geopolitical future and to legitimate Russian national security interests.

Russia's relationship with Syria has always hung on a pendulum, swinging from relatively close to relatively cool over the past half century. What remains constant for Russia's dealings with Syria, however, is its desire to ensure America is not the only legitimate actor with international influence in the region. To that end, Syria is an arena to help facilitate those endeavors. This goal of global recognition and legitimacy has a long and documented history within the Russian diplomatic psyche. Discussions about Russian material interests in Syria create significant scholarly debate. Many consider the commercial investments to be relatively modest and not part of any larger Syrian strategy. This view, however, is too economically quantitative, missing the greater esoteric foreign-policy point behind Russia's commercial dealings: if the greatest national security objective for Russia is to maintain global diplomatic significance and international influence, then maintaining relevance within the Middle East must be a crucial part of the master plan. Syria is by far the most convenient partner for Russia in this endeavor. As such,

Russian commercial initiatives are more about strategic allegiance and perceived political dependence and less about profit. This helps explain why Russia agreed to renegotiate Assad's debt repayment in a manner that was extremely generous and beneficial to Syria: rather than a sign of weakness or incompetence, it was an effective strategic measure that tied Syria more tightly to the Russian sphere of influence, thereby keeping a Middle East doorway open. Commercial investiture in Syria is just one tool in the Russian diplomatic pouch to keep active and engaged within the Middle Eastern sphere. With this in mind, the expansiveness of Russia's economic engagement with Syria becomes quite impressive.

In addition to the Arab Spring and commercial activity, foreign policy is a third aspect that elucidates a more nuanced analysis of Russia's position on Syria. Russian foreign policy is witness to a much larger vision than simply fostering anti-American sentiment. Again, by no means do these foreign-policy positions bind Russia inextricably to Assad. On the contrary, Russian foreign policy seems more pragmatic: it would not hesitate to drop support for his regime if it could see that it was ultimately going to fall. In other words, what was most important to Russia was its overall relevance in the region and that the region remained at peace and not vulnerable to radical Islamists. How close its friendship was with a particular leader or whether that particular leader remained in power was not nearly as relevant. Indeed, in 2013 President Putin himself declared, "We are not concerned about the fate of Assad's regime. . . . We are worried about . . . what next?" He added that Russia's position is "not to leave Assad's regime in power at any price, but to first let Syrians agree among themselves how they should live next. Only then should we start looking at ways to change the existing order."

When dealing with Syria, Russia is for Russia far more than for Assad. In addition, when Russia looked to the dilemmas and crises rising out of Damascus and across the Syrian countryside, it did not see other interested actors, like Iran and China for example, lining up to take a leading role in conflict resolution. American infatuation with seeing Assad deposed was regarded by the Russians as an incredibly rash and poorly thought-out action that did not consider the long-term strategic consequences across the region. This alone was powerful reasoning that compelled many in the corridors of power in Moscow to act as they did.

What is most remarkable in all of these considerations is how little anti-Americanism factors as a foundational element. Russia's interactions and support for Syria have more to do with its desire for diplomatic/political influence and legitimate national security objectives than they do with Cold War nostalgia or knee-jerk anti-Americanism. Russia sees its rightful place as a diplomatic player with independent operating power and as the only state truly able to balance the influence of America in the Middle East. Though difficult for observers in the West to believe, many outside of Washington and the European Union did not see American positions toward Syria as generally promoting peace but saw them rather exacerbating the violence further by blindly supporting questionable opposition groups that may have been against Assad but were also not for democracy. When Russia voiced its opposition against such groups, it saw itself not as a force that worsened the conflict but rather as the one state truly trying to contain the violence from exploding uncontrollably. Many Western diplomats tended to just assume anti-American sentiment always informed such Russian strategy. Still others backed up the perception by emphasizing how

Russia defended the Syrian regime against Western pressure, used delay tactics, and disrupted repeated US efforts to "resolve" the crisis. These arguments are overstated, as is the conventional wisdom that supposes many of Russia's contemporary positions have not evolved beyond the residue of Cold War mentalities. That residue, quite honestly, seems to exist more in the minds of scholars and practitioners *in the West* rather than in the diplomatic institutions of Russia itself.

Ultimately, what has been largely missed in contemporary debates about Syria in the West is how Russia views the conflict from perspectives that do not place America and American interests as the chief priorities. Concern over long-term American visions in Syria is real for Russia not because it must automatically oppose America but because Russia thinks America is absentmindedly pushing Syria into chaos. When American analysts downplay these concerns and focus instead on perceived anti-Americanism as the primary motivating factor, they lessen the ability to properly understand how the Syrian crisis continues to evolve and how major players may react to and interact with certain crisis stimuli. In other words, the American tendency to make itself the sun in a Copernican foreign-policy universe handicaps the United States by impairing its diplomatic vision and retarding its options for real interaction and cooperation. There is indeed a Cold War residue in the world today. But that residue, unfortunately, is not being pushed by the Russians.

Putin-Mongering

JULY 15, 2015

If you spend some time listening to reputable news shows all across the West, you will start to notice several recurring "interpretations" that explain all things Russian and Vladimir Putin. Rather than being enlightening about this complex country and its perhaps even more complex leader, a series of increasingly incredulous pop-psychology analyses emerge instead. What follows are just five of the most commonly touted, with subsequent breakdowns for those who wish to read more accurate alternative considerations.

1. **Putin fantasizes about returning to the "glorious Soviet" past. Ukraine is just the first step.**
   Putin has made many comments and started many symbolic initiatives over the last decade that in some ways have reclaimed the accomplishments and history of the Soviet Union. What most in the West miss about this is the internal perception in Russia that the dissolution of the Soviet Union in 1991 was not just a historical and political transition to a new stage or a new evolution for the state as a whole. Since the dissolution took place within the context of the Cold War and the ideological war that was capitalism versus communism, with communism losing, most of the world felt the dissolution was also an erasing of history, as in, nothing that took place from 1918 to 1991 was worth remembering, commemorating, or observing. Many of the leaders in the initial Yeltsin years at least partially supported

this, if not directly then by simple omission. In short, the ways in which Putin has reclaimed the partially erased Soviet history can be viewed as his denial of the Western demand that losing the Cold War means nearly seventy-five years of history no longer counts for Russia, unless it is to emphasize negative events and incidents done by the Soviet Union. Putin rejects that concept, which he considers a sort of emotional Treaty of Versailles put upon Russia unfairly by the West. But there is nothing about Ukraine that connects to this reclamation of history. The concept is actually rather absurd: if the Russian Federation truly wanted to reinstitute the Soviet Union in full, there are few competent strategic plans that get there by first taking over Eastern Ukraine and causing that country to disintegrate into chaos.

2. **Putin is obsessed with getting attention from the United States. This is just his way of acting out.**
   I like to call this the "infantilist theory" of Russian politics here in the United States. It is littered with the breathless condemnations of so-called experts who have spent little time actually in Russia, have questionable language skills when it comes to Russian, and most certainly have never spent significant time with Putin or anyone within his close circle. Despite these rather daunting limitations, these experts do not hesitate to appear on numerous radio and television talk shows and write countless newspaper and magazine op-ed pieces, giving a detailed and intimate psychological profile of the Russian leader that basically amounts to characterizing the Russian president as a petulant child who is hopelessly needy and demands that the United

States recognize him as an "unequal equal partner." What most in this camp fail to see is that the position of Russia in Ukraine has been largely based on a strategic plan that *ignores* the relevance or power of the United States. If the so-called Ukraine initiative was about Russia getting attention from the United States, then Russia seems to be doing an outstanding job of misdirection, feigning total ambivalence on statements, sanctions, and initiatives coming out of Washington, DC.

3. **Putin demands the rest of the world accord Russia "superpower" status. Ukraine is his reminder to the rest of the world.** This leans a bit on the logic of the first rumor in that it is unclear how any initiative in Ukraine signals superpower status to anyone anywhere. By now even the most hardened Russian critics in the West have admitted that Ukraine basically squandered two decades of political, economic, and geostrategic promise with complete mismanagement and dysfunctional governance. To admit that on the one hand and then try to connect Russian initiatives within Ukraine as a so-called grand-plan springboard to being taken more seriously by the global community is inane and lacking in strategic common sense. This is even more ridiculous when one simply looks to other areas of Russian hard power that have monumentally increased under Putin since 2000, whether that be in military restructuring, federal budgetary strengthening, or natural resource development. If Putin was going to lean on something to make the world understand Russia should remain or once again be considered a superpower in the twenty-first century, it is those areas of real domestic strength that would power the argument. Getting involved with

Ukraine after the Maidan revolution has absolutely zero chance of accomplishing that goal. Putin clearly acknowledges this, so it is a mystery why the West won't as well.

4. **Putin is violating international law by interfering with Ukrainian affairs.**

   One of the most successful movie franchises in history, Pirates of the Caribbean, is actually a fantastic teaching tool for this accusation. In the very first film, when Elizabeth is taken aboard the *Black Pearl* to face the dreaded Captain Barbossa, she is dismayed to learn he is not going to follow the so-called holy pirate's code. To which, rather bemusedly, Captain Barbossa explains that the pirate's code is not so much a code as a set of guidelines. And guidelines are to be followed pretty much as one sees fit . . . or sees not to, as the case may be. This is an absolutely spot-on description of how international law measures up against actual strategic foreign policy and global affairs: states would like to follow international law, may even prefer to follow it, and for the most part do follow it. *Until*, that is, international law comes in direct opposition to national interest and foreign-policy priorities. At which time international law can pretty much be told to go hang. Now, the part of this that always gives the United States consternation (or is it political indigestion?) is when Russia is adamant that the chief model for this semirespectful, semidismissive attitude toward international law is none other than the United States. If you want to stop a dinner party dead in its tracks in Washington, casually mention how Putin feels absolutely certain that his actions in Ukraine are a perfect mirror to how the United States has conducted its business in other areas, like Iraq, Afghanistan, and Libya—just to name a few. Only Putin believes his interference in Ukraine is *far* more justified and explainable than American interference in those aforementioned countries. In short, international law is a grab bag of mysterious and contradictory interpretations based on power and priority. Russia simply admits it more readily, and more publicly, than the United States.

5. **Putin has put hundreds, if not thousands, of intelligence agents into Eastern Ukraine, and they are causing all of the unrest.**

This last one is disheartening simply because it is an avoidance of political and military reality on the ground in Ukraine and, as a result, could be influential in the continuing violence and bloodshed. There is no doubt that Russia has an intelligence presence inside of Ukraine. Russia has always had one. So has the United States. The United States also has an intelligence presence inside of Russia, some of it with permission, some of it without. But to take this basic principle of intelligence reality all around the world (for example, China has intelligence agents in Taiwan, Japan has agents in China, India has them in Pakistan and Pakistan in India, and the United States basically has agents everywhere) and distort it so that it is the chief culprit of events spiraling out of control in Eastern Ukraine is irresponsible. Dissembling of this sort removes most of the focus from the Ukrainian authorities who are struggling to regain control across their territory, sometimes wisely, sometimes foolishly, sometimes peacefully, and sometimes violently. It also eliminates the existence of actual pro-Russian factions

> within Ukraine that no longer wish to be part of it. The West is dominated by stories of pro-Russian groups engaging in violence in Ukraine, and within a day those pro-Russian factions are magically "littered with Russian agents and/or provocateurs," i.e., there is no legitimate anti-Ukrainian authority movement, there are only Russian intelligence forces manipulating events on the ground to the detriment of Ukrainian territorial integrity. This is overstatement at best, political fabrication at worst, as the West has made it clear it does not want to see any disintegration of Ukraine. What's not being said is how that position is not so much based on the desire for peace and tranquility as it is based on the fact that any dissolution of Ukraine will undoubtedly end up benefiting Russia. And that has been silently acknowledged as the least-optimal outcome to the West.

Russia is not perfect. Russia is not blameless. No country is. But when reputable news sources and so-called experts with decades of experience examining Russia all seem to cater to the same storyboard, and that storyboard seems a bit far-fetched if not actually fantastical, then it is time to signal the call for a new generation of leaders and experts who are willing to examine not just from old prejudices but from coldhearted, objective foreign-policy reality. In that crucible, no one is absolved, but no one is unfairly prejudged. Right now the future of Russian-American relations depends on the emergence of these new voices.

America's National Security Schizophrenia

Damning Russia with "Partnership"

FEBRUARY 24, 2015

There is no stronger example of the schizophrenic nature of American foreign policy toward Russia than comparing statements written in the formal National Security Strategy (NSS) of President Obama with actual testimony given by Director of National Intelligence James Clapper. In 2010 the NSS asserted that the United States would endeavor to "build a stable, substantive, multidimensional relationship with Russia, based on mutual interests." What's more, the NSS called Russia a twenty-first-century center of influence in the world and a country with whom America should build bilateral cooperation on a host of issues, including forging global nonproliferation; confronting violent extremism; fostering new trade and development arrangements; promoting the rule of law, accountability in government, and universal values in Russia; and cooperating as a partner in Europe and Asia.

Now take into account Director James Clapper's speech while appearing before Congress in 2013 to discuss global threats. He described Russian foreign policy as a nexus of organized crime, state policy, and business interests. (Let it be noted that all three of these descriptors were said pejoratively. It wasn't just the organized crime reference that was considered bad.) Clapper went on to warn that both China and Russia represented the most persistent intelligence threats to the United States and that Russia could even face social discontent (read: political disorder and revolution) because of a sluggish economy, the constraint of political pluralism, and pervasive corruption.

At first blush these two accounts seem to offer completely incompatible attitudes toward Russia. But this is only at first blush. Reading deeper between the lines of the NSS reveals key words that always trigger contempt from Russian actors in the Kremlin. When the NSS speaks of the ideal of promoting rule of law, government accountability, and universal values, they do not extend an olive branch offering Russia the chance to team up with America to achieve these goals in problem areas around the world. These things are mentioned as not needing to happen *with* Russia but *in* Russia. To follow that goal up with being a cooperative partner in Europe and Asia has always signaled to Russian ears an American skepticism about Russia's ability to be a nonmeddler. In other words, the NSS comes across not as a mechanism to promote deeper, equal ties between the two countries but rather as a snobbish slap across the face about how the United States needs to engage Russia to stop it from getting in its own and others' way.

Clapper's comments in some ways garner even more derision from Moscow. Although Russia has always been rather indifferent to the complaints about centralized power and corruption since Yeltsin first came down off the tanks after the August coup in 1991, Clapper's comments about the possibility of social discontent and unrest, placing that possibility at the feet of the Russian government because of repression and incompetence, always come off as a red flag to the bulk of Russian conspiracy theorists: they are quick to see American interference in any and all things that go wrong in Russia. And even if the more rational voices in Russian political power dismiss conspiracy theories, there is still the obvious interpretation that while America might not try to personally foment unrest, it would welcome instability if it happened.

Americans at times can play too fast and loose with semantics: as long as the United States does not actively try to create such discord, it thinks it cannot possibly be seen as a source of such discord. There are simply no Russian actors that would agree with that interpretation. Russians to this day point to Georgia, to Ukraine, to the countries of the Arab Spring, to Syria, and believe the buildup to the unrest was either directly orchestrated by the United States or at least subtly fostered by America. Indeed, it is surprising there is not more analysis comparing the US National Security Strategy with the subsequent Russian foreign-policy concept that came out in 2013 on the heels of Clapper's testimony. It affirms the Putin criticism that US-Russia relations will always remain complicated because of fundamental cultural differences. What might these cultural differences be? According to Putin, that American identity is based on individual wants, racism, and genocidal and other extreme forms of violence, and this will always conflict with Russian identity, which is based on "loftier ambitions, more of a spiritual kind." This foreign-policy concept was elaborated upon on September 11 of the same year, when Putin published a letter to the *New York Times* making the following points:

- The United Nations could collapse, and international law would suffer if nations take military action without UN approval.
- Such action in Syria would only result in a total destabilization of the area and a widening of conflict and terrorism.

- Russia is protecting, therefore, international law rather than the Assad regime.
- Many in the world are beginning to see the United States as relying solely on brute force and that such US reliance has proven ineffective and pointless.
- President Obama's statement that the United States should act when possible to uphold international norms was "extremely dangerous," arguing that all countries are equal already under international law.

Rightly or wrongly, Russia is convinced that America has a global agenda that pushes a single unilateral superpower with special attention paid to keeping Russia on the sidelines, politically and militarily marginalized. Most analysts in the West take these reactions from Russia as an example of Moscow's innate instability and political unreliability. What they unfortunately fail to realize, however, is how much of that so-called instability comes as a reaction to what the Kremlin feels is the national security schizophrenia of the United States, a country fully smitten with its own image as a white knight to the world while also being fairly quick to tell the same world it is saving exactly how it is misbehaving and how it needs to change.

US-Russia Redux

The Problem with Intellectual Insincerity

OCTOBER 21, 2015

There are numerous intellectual sources, from think tanks to governmental agencies in both the United States and Russia, that are deeply concerned about the state of Russian-American relations. Places like the Moscow Carnegie Centre or the Brookings Institution in Washington, DC, are regular go-to places for the media when seeking expert opinion and analysis. However, these centers of independent knowledge production have had a decided slant in allocating blame for the poor bilateral relations to the Russian side, with the explanations ranging from the fairly simple to the rather mystically esoteric.

> If America did not exist, Russia would have to invent it. In a sense it already has: first as a dream, then as a nightmare. No other country looms so large in the Russian psyche. To Kremlin ideologists, the very concept of Russia's sovereignty depends on being free of America's influence.
>
> Anti-Americanism has long been a staple of Vladimir Putin, but it has undergone an important shift. Gone are the days when the Kremlin craved recognition and lashed out at the West for not recognizing Russia as one of its own. Now it neither pretends nor aspires to be like the

> West. Instead, it wants to exorcise all traces of American influence.[1]

It is not difficult to find this Freudian type of political psychobabble today when it comes to analyzing Russian positions. The United States tries to portray itself as the victim of a global oedipal complex when it comes to Russia: first Putin desperately craves Daddy's attention; then defiantly and recklessly rejects him; only to then petulantly try to run away from home. Most countries around the world would actually find it dangerously myopic and unhealthy to base their foreign policy on earning the approval of another country. The far more standard approach to foreign-policy formulation is to determine a country's own national interests and craft an independent position best able to achieve its own optimal goals.

And that, incredulously, is what is being described above in America as a "shift": from craving attention to striving to exorcise American demons. In reality there is no shift at all: Russia has always been about Russia, as it expects America to be about America, France to be about France, Nigeria to be about Nigeria, and so forth and so on. What Russia finds so irksome is that when it does what everyone else does on the issue of global positioning, it is judged as psychologically unstable or mentally deficient. What the American media outlets and think-tank personalities fail to recognize is how much of this judgment is not from observable behavior or direct

1 "The Dread of the Other," *Economist*, February 16, 2013, https://www.economist.com/news/europe/21571904-leading-role-played-anti-americanism-todays-russia-dread-other?fsrc=scn/rd_ec/the_dread_of_the_other.

quotes from relevant actors but is instead from so-called experts pushing a decidedly one-sided interpretation of the agenda.

Russia is not supposed to aspire to be a copy of or mimic for the West. Nor should it be allowing any particular American influence over its policy decisions. This is not said as an anti-American statement but rather as simple foreign-policy logic: America would never strive to copy another country, and it most certainly does not endorse another country trying to force or influence its foreign policy. So why should Russia? It is this very straightforward question that seems to never be asked by what are otherwise august media institutions and impressive political think tanks in the West.

Sometimes this tendency can reach near farcical levels. When Alexei Pushkov, chairman of the Russian parliament's foreign-relations committee, spoke about ridding Russia of dependence on America and even ridiculously commented about fining cinemas that show too many foreign films, it was up to Western experts on Russia to recognize the absurd for what it is: just absurdity. Failure to do so is especially egregious given that so much Western political analysis over the past fifteen years has lamented the strengthening and deepening of Putin's own presidential power system. Decrying how little power sits within the legislative or judiciary branches of Russian government means it is nonsensical to then highlight parliamentarians as having real impact and relevance on Russian-American relations. But this happens quite a bit in American media outlets and think tanks without anyone ever taking the time to point out the blatant contradiction.

This bias is only more pronounced when you leave academically oriented think tanks / news monitors and observe opinions within the corridors of American power. Traditionally, this decidedly anti-Russian fervor came from the Republican Party. However, this analysis would argue that except for a very brief and ultimately dashed Obama "reset," attitudes about Russian-American interaction within Washington, DC, have always been dominated in *both* parties by a largely Republican mind-set.

That mind-set sets a fairly stark characterization: Russia is an aggressive and untrustworthy dictatorship that is an innate contradiction to American values. As such it will inevitably always be a threat to US interests and global security. By all indicators, Russia is a threat not just to itself and its immediate neighbors but to the entire world, masking its own domestic failings and instabilities with an aggressive foreign policy that will never acquiesce to a more peaceful and cooperative global community. Indeed, when American politicians specialize in ambiguous statements and plausible deniability, it is rather remarkable how freely the American Congress seems to deride Russia:

John Boehner: "It is increasingly evident that Russia is intent on expanding its boundaries and power through hostile acts."

Ted Poe: "The Russian bear is coming out of its cave because it got its feelings hurt because of the fall of the Soviet Union, and now it is trying to regain its territories."

Chris Smith: accused a "repressive Russian regime" of "coddling dictators" around the globe from Central Asia to Syria to Cuba and Venezuela.

Trent Franks: After the conclusion of an arms deal between Russia and Venezuela, President Putin was called a "thugocrat" engaged in "dangerous alliances."

Keep in mind all of the above statements were uttered *before* the 2014 crisis in Ukraine even broke out. So before the US Congress saw what it considers undeniable and irrefutable proof of Russian aggression, it already viewed Russia as a corrupt kleptocracy willfully abusing human rights, powered by an irrational and paranoid hatred of the United States.

There also tends to be a failure to place Russian analysis through the looking glass of reciprocity. What this means is that current American thinking emphasizes how untrustworthy Moscow decision makers are or how there is no real point in talking with the Kremlin while completely ignoring or dismissing the very real Russian criticism that lobs the same complaints back at Washington. President Putin openly and publicly discusses his lack of trust in American power and in the specific policy decisions emanating from the White House. It is this skepticism, even cynicism, that he claims forces his own lack of desire to engage the United States. There are simply too few voices at present trying to analyze this declared mind-set as a legitimate position. As far as can be determined, the only reason this is not analyzed more seriously is because the competing alternative—that Putin is untrustworthy and Moscow is the cause of all communication breakdowns—is simply too powerfully accepted as a de facto axiom.

In short, if the United States does not trust Russia, it is because of how Russia behaves on the global stage and because of its own history on said stage. If Russia does not trust the United States, that is simply Russian posturing and a case of political transference, wanting to blame its own self-made problems on someone else so that it can avoid any accountability or being held responsible for poor performance. The issue at hand is how this is simply accepted rather than investigated. And how few so-called Russian experts are at present willing to step forward and shine a light on this intellectual insincerity. There are voices that decry a picture being painted that combines inaccuracy with heightened rhetoric while purposely ignoring mitigating contexts and less negative observations. However, those voices are extremely rare and at the moment easily drowned out by the drumbeat of Russian derision. Until those voices get louder or strive to become more prominent public figures in Washington, it seems there is little hope for an improvement in relations between the United States and Russia based on actual events in the real world.

Obama v. Putin

A Tale of the Posturing President

AUGUST 15, 2014

Less than two weeks ago President Obama, sitting for an interview with *The Economist*, basically went "old school" on President Putin, dismissing his presidency, his country, and the future of both. While his words were certainly blatant and blunt, what might be even more revealing is the subtle subtext hidden inside his cavalier attitude: apparently even presidents are not above being petulant.

There can be little debate about President Obama's intent to insult and offend, declaring that "it was important to keep things in perspective. Russia doesn't make anything. . . . Immigrants aren't rushing to Moscow in search of opportunity. The life expectancy of the Russian male is around sixty years old. The population is shrinking." Judging by these rather truculent comments, it is a wonder Russia is not presently a ghost town, full of nothing but garment-rending females desperately in search of goods from empty shelves. The reality behind these comments is far more interesting, however: Russia is the world's third-largest oil producer and second-largest natural gas producer. It is true Russia's domestic goods production is no doubt not where Putin would like, but last time anyone checked, the president of the United States was not criticizing Saudi Arabia for failing to manufacture more tchotchkes for Walmarts all over America. To be more completely honest, the United States doesn't do all that great a job of manufacturing things either, given Americans have been complaining about the exporting of such jobs to Asia for the last three decades. So while America leans on other countries by pure force of political will and diplomatic power, Russia could technically shut off its natural resource spigots, if it wanted to be just as petulant and truculent as Obama's interview, and pretty much send all of Europe into a total energy panic and crisis. So yes, Mr. President, it might be a good idea indeed to keep things in perspective: like not taking cheap potshots at a country that actually has real political power and admittedly has a rich cultural history of doing things that might be construed as politically rash at times.

Obama went on to describe Putin's presidency as an office causing "short-term trouble for political gain that will cause long-term trouble for Russia." There is a bit of incredulity when examining this simple, provocative statement. In the past I have called this "Wonka Vision" politics, from the famous movie *Willy Wonka & the Chocolate Factory*. Wonka Vision politics is when a country basically ignores facts on the ground and reality in diplomacy in order to focus exclusively on the talking points, on the political vision it wishes to force onto the global stage. There is a strong element of this when looking at how the United States is characterizing Russia over the Eastern Ukraine crisis. Today in Washington, DC, you will find more people who think Russia has already openly invaded Eastern Ukraine and is trying to steal the rest of the country for itself, causing mayhem and destruction along the way, rather than people who understand that a convoy of 250 humanitarian aid trucks are driving in to the region to donate aid and assistance, even allowing Ukrainian authorities to inspect the trucks before they reach their final destinations.

Keep in mind, Obama's interview is with a respected international news magazine. He is crafting an image of Russia that is not in fact in line with actual Russian maneuvers on the ground but is in line instead with the talking points America wants the world to believe. This diplomatic massaging is not just cavalier: it is dangerous, because it inspires like-minded recalcitrance from the Russian side, breaks down opportunities for open discussion and negotiation, and signals to outside actors and third parties to choose sides, thus exacerbating the crisis rather than defusing it. All of this because of poor words chosen by the "leader of the free world." So far the meaning behind this war of words has been ignored: President Obama is quite frankly flummoxed that President Putin has dismissively laughed off his positions, his entreaties, and his sanctions. This, in real terms, is nothing more than a schoolyard standoff, with the two popular boys standing opposite one another and firing taunts back and forth. The rest of the school is on the playground, watching, fascinated, intrigued to see how it actually plays out. Will it go beyond simple taunting? How bad will the insults get? With punches be thrown? Who will be the first to blink? Oh, the hyperbole and hype when schoolyard drama becomes a giant metaphor for the global stage.

What is disappointing is that this drama, this war of fake words and childish insults, is originating from the United States, not Russia. Even worse, the world is subconsciously relying on Russia to be the one to show restraint and diplomatic maturity! And even though the world is particularly slow to recognize this fact, truth be told, Russia has risen to the challenge and has shown restraint. Let us hope that in this particular schoolyard media showdown, some of this will actually start to rub off on President Obama. For if it does, then real discussions and negotiations can begin anew, and American-Russian relations can once more get serious and move beyond these lame attempts to conjure a neo–Cold War that is in the interests and objectives of no one. Well, at least, not in the interests and objectives of anyone who desires peace and tranquility between two old rivals. This playground certainly *is* big enough for the two of them. Someone might just want to whisper that fact into the ear of Obama.

The Ass and the Elephant

Russia and the American Presidency

JULY 8, 2016

Whether one truly believes in the old adages that the president of the United States is the "leader of the free world" and "the most powerful person on the global stage," it is unquestionable that whoever holds the Oval Office in the White House wields tremendous influence and impact, far beyond the borders of America. As the world looks on with fascination in 2016 at the coming confrontation between Hillary Clinton and Donald Trump, questions remain as to which candidate is favored by which foreign leaders.

While mainstream American media is still basically covering the race with an intense if also somewhat incredulous fascination at the popularity and perseverance of the Trump campaign, the reality beyond America seems to show his candidacy is being taken quite seriously by other countries. Some may even be taking it not just seriously but favorably when compared to the anticipated presidency of another Clinton.

At the moment, Russia seems to be one of those countries. However, deeper analysis shows this support might be more of an indictment against past positions of Hillary Clinton and statements rather than based on real evidence that accurately predicts what a Trump presidency might mean for Moscow. In fact, looking at both candidates strictly from a "what this means for Russia" perspective reveals that the next four years of White House–Kremlin relations could be rather problematic no matter who wins.

HILLARY CLINTON

Before some of the specific statements and positions of Hillary Clinton on Russia are considered, a subtle comment needs to be made about the state of foreign policy within the Democratic Party, especially when it comes to potential candidates for president. Approximately four years ago I published a very popular piece that argued how the foreign policy of President Barack Obama was by and large Republican in its conservative orthodoxy. While I admitted that this traditionalist approach could be partially explained by the personal comfort level of the president himself, American presidential race history also weighed heavily in explaining these right-of-center positions for a left-of-center president. This same heavy weight affects Secretary Clinton just as much as Obama and therefore bears repeating.

Why do liberal leaders in America become largely conservative statesmen when it comes to real decision-making on the global stage? Some of this is undoubtedly tied to the accusation Democrats have had to fend off as an entire party in the past generation of presidential races: that Democrats are too focused on domestic affairs and are unfit or inexperienced to handle world affairs. In essence, Democrats always have to defend against the accusation of being foreign-policy weaklings. This accusation is never leveled against Republican candidates. (Even when a particular candidate may appear amateurish to the international community, his party's reputational legacy is apparently automatically transferred to him. This is clearly happening today with Trump.)

This "Chamberlain Syndrome" (Democrat-as-global-appeaser) has existed for quite some time, but it was surely exacerbated by 9/11 and the new emphasis on national security. It was a major part of the lead-up to the 2004 election, when some analysts warned, "If Democrats are to have any hope of returning to power in 2004, or even of running competitively and keeping the US two-party system healthy and balanced in the coming decade, they will have to convince the American people that they are as capable as Republicans of protecting the United States from terrorism and other security threats." While it was assumed that it would be quite some time before Democrats could actually win national elections based on their national security and foreign-policy stances, the big hope was to have the party advance far enough so that it would stop losing national elections solely because of these two factors. This was arguably the biggest lesson learned from the Democratic failure of 2004, when Vietnam war veteran, Purple Heart winner, and longtime Foreign Affairs Senate stalwart John Kerry lost to Bush, who had no such international military service accolades to lean on.

While in the past Democrats could always criticize Republicans for being too eager to consider war (all stick, no carrot), the reverse accusation thrown back at Democrats post-9/11 seemed more damning (all carrot, no stick). What Democrats as a party needed to ensure was that Americans could see them as not too weak or awkward when it came to handling said stick. Undoubtedly this was a legacy lesson made disturbingly eternal when Massachusetts governor Michael Dukakis stuck his head out of a tank in 1988, ostensibly to make people believe in his toughness, and instead became the butt of such jokes and ridicule that it arguably led to his loss to George H. W. Bush.

It seems clear that ever since that debacle Democrats have been quick to overreact to such criticism. They thus tend to be even quicker than Republicans to line up and show the military chevrons symbolically tattooed on their arms, signifying their willingness and capability to defend America as aggressively as the opposing party. This historical weight was prominent on Obama because his past experience as a Chicago community organizer, followed by very limited service as a single-term senator, created a hyper-sensitivity to not being internationally ready. If anything, this same weight is heavier on Secretary Clinton: not only must she fight the traditionally sexist accusations made against all women politicians as being peacemakers and not war-makers but she also must fight her own personal history, which if anything began as classically feminist and liberal, two things never commonly associated with the military or the utilization of hard power. Given this background, both within the party in general and her personality in particular, it becomes much easier to understand why Secretary Clinton's comments and positions over the years have been so decidedly skeptical and critical toward Russia. Easier to understand, however, does not necessarily translate into easier to accept.

Many of Secretary Clinton's critics tend to cite her steadfast belief in the mythology of American exceptionalism and the country's self-proclaimed role as leader of the free world. To be fair, most Washington politicians will at least give public voice to these same ideas, but few have also been secretary of state and maintain very close ties to the military-security complex. It was Ralph Nader who decried her as both a "deep corporatist and deep militarist . . . never having met a weapons system she didn't like." Perhaps most significantly, this characterization would have been impossible to imagine when she began in Washington as First Lady. One only need look at the failed managed-health-care initiative Bill Clinton gave to her charge during his first term to see how dramatically her issue foci and temperament have adapted over time.

Secretary Clinton still maintains unofficial and official contacts within her Eastern European team that are, amazingly, highly adaptable neoconservative holdovers from the Bush administration and have succeeded in staying near to the ears of Obama, Clinton, and Kerry over time. Anatol Lieven, the renowned scholar at King's College London, has openly decried that too many of the figures currently surrounding Secretary Clinton are old-school members of the military, foreign-policy, and security establishment that chronically view Russia with Cold War attitudes, regardless of evidence.

During the Crimea crisis in 2014, Secretary Clinton tried to make a connection between the Putin policy on the secession/annexation issue and policies pursued by Adolf Hitler in the 1930s. Given that over twenty million Russians died fighting Hitler, a sacrifice many historians the world over consider the crucial lynchpin that ultimately led to Hitler's defeat, and that WWII in Russia is officially known instead as the "Great Fatherland War," it was incredibly rash and ill-thought to make such flippantly inaccurate connections given how important Russian-American relations will continue to be to the office Secretary Clinton is pursuing.

At the powerful and influential Brookings Institution, Secretary Clinton stated that more needed to be done to "up the costs" on Russia in general and Putin in particular because of Russian action in Syria. These comments were, of course, made under the aegis of honoring international law and wanting an end to conflict, even though Russia was formally invited to enter Syria and its intervention was technically in line with said international law. Neither statement can be formally applied to the American assistance given to the chaotically diverse opposition groups trying to overthrow Assad. This type of reworking of the narrative is continually irritating to Russia: what it considers to be blatant and untruthful manipulation of the global media covering events actually transpiring on the ground.

Secretary Clinton has not been very gracious when discussing her personal opinion of Putin as a man, having once even described him as having "no soul." In her book *Hard Choices*, she called him "thin-skinned and autocratic." This fuels a general perception within the corridors of power in Russia that perhaps Secretary Clinton views this relationship too personally: that as long as Vladimir Putin is president of Russia (which could very well be for the entirety of a Hillary Clinton presidency), then she will not strive to achieve better relations with the country, nor will she even treat Russia as an equal partner on areas of global mutual interest.

Secretary Clinton has maintained self-serving double standards in interviews, drawing false distinctions between the presidency of Medvedev from 2008 to 2012 and the return of Putin after 2012. On the one hand, she would decry Medvedev of simply doing the bidding of Prime Minister Putin, but then on the other hand would praise her ability to work and get things done with Medvedev. Medvedev, therefore, has been both a puppet who does nothing and a puppet master who let the United States achieve a nuclear arms deal, Iranian sanctions, and facilitate further operations in Afghanistan. In a massively publicized interview with the famous television journalist Judy Woodruff, Secretary Clinton clearly established a stance marked by distrust and wariness toward Russia, even if begrudgingly acknowledging that it was still a country that had to be worked with.

While many traditional liberals within the Democratic Party have issues with what they consider to be the blatantly "far right" conservative foreign-policy positions of Secretary Clinton, the real concern for the Russian Federation is that it sees her as a candidate that, correctly or incorrectly, wants to use Russia and Putin as a convenient scapegoat and whipping boy to establish her own toughness on the global stage and leans on outdated Cold War rhetoric to analyze contemporary strategies and initiatives. If Russia is interested in establishing new twenty-first-century relations with the United States not beholden instinctively to the legacies of the twentieth, then it is hard-pressed to view Secretary Clinton as the president who would be willing to create such an environment. This is what likely fuels the positive statements coming from Russia about Donald Trump. Unfortunately, Russia should be wary of wanting a president just because he isn't Hillary Clinton. While Trump brings a different style and approach to potential relations with Russia, it does not mean those relations will produce anything new and innovative.

DONALD TRUMP

Having examined some of the more strident comments and commentaries made by Secretary Clinton toward Russia, it is hard to avoid the impression that Russia may be supporting a Trump presidency in very much the same way so many Americans are: they simply do not want a Clinton presidency. In my university classes I often caution students from engaging in what I call "negative voting": voting not so much *for* a particular candidate but rather *against* the opposing one. When citizens cast votes based on negation rather than affirmation, then it is not uncommon that the succeeding presidency is ultimately disappointing. I believe this will be applicable to

Russia as well if it thinks simply preventing Secretary Clinton results automatically in a better presidency for Russian-American relations.

Within Mr. Trump's campaign has been a penchant for making bold statements that subsequently get walked back soon after. He did it with the building of a wall against Mexicans; did it with the promise to tax the superrich; did it with the promise to raise the minimum wage; did it with the proposal to simply ban all self-declared Muslims from entering the country. While many Democrats (and Republicans for that matter) lament this as making it impossible to understand just what a Trump presidency will truly look like, many former business associates have warned that this spinning and counterspinning is what his administration will be: no solid principles, simply a willingness to jump back and forth across diametrically opposed positions with no real logic as to why. Ultimately, the accusation is one of being supremely self-serving. Russia may think this is a personality it can work with, but that makes an assumption that the self-serving egotism will be rational and predictable. Moscow seems to emphasize the word "pragmatism" with Mr. Trump. But the policy spins, flip-flops, and contradictions do not indicate pragmatism. They indicate unreliability.

Mr. Trump has made headlines by saying he is willing to work with Russia, "but only from a position of strength," while also adding that the United States should be willing to walk away from Russia if it is "too demanding." Since Secretary Clinton has so clearly staked out a position openly antagonistic toward Russia, comments like these from Mr. Trump make it seem like a dramatically different policy. In real terms, it is not. The key is cluing in to the code words. Whenever a politician in America speaks about positions of strength and not wanting to see an opponent too demanding, it is basically arguing for the very same position crafted by Secretary Clinton: the preferences of the United States will take priority, and working together only takes place if America is granted the clear leadership role. This attitudinal arrogance has been sanctified in Russian-American relations since the dissolution of the Soviet Union, and no president so far has seemed willing to blaze a new path. Mr. Trump's comments are not trailblazing: they are secretly masked to hide what will simply be more of the status quo. He will be partner to Putin as long as Putin accepts a subordinate role, which, obviously, seems highly unlikely.

The previous point is a perfect segue to what will likely be the real fuel between Trump and Putin—ego and machismo. These two things are currency to Mr. Trump. It is clearly what he admires about Putin: whether countries around the world approve or disapprove of Putin policies and initiatives, one thing is never denied—his power and undeniable sense of authority over his administration and system. That Mr. Trump sees this as something to admire does not in fact indicate a willingness to be "mentored" by Putin. Rather, it is far more plausible that the relationship will devolve quickly into a battle of egos. In America, this is often denigrated as a "pissing contest." When Putin called Mr. Trump a "bright person, talented without a doubt," it inspired Trump to respond: "I like him because he called me a genius. He said Trump is the real leader." In other words, substance matters not. Just be sure to stroke Mr. Trump's ego, and he will consider you a friend and partner. But what will his mercurial personality do when a disagreement on substance overrides any mutual-admiration society based on style? For Mr. Trump, it will be the end of partnership, the end of friendship, and thus, the end of "new" Russian-American relations. Ironically, Russia may find out that only Putin is the pragmatist. Mr. Trump is simply a narcissist.

In a bit of reverse psychology, Russia should be wary when one of the most biting opponents of Putin, the former world chess champion Garry Kasparov, vociferously proclaims how Trump is the American version of "Putinism" and that Mr. Trump's presidency would be the "best hope" for Russia. Kasparov's logic is that the election of Mr. Trump would severely weaken American democracy and rip apart positive trans-Atlantic relations. Put simply, Kasparov treats Mr. Trump like a de facto agent of Russian interests, i.e., Mr. Trump would be willingly subordinate to Putin. As mentioned before, ego and narcissism will not allow that. In the current state of Russian-American relations, when so many Americans are being fed stories about the adversarial aggressiveness of Russia, there simply is no evidence-based thought process to make someone believe Mr. Trump would buck American opinion about a so-called enemy. Rather, he is much more likely to sycophantically cater to American paranoia, in order to guarantee his own need for self-aggrandizement.

Finally, the comments of Konstantin Kosachev, chairman of the Upper House Committee for Foreign Affairs, illustrate perfectly how much of the hope on Mr. Trump is really just about the lack of hope with Secretary Clinton:

"New chances may appear only as radically new tendencies in the White House, and we are talking not only about pro-Russian sentiments, we simply need some fresh air, some 'wind of change' in Washington. Then, we can reset certain things and agree on continuation of the dialogue. . . . In the context of these two factors Trump looks slightly more promising. . . . At least, he is capable of giving a shake to Washington. He is certainly a pragmatist and not a missionary like his main opponent Clinton."

What this article has established is how misplaced such faith tends to be when considering Mr. Trump. People in Russia are making false connections: if you are not a missionary, then you must be a pragmatist. There are other more dangerous and damaging options in that equation. It is not binomial, 0 or 1. To repeat: just because Mr. Trump is not Secretary Clinton does not mean he is better or more approachable for Russia. His track record and personality indicate otherwise.

There are in fact some figures of cautious moderation in Russia, and they are offering wisdom on the coming election. People like Aleksey Pushkov, head of the Lower House Committee for Foreign Relations, and Fyodor Lukyanov, head of the Russian Council on Foreign and Defense Policy, while admitting their understanding of the immediate Russian attraction of Mr. Trump over Secretary Clinton, also emphasize how the system of Washington politics tends to bring any incoming president quickly to heel and that it is impossible to truly know what to expect from a Trump presidency. I think it is possible to reliably guess, however. For Russian-American relations to significantly change from its current negative status quo, the incoming president would have to be eager and intellectually motivated to instill innovative new political thinking and diplomatic pathways. Secretary Clinton has clearly staked her position in the ranks of the old guard of suspicion, skepticism, and distrust. Mr. Trump perhaps has not done this publicly. But his need to be adored and admired by the American public (an American public constantly fed a steady stream of negative perception and analysis about Russia and Russian leadership) means he would have to be willing to abandon the feeding of his narcissism for the sake of improved Russian relations. And while there are many mysteries in this world, one thing is most certainly *not* a mystery: the person whom Mr. Trump has always loved most of all is . . . Mr. Trump. Thus, Russia needs to be careful as it approaches the coming 2016 American presidential elections. Some loose assumptions and false connections are driving apparent loyalty to a candidate that is unlikely to offer anything close to what is hoped for. Indeed, it may just be the sad news that 2016 goes down simply as the American election that offers Russia option *C* as the best choice: none of the above.

Resisting Globalistan

Why Putin Is Winning the New Cold War

RAKESH KRISHNAN SIMHA DECEMBER 18, 2014

If history has taught us anything it is that Russia has a habit of grinding down its enemies. There are 7.2 billion people on this planet, but the United States fears only one man apparently—Vladimir Putin. That's because on virtually every front of the new Cold War, the Russian president is walloping the collective challenge of the West. Fear can make you do strange things—for the second year running, *Forbes* magazine has named Putin as the world's most powerful person. This piece documents how many non-Western countries and citizens outside the so-called Anglosphere regard all things Russian and American on the global competitive stage.

An old proverb says about the Russians that they take a long time to saddle their horses, but they ride awfully fast. After patiently nursing the collapsed Russian economy back to health from 1999 to 2007, Putin started pushing back against what he perceived to be the Western encirclement of his country. In Syria, Crimea, and Ukraine, the West has faced humiliating setbacks and melted away at his approach. In the high-stakes game of energy, it will be Russian—not Western—pipelines that will dominate the Eurasian landmass.

But instead of scorekeeping, a more instructive exercise would be to try and understand how Putin has managed to keep Russia ahead in the game. More than any other leader, the Russian president seems to deftly understand how the United States operates.

The American modus operandi—in sync with the British—is to organize coups, rebellions, and counterrevolutions in countries where nationalist leaders come to power. Iran, Chile, Ecuador, Venezuela, Panama, and Ukraine are some of the classic examples.

John Perkins writes in *Confessions of an Economic Hitman* (2004) how he and other "hitmen" like him were sent to developing countries as consultants to bribe or coerce diplomats, economists, administrators, and politicians to do the bidding of the United States. Often, they succeeded, but if they failed then the CIA would send in the "jackals"—professionally trained assassins who would engineer the deaths of those who stood in the way of strategic American interests. (Chilean prime minister Salvador Allende's assassination—the result of a request by PepsiCo chairman Donald Kendall to the company's former lawyer president Richard Nixon—is a classic example of a CIA jackal job.)

This one-two punch by economic hitmen and assassins was so effective in creating banana republics that the United States rarely had to up the ante. Among the rare occasions the United States had to use the formal military in pursuit of commercial aims was in Iraq and to a limited extent in Libya. Putin feels strongly that the United States has attempted—and will continue to attempt—regime change in Russia. As a former KGB officer stationed in East Germany, he knows the hitmen are looking for an opportunity. That's why he kicked out and labeled as rogue agencies such institutions as the USAID and British Council, both of which are deemed by many everyday Russians and decision makers in the Kremlin as fronts for Anglo-American secret services.

"One of the things to understand is that Putin in particular studied counter-intelligence, which is key in understanding why he's a critical player," writes Joaquin Flores in the Center for Syncretic Studies. "Counter-intelligence is not just finding spies, but it's actually countering the work of other agents who are embedded or whose work involves embedding themselves to destroy institutions from within." Parallel to American black ops is naked war. The US economy—and that of its sidekick, Britain—is a war economy. Kremlin adviser Sergei Glazyev said at a June round table in Moscow: "The Americans have gained from every war in Europe—World War I, World War II, the Cold War. The wars in Europe are the means of their economic miracle, their own prosperity."

The Nobel committee's choice of Obama sparked bitter controversies—he was the only Peace Prize winner waging two wars at the time of being awarded. Believe or not, Obama was praising war as an instrument of conduct even during the Nobel ceremony. "Clear-eyed, we can understand that there will be war, and still strive for peace." Waging war is not a way of imposing the will of the United States on the world, he said, but a way of seeking a better future for its people. "The instruments of war do have a role to play in preserving the peace," the Nobel laureate said, thanking the Committee.

The ongoing skirmishes in Ukraine are seen by Russians as a clear pretext to pull Russia into a direct military confrontation with Ukrainian armed forces, in order to create a regional war in Europe. Russia's response is two-pronged. One, by refusing to get into a shooting war with ostensibly Ukrainian thugs, it keeps the Americans frustrated. Washington's inaction in Ukraine was brilliantly described by a Chinese general as a symptom of America's strategic "erectile dysfunction." Secondly, Putin is employing asymmetrical strategies to stop—and ultimately bring down—American hegemony. A key element of this strategy is to strike at the key pillar of American power—the dollar. Russia—with support from fellow BRICS members China, India, Brazil, and South Africa—is moving away from dollar-denominated trade, a step that is aimed to seriously impact the barely growing American economy.

According to financial portal Zero Hedge, "Glazyev's set of counter-measures specifically targets the core strength of the US war machine, i.e., the Fed's printing press. Putin's advisor proposes the creation of a 'broad anti-dollar alliance' of countries willing and able to drop the dollar from their international trade initiatives. Members of the alliance would also refrain from keeping currency reserves in dollar-denominated instruments. An anti-dollar coalition would be the first step for the creation of an anti-war coalition that can help stop American aggression." Ukraine could eventually turn out to be the catalyst for Europe's divorce from the United States. This is because sanctions against Russia are threatening business houses in Germany and other western European countries, which have over the past two decades developed deep links with the Russian economy. "Somewhat surprisingly for Washington, the war for Ukraine may soon become the war for Europe's independence from the US and a war against the dollar," says Zero Hedge. Moscow is also pushing for institutional changes. The $100 billion New Development Bank, co-owned by the BRICS, will not only try to counter the influence of western lending institutions but also strive to stop the flow of cash from developing countries to the West exclusively.

The current lending system is skewed in favor of western countries because loans by the World Bank and the International

Monetary Fund come with a basket full of conditions. For instance, when these two outfits offer a loan, it can be used to purchase goods and services only from the West or the loan can be used only for building dams but not for, say, drinking water utilities.

Of course, the expertise and material for building dams will have to come from the United States and Europe. And when the drinking water supply remains poor, it creates demand for—mostly western-owned—colas and bottled water. The New Development Bank will, therefore, hit the West where it hurts most—in the business development–new markets pocket. Even as Putin has been making strong moves on the geopolitical chessboard, his opponents aren't sitting idle. The Russian ruble is getting hammered even as the price of oil is being driven into the ground by the Saudis at the bidding of their American partners. No surprises here—the Americans will relentlessly try to weaken Russia as it is the only country that stands between Washington and world domination. However, Putin is a judoka who knows how to use his opponent's force against the opponent itself. He's content to watch the Americans commit strategic overreach—taking on Russia and simultaneously trying to contain the rise of the BRICS nations.

Putin is fortunate that his heavyweight partners in the BRICS continue to back Russia in its tussle with the West. Both India and China agree Moscow has legitimate interests in Ukraine and Crimea. Recently, the BRICS challenged Australia for its foolhardy proposal to ban Putin from the G20 summit. Such assurances of support have emboldened Putin to show the West further defiance. In 2012, he nonchalantly skipped the G8 summit, and earlier this year he merely shrugged when the G8 went back to a G7—the pre–Cold War configuration.

If history has taught us anything, it is that Russia has a habit of grinding down its enemies. After Napoleon and Hitler, it could be the turn of the Americans to realize the dangers of bear-baiting.

(This is an updated version of an article that appeared in Tehelka *magazine, December 2014. It is purposely left in its strident tone so as to let Westerners read the attitude often found outside of the United States and the European Union.)*

The Real Estate Cold War

Russia and America Fighting over "Parity"

SEPTEMBER 1, 2017

This past week the United States informed the Russian Federation that it was going to immediately close the Russian consulate in San Francisco as well as two other properties that house trade missions in Washington, DC, and New York City, respectively. The Russian Foreign Ministry was told this was a tit-for-tat response to the maneuver done earlier in the summer when Russia literally evicted nearly half of the diplomatic and technical corps of the United States, dropping its number down to 455.

Not coincidentally, this number was chosen by Russia because it meant the number of American diplomats working in Russia would exactly equal the number of Russian diplomats working in America. Call it a personnel parity war. But it is when you look below the surface and follow the thread backward in time that one sees a conflict that borders on the farcically absurd.

Back in December, then-President Barack Obama actually closed, without much media fanfare, two Russian holiday retreats for diplomatic staff that were located in Maryland and New York, stating that the residences were instead being used for intelligence initiatives. In addition, thirty-five diplomatic corps members were expelled from the United States. Most of them were technical members and were at least suspected of being likely involved in the attempts to hack and disrupt the 2016 American presidential election. The Kremlin, of course, denied these allegations but by and large did not respond to these maneuvers. Given how tense and strained Russian-American relations were even then, it is plausible the Russians felt it would be better to simply wait out the exiting Obama administration and see what would come from the incoming President Trump. It is even more likely they considered the possibility of reversing these Obama decisions quite high, given Trump was declaring the need to reestablish positive relations with Russia and his overt passion to overturn just about anything done by Obama. But this is where the stability of American democracy and its system of checks and balances got in the way.

As more convoluted and confusing information emerged throughout the first half of 2017 about potential preelection interactions between Russian officials and Trump go-betweens, it became apparent that Trump dare not risk any major overt initiative toward Russia. Meanwhile, the Republican-controlled Congress has grown ever more hostile toward the mounting evidence of Russian electoral interference. It was this hostility that resulted in new sanctions being put upon Russia this summer, basically doubling down on the still-in-place sanctions over the events in Ukraine that have hampered the Russian economy for the last few years. It was this double-up that forced Russia to finally react and eject several hundred American diplomats from the country (although it is interesting to note that hardly anyone in the media here in the United States has asked why it was necessary for the United States to have nearly double the amount of diplomats than Russia had in America). Laughably, this most recent real estate closure initiative does not involve any diplomatic personnel leaving the United States: the only thing effected is the closure of the real estate. People working there can be reshuffled to other diplomatic assets in the United States.

Unbelievably, the State Department has officially said this was done so as to not just maintain the 455 to 455 parity in personnel but so now there will be closer parity between the two nations in terms of *property holdings within each country.* Even more unbelievably, the United States has said not ejecting the personnel from the closed properties was done "in an effort to stop the downward spiral in Russian-American relations." So, uprooting dozens of people and forcing them to move to another part of the country, where their jobs are likely already occupied by people, for example, in Houston, New York, or Seattle (the other places where Russian consulates are located), is not a worsening of relations? This is horrifically flawed diplomatic logic to say the least. So instead of a personnel parity conflict we have a real estate Cold War, and we are supposed to consider it an opportunity for improvement in Russian-American relations.

What we have now is a petulant schoolyard tête-à-tête more focused on each side trying its best to humiliate and hinder the other, while still officially stating before press conference microphones that there is hope relations will improve. Not likely. As is often the case in America, the United States government tends to be highly selective in its use of historical precedent. It traces problems in Russian-American relations currently to the actions involving the secession and reintegration of Crimea into the Russian Federation. Russia, of course, considers the Maidan revolution (which directly preceded and ostensibly caused the Crimea secession referendum) to be a fairly obvious attempt by the United States and the European Union to put adversarial authorities and policies right on the very borders of the Russian Federation. Follow that up with the original Crimea sanctions, which have devastated the income and buying power of most ordinary Russians, who have seen the ruble lose 100 percent of its value over a single year. The Kremlin, if you can get it to speak privately behind closed doors, will admit it considers this to be open interference in their domestic peace and prosperity by a foreign power, and thus the United States "earned" the cyber interference effort in 2016. We have a fundamental historical analysis problem between the two countries.

Foreign Minister Lavrov expressed his disappointment with the real estate closures but was hesitant to speak in any concrete terms about consequences or repercussions. But if precedent is any indication over the last five years, we can expect some strange countermeasure within a few months that involves the shuttering of American diplomatic offices or the like in Russia. It will not signal either side moving closer to out-and-out war, but it will also show that the opportunity for the two sides to find new ground for collaboration is purely symbolic. The Real Estate Cold War is in full effect. It won't bring about the end of the world in nuclear apocalypse, which is a good thing. But it does keep two major global powers acting like seven-year-old schoolyard bullies trying to one-up each other while the rest of the school suffers the consequences, which is a very bad thing indeed.

PART II

THE UKRAINE CONFLICT

Viva la Revolutsione!

Now, Don't Mess It Up Like Everyone Else, Ukraine!

FEBRUARY 24, 2014

When a leadership neglects the best interests of its own population, it is well within the rights of the people to attempt to remove this leadership from power. Ukraine is now in the subsequent stages of a revolution that has ousted the former president from power. Now, though, careful deliberation and planning is vital. Opposition leaders must not rush into conducting immediate elections, or they risk jeopardizing the very gains they have fought so hard to achieve.

I have no problem with revolutions. There is no shame in people taking to their own streets and overthrowing decrepit, negligent, corrupt, or evil national governments. Since most corrupt and authoritarian governments usually take great pride in how much they control and commandeer the collective methods of state violence, I have no sympathy when one cannot govern properly and resorts to putting down what is usually, relatively speaking, small pockets of unrest. I do, however, have major problems with a mistake that now seems to be common to every single revolutionary country in the twenty-first century: bending to pressure (often Western-initiated) to hold *immediate* new presidential elections on a very dubious and unrealistic timetable. This timetable in Ukraine, apparently set for May 25, is one of the fastest I have come across.

When you launch full tilt into new elections in a state that heretofore has been nothing but quasi-authoritarian—crippled by rampant corruption, poor institutions, controlled media, and crushed political dissent—then you are ignorantly creating the very recipe to make those new elections possibly detrimental to the very soul of the revolution itself. Think about it: in a country with no real sense of multiparty health, free media, measured political opposition, or robust civil society, what results can possibly come from a rush to hold elections? Only poor results.

Elections after a revolution in the twenty-first century seem to have basically become a great and mighty symbolic maneuver signifying nothing (at best). At worst, they collapse in on themselves or stunt the great success and hope felt by the initial revolutionary stimulus. Why does one think the joy and jubilation of the Arab Spring has already sprung a cottage scholarly industry on the new "Arab Winter"? There is a difference between the power, wisdom, cunning, and courage needed to undertake a revolution successfully and the same qualities that are required for successful democratic development. The world should not be so naïve as to think that these revolutionary qualities can then capitalize on the aftermath of that revolution and truly build long-term, stable, and healthy foundations for a better government and society. The latter is a new phase resting upon the shoulders of the former but requiring new talents and insights to truly succeed.

It does not matter if we are talking about places where revolutions have taken place or where the West might wish to see a revolution take place. It does not matter if we are discussing Tunisia, Libya, Egypt, Syria, Bahrain, Yemen, Iran, Kyrgyzstan, Venezuela, or Ukraine. Crucially, in the midst of the passion and self-righteousness of the victors, someone must step forward and push for careful deliberation and well-reasoned planning. The lack of such a strong organizational presence in all of these revolutionary venues is what inevitably spells doom for their hard-earned win. And given how tragic and self-sacrificing revolutions tend to be, that is always unforgivable.

So take a breath, Ukraine. Step wisely. Think thoughtfully and carefully. Ignore the Monday-morning-revolution couch quarter-backs in the West who will try to push and pull you in every which way, continuously emphasizing speed and tempo. It may bother many if you wait to hold elections, perhaps for another year. But it will bother everyone, ultimately, when they see how poorly your country fares because you rushed into new elections in just two and a half months. Breathe. And don't mess up in the same way everyone else seems to be doing.

The Dilemma of Duplicity

The Three Maestros of the Crimea

MARCH 8, 2014

The events transpiring in the aftermath of the "EuroMaidan" Revolution in Kiev are clearly multifaceted and complex. What is clearly not helping matters, however, is a pervasive duplicity reflected in each of the three main sides' behavior. The idea of duplicity being an integral part of any conflict and even a fundamentally basic aspect of foreign policy is not a new or radical idea. What's distressing, however, is the lack of clarity from the media, which is failing to consistently expose the duplicity, thus keeping a more accurate view of the Kiev/Crimea crisis distant from all concerned. Below are not the only examples of duplicitous behavior emanating from each side. Rather, they are just prime examples of *blatant duplicity* so egregious they stretch the bounds of credulity. Until each side rids itself of such insincere posturing, and until world media does a better job, the optimal resolution in Ukraine will remain out of reach.

UNITED STATES

The revolution has been presented in the West as the ongoing battle for Ukraine's political soul: Will it move west with the EU or east and back to Russia? Maidan is portrayed as an action against President Yanukovych siding with Russia and turning down a stronger EU trade relationship back in November 2013. What the United States seems to ignore in that decision was Yanukovych brokering a *$15 billion* Russian benefit package for Ukraine by not accepting the cozy EU relationship. Right or wrong, good or bad, semimanipulated or willingly volunteered, whatever one's position on that decision may be, it is irresponsible to underemphasize such a huge monetary gain. The United States has been fairly persistent in presenting that fall 2013 decision as an example of diplomatic stupidity on the part of the Ukrainian president, when in fact it was more reflective of a cold and calculated short-term decision being chosen over a longer-term vision. Perhaps it was not the best, ultimate deal for Ukraine's future. But it was also not a decision entirely absent diplomatic or economic merit.

The United States has also been quite happy to propagate an image of Russian troops entering into Crimea as a bold and blatant maneuver of Russian neoimperialism. This is not only underemphasizing the critically strategic presence of the Russian Black Sea Naval Base and Fleet, it is also conveniently ignoring the fact that Russia and Ukraine had previously signed an agreement approving a significant increase in Russian military boots on the ground in Crimea. The timing of the Russian entrance was certainly no coincidence and not done in a manner to put anyone at ease, but it is also not entirely without merit that Russia might have been concerned about its own previously signed accords (done to maximize its own global strategic interests). Pushing an image of Russia "trying to swallow Ukraine whole" is not only inaccurate, it runs the risk of being reckless exacerbation. Such a role should not be the United States' priority.

UKRAINE

While the new government in Kiev has been eager to capitalize on the tendency in the West to portray it somewhat like the innocent victim caught unawares by a menacing neighbor, it is not entirely without blame in this game of mutually reinforced duplicity. One of the final things Yanukovych was able to achieve before events in Maidan overtook him was a basic debt-forgiveness agreement between Ukraine and Russia for natural gas deliveries that could have ended up nearing an additional $2 billion. Russia was clearly amenable to the deal in return for the expected loyalty of a Yanukovych presidency. Despite leading a popular uprising that resulted in Russia's man being rudely deposited out of the Presidential Palace, despite voicing numerous protests in Western media about how its new government was being taken advantage of by Russia, and despite eagerly supporting a Western image that has portrayed Russia as everything from the "Old Soviet bear" to Hitler, the new authorities in Kiev still managed to release a press statement (little reported in the West) that it hoped Russia would honor its previous agreements with Ukraine, namely forgiving the near $2 billion in natural gas debt. Amazingly, the comments that came from Prime Minister Medvedev's office and the chairman of the Russian gas giant Gazprom were actually fairly demure—emphasizing that continuing the original deal made with Yanukovych was likely the best move for both sides. The question to be considered, therefore, is just how calamitous and WWII-like can a situation truly be when both sides are making nice behind the scenes over nearly $2 billion of debt?

RUSSIA

Russia is not immune to the criticism of duplicity. Some examples of its duplicity have been well documented and pushed in the West. The supposed inability to control pro-Russia militia members running around Crimea and it entering Crimea in order to safeguard ethnic Russians from violence and chaos are just two of the more ridiculous positions heard over and over again across Western media outlets. But a more subtle and substantive example can be seen in the fascinating and biting hour-long interview Putin gave to Russian reporters in his residence approximately one week after Russian troops entered Crimea. In this somewhat rambling speech, Putin said that Russia felt the events in Maidan constituted an unconstitutional coup and therefore not something to be supported. If the people wanted a change in leadership (and Putin even agreed in this interview that it was probably necessary), then they should use the proper democratic institutions to enact that change. This is entirely logical, well reasoned, and the proper line of action within any mature democracy. It is also, alas, utterly deceptive on the part of Putin. The democratic institutions in Ukraine are not exemplified by a vibrant civil society, an independent judiciary, a counterbalancing legislative, and a probing free press. Asking the people to utilize democratic institutions for change in a country that strives to be as hyperpresidential as Russia itself really means you are basically just telling the people to sit down, be quiet, and stop interfering with the elite decision makers.

Again, this summary of duplicity is not an exhaustive list. The importance in highlighting these more ridiculous and egregious examples is to show how often a conflict is exacerbated by the very parties most responsible for its amelioration. If Ukraine, Russia, and the United States truly want this situation resolved quickly and peacefully, they will do well to begin eliminating the gamesmanship each has been using so far to promulgate a vision of the conflict that is neither accurate nor peace inducing. In addition, continued failure to accurately emphasize and report this duplicity across the media is not just unacceptable; it is insulting to the interest and intelligence of all those who sincerely wish to see this dilemma resolved without bloodshed and violence.

Что делать, или, куда дальше?

What Is to Be Done, or, What Happens Now beyond Crimea?

MARCH 29, 2014

Why Ukraine should be disappointed: Crimea is done. As the famous Southern saying in America goes, "closing the barn door after the horses have left doesn't do much good." Authorities in Kiev are understandably displeased. They will remain displeased. They must learn to make peace with this defeat. And let's be honest: it is a defeat. A relevant piece of territory is now going to be part of the Russian Federation and no longer part of Ukraine. But Russia has the superior military force in Crimea, and the Crimean people have voted their own political will in a referendum that supports Russia. And please, no more discussions about its legitimacy. It was unfortunately laughable when the US Ambassador to the United Nations Samantha Power mentioned that such a vote would have to take place across all of Ukraine in order to be legitimate. If such logic is broken down it means the only way for such initiatives to be acceptable is when the entire state agrees to remove part of itself and give it to another country. This is not how secession usually transpires, anywhere, anytime. If the authorities in Kiev are guilty of anything, it's not understanding that revolutions do not happen in a vacuum: the assumption that their success in removing Yanukovich would be universally lauded and not considered from the strategic interests of other powers is beyond naïve. Western powers agreed the Maidan revolution was likely to be in their favor (keep in mind this is also an assumption not proven; just view Egypt and the situation of President Morsi for a recent example of a revolution's unintended consequences and how quickly positive assumptions can turn into negative reality). Russia could not make such automatic positive assumptions about the Maidan revolution, and so it made maneuvers to solidify its interests and future objectives, regardless of those in Kiev or Brussels or Washington. Any half-measured, ill-conceived attempts to retake Crimea would be counterproductive and potentially dangerous.

Why the United States should be disappointed: Russia outplayed it. Not only did the United States not anticipate the initial Russian maneuvers into Crimea, subsequent threats and warnings from American authorities have not so much fallen on deaf ears as amused ones: when a presidential aide to Vladimir Putin reacts to sanctions by saying the only thing relevant to him about America is the deceased iconic rapper Tupac Shakur, Allen Ginsberg, and Jackson Pollock (and he doesn't need to go to America to enjoy them), then you can rest assured the deterring power of your sanctions have long since jumped the shark. Present efforts to lend support to Poland and the Baltics are not actually about American power preventing further Russian aggression but are a rather deft maneuver to take attention off of Crimea and move the focus to Eastern Europe. Why would America do this? Because it is an unspoken acceptance of the fact that Crimea is over and the United States lost. If the focus can be moved to Poland and the Baltics, where Russia has no intention of invading, it is a small face-saving gesture for the United States: it may not have "saved" Crimea, but at least it prevented the conflict from spreading to neighboring countries. I have no doubt Russian authorities find this interpretive logic as laughable as the Power comment above, but saving face is also a major element of foreign policy, and so hopefully Russia will let it pass. Thus, the American disappointment, but it must be accepting if it wants further peace and stability. Any forced argument that tries to physically eject the Russian military presence in Crimea or tries to undo the Crimean referendum would be counterproductive and potentially dangerous.

Why NATO should be disappointed: Who is NATO anyway? These events have only affirmed how lifeless the organization seems to presently be. It really hoped events in Crimea would provide its main members in Western Europe evidence as to its continued value and relevance. But it has been a nonentity in Ukraine, and its focus now on "shoring up Eastern Europe and bringing Russian power to heel" is shocking to me in just how empty it is. It is not so much that Russia outmaneuvered NATO (which it did, going back in this situation all the way to 2008, when it basically put the kibosh on preliminary talks about Ukraine becoming a NATO member). Rather, if you want to know why NATO has no teeth and seems a bit aimless today, then you need to look accusingly at Western Europe, which really didn't want "too much" of a continued American military influence over the continent once the Soviet Union disappeared. The dominant Western European thinking at the time was that the "peace dividend" of the 1990s made NATO superfluous. That is why NATO is the emperor with no clothes. Russian strategic maneuvering in Crimea perhaps flashed a light on this reality, but it did not create the reality. Thus, the NATO disappointment, but it must be accepting if it wants further peace and stability. Any explicit initiatives where it tries to actually provoke or incite Russian reaction with hyperbolic posturing would be counterproductive and potentially dangerous.

Why Russia should be disappointed: it should not bite the apple. Attempts at Western posturing and redefining events aside, it is hard to overstate just how complete the Russian victory on Crimea has been, despite attempts in the West to understate it. Putin followed his own country's constitutional protocols and caught potential adversaries completely off guard in terms of his intentions, efforts to reverse his gains are weak, his maneuvers were ultimately affirmed by the very people of Crimea, and his military forces didn't suffer a single casualty. In American football terms, this would be a blowout. But despite this complete strategic domination, Russia is best off if it doesn't bite the apple of political temptation and try to further capitalize on this victory. One of the key elements of strategic superiority is understanding when to press forward and when to magnanimously pull back, satisfied with your winnings. This is that time for Russia. It must not give in to the seduction that might be the eastern half of Ukraine or, even worse, affirm Western suspicions about its intentions in Poland or the Baltics. The oft-quoted proverb about it being better to keep your mouth shut and have people think you are a fool than to open your mouth and remove all doubt applies here: it is better to have people think you are a menacing, militaristic, imperialist wannabe—while doing nothing—than to act and confirm for people their worst suspicions. Thus, the Russian disappointment, but it must be accepting if it wants further peace and stability. Any rash overreaching or impolitic grandstanding that would only portray Russia in a more intensified, negative global light would be counterproductive and potentially dangerous.

And so here we are. As all sides move forward and consider the eternally prophetic Chernyshevsky question—What is to be done?—hopefully everyone will heed the argument that sometimes disappointment can be the most productive and least dangerous path. At least it is in this case for all the sides mentioned.

Beware the Sheep with Fangs

MARCH 30, 2014

Starting to heat up the internet (well, at least in Russia and Eastern Ukraine, though it will likely not even be acknowledged in Western Europe) is a hacked telephone call last week between the former deputy secretary of the National Security and Defense Council Nestor Shufrich and the former prime minister, recently-freed-from-prison media darling Yulia Tymoshenko. The recording, which lasts just over two minutes, pulls no punches as Tymoshenko and Shufrych basically excoriate everyone associated with the events in Crimea, regretting they are not able to, in turn, shoot people in the head, fire nuclear weapons on them, and march down to Crimea themselves and start an armed retaliation campaign against all those who were for the referendum to secede from Ukraine and rejoin Russia. Tymoshenko is especially intense in her bravado, claiming that if she had been able to get down to Crimea the people would have been eating (expletive deleted) instead of succeeding in holding the referendum.

I am not able to say at this early time that there can be no doubt whatsoever about the recording. Reliable sources in both Ukraine and Russia have authenticated it, but competing opponents have decried that it is either fake or—that famous Western media lament—"was taken out of context." Personally, I'm not really sure how making the region eat excrement or threatening to use nuclear weapons on people or shooting them in the face with automatic weapons can actually be taken out of context. Such threats are fairly explicit no matter what words precede or follow them. Interestingly, whether the recording is a perfect representation of the conversation between Shufrych and Tymoshenko or a total fabrication is actually not as relevant to me as a more subtle issue: just how poor Ukrainian leadership is at the moment and how this does not bode well for its immediate future.

I have written in the past as to how I am no fan of Yanukovych. One of the motivating factors that pushed Yanukovych to accept the more immediate, short-term oil and gas deal with Russia (which many attribute as the empirical factor that launched the Maidan revolution to begin with) over a more speculative, long-term trade relationship with the European Union was how poorly his country had been fairing economically. Quite frankly, Ukraine had become such a disorganized economic mess that it needed the money in real terms then rather than in more prospective terms later.

What perplexes me is how people in the West continue to blame Yanukovych for this decision while remaining so quick to point out how much unfair suffering Tymoshenko has had to endure, sent to jail in 2011, charged with exceeding her authority as prime minister by signing a new gas deal with Russia in 2009 that the rest of the cabinet opposed. Many claimed the charges were ludicrous: Tymoshenko may have made a poor decision, but not an illegal one. Yet the West makes an angelic quasi-martyr out of Tymoshenko *for the exact same action* that forced Yanukovych to flee a revolution? Why is Tymoshenko's deal "bad but not criminal" while Yanukovych's deal is worthy of forcibly ending his electoral term without new elections? *Both* deals were economic agreements signed with Russia. Is it just the fact that Tymoshenko's was not done against a backdrop of possible EU collaboration (and so the

West didn't care) while Yanukovych explicitly turned away from an EU gesture (and so the West suddenly found an interest)?

Again, please allow me to repeat that I really don't care about Yanukovych losing his seat of power. As Machiavelli himself made clear centuries ago, if you can't hold it, you don't deserve it. The fact that Yanukovych can get his main political opponent sent to jail for doing the exact same maneuver that he hoped would save his claw-hold on power three years later shows what a self-serving and manipulative "leader" he actually was. I think Putin himself has made it clear in subtle terms that he doesn't really care who governs Ukraine as long as positive, normalized relations with Russia continue (call it the Syrian Assad Gambit, if you will). He favored Yanukovych over Maidan leaders in Kiev because his assessment was that those leaders would likely try to kowtow to Brussels and not Moscow.

But this gets us back to the original point: the horrible options available for Ukrainian governance. While most in the West won't bother to go back far enough to see the extent of the Tymoshenko career arc, the former "Gas Princess," quasi-oligarch, disgraced former prime minister even changed her physical appearance over the years, discarding the Alpha Business Queen dark chic she preferred to the lighter, halo-plait, blonde-crown Ukrainian Princess brand that has been her political alter ego. Always a firebrand with a mouth to match her temper, this vulgar verbal history might be the thing that makes the hacked phone conversation so believable: it simply sounds like something Tymoshenko would say. And that is indeed a problem. It hints at narcissistic egomania that cares nothing for diplomatic statesmanship and rising above the fray, something most in the West would say is essential for effective leadership in an open democracy. After all, there are no such hacked phone conversations with Obama screaming obscenities about all the nasty and horrific things he would like to do to House Republicans in Congress for how they constantly try to derail Obamacare. You can rest assured he would like to do that very thing but understands true statesmanship forbids it.

And so here we sit. Yanukovych was no leader and helped run Ukraine into the ground while having gilded toiletries installed in his presidential residence. Tymoshenko emerges from prison and clings to a Western media image that paints her as some modern version of Joan of Arc when in reality she is more likely to be Yanukovych with a braid: wanting the presidency just because she thinks it's her right rather than because she believes she can better the plight of the Ukrainian people. I don't take the hacked recording seriously, even if real, simply because it comes off not so much as a viable threat—Ukrainians being incited to kill Crimeans—as it does whining from the political losers. But that doesn't make it any less relevant that Tymoshenko felt empowered to speak that way and formulate her thoughts in such barbaric and base terms. Beware the sheep with fangs, Ukraine. In the end the blood it spills might just be your own and for no good reason other than to satisfy its own power lust.

The Unintended Precedent of Maidan

MAY 5, 2014

Oh, how fickle and strange revolutions can be. Perhaps the Western academic world can be forgiven for its presumptuousness. After all, it has been nearly a generation since the dissolution of the Soviet Union and the subsequent march of "democratic revolutions" all over the globe. Or what has been hailed as a march of democratic revolutions. What has erupted all over the globe has largely been the triumph of democratic language: most regimes, whether they truly resemble democratic best practices or not being of a secondary concern, have usually couched their activities in decorative democratic language. Naturally, opposition movements emerge and challenge the status quo by claiming to be "more democratic" or "truly democratic," thereby setting the stage for the outside world to decide which side is telling the truth more accurately. It is not always an easy choice. Whether it has been in Southeast Asia, Africa, Latin America, Central Asia, or the Caucasus, what the world has usually seen is a corrupt and/or dysfunctional regime replaced ultimately by opposition figures or parties that come to be almost as corrupt and dysfunctional, if not more so. The momentous events that have been characterized as the Arab Spring have not led to waves of Arab democracy providing new hope and prosperity to peoples and communities that were downtrodden and ignored. Rather, there has been a grinding, inexorable, plodding progress, at best, of countries that discovered soon enough that identifying the problems was far easier than actually solving them. In that, I suspect Ukraine will be no different, no matter how many elections, reforms, or "repositions" the country goes through. But that is not what is most interesting from an academic perspective. Rather, it is the fairly unique set of structural circumstances in and around the Maidan revolution that can be largely to blame for how poorly things have gone for the Maidan revolutionaries.

Consider: most revolutions in the twenty-first century have been positioned as protests against corrupt regimes and thus have themselves largely escaped the microscope of political analysis until much later. Georgia, Kyrgyzstan, the first Ukraine (the "Orange" one), Egypt, Libya, Yemen—all of these protest movements were first and foremost lauded for their ability to overcome entrenched regimes that seemed more interested in personal enrichment and cronyism than functional governance. As it turned out, none of the revolutionary movements created great governing regimes themselves, with a few even ending up victims of additional revolutions later on. The Maidan revolution is quite different from this twenty-first-century Western academic trend of analytic largesse, however, in that there was a geopolitically powerful neighbor right next to the revolution that happened to have a very great interest in how things evolved. Think on it: in the aforementioned revolutions there was either no strong power nearby deeply interested in how affairs on the ground played out, or the strongest power was the United States from a great distance just hoping an autocratic regime would fall one way or another. In the Maidan revolution this was not the case: Russia was very much interested in the long-term, geostrategic consequences of regime change, and it was the blind laziness of Western academia that simply missed the obvious reasons as to why that would be so. Or, again, because of an intellectual presumptuousness that had come to afflict most Western scholars to believe any toppling of a crony-like regime would only be applauded by all players, regardless of long-term consequences. To this day you will be hard pressed to find much Western media/academic coverage analyzing or considering legitimate Russian interests in long-term Ukrainian political affairs. Those responsible for leading the Maidan revolution were equally blind or presumptuous: while they are quick to lay blame on Russia now, it is obvious going back two months that they were completely caught unaware and off guard that anyone on the outside would have words or actions for their behavior other than simple congratulatory phone calls. Obviously this has proven to be a rather large mistake.

A second aspect to play out from the Maidan revolution (the Crimean referendum) is also rather unique and an academic special case study worthy of greater attention that as of yet has failed to be recognized here in the West. Most of our studies dealing with regions trying to secede tend to be examples of true secessionist activity, i.e., the region wants to become its own country. Crimea not only went against trend in that it wanted to join another country instead, it went far against trend by wanting to join a country that was superior to the original host country in every political, financial, military, and geostrategic way. Just because no one talks about it doesn't eliminate its crucial relevance: What is one to do when a region with a long history, ethnic connection, cultural ties, and geostrategic relevance to a larger, richer, and more powerful country next door wants to leave the chaos of its current host nation for the more peaceful pastures of the bigger, badder brother? As far as I can tell, most in the West bypass this question by focusing on concepts like "territorial integrity" and "national sovereignty," when we all know these concepts, though undoubtedly sound and unoffending, are not exactly universally acted upon. They are universally spoken about but not always universally supported in all cases or even always in the United States. So I am not sure if I should be so stunned or bothered by the fact that Russia might not support these concepts either. Indeed, one can feel sorry for Ukraine. It has been dealt a rather bad hand, one it could never have expected as the reveling on Maidan Square took place so many weeks ago. But the people of Crimea, and in turn now the people of Eastern Ukraine and Odessa, seem to be basically saying, "You can have your traditions of international law for all we care. What we really want are the traditions of international *dating*. Why should we be forced to keep dancing with the partner we don't want when the partner we truly want to dance with is standing there waiting to tango?" As silly as that analogy may seem, its logic makes more sense to the people of Eastern Ukraine today than any discussion about territorial integrity and national sovereignty. If these regions were looking to become independent states, then it would indeed be a biting criticism to ask them if they were better off remaining a part of Ukraine. But what is the answer to the question these regions actually want posed: "Aren't you better off becoming a part of the Russian Federation?" Just because the West and Kiev want that question obliterated from the news doesn't mean it is any less relevant to the actual people in the eastern half of the country.

And so here we sit. Eastern Ukraine remains unsettled. More casualties mount. Accusations fly about Russian subterfuge as authorities in Kiev violently struggle to preserve Ukraine's larger territorial mass. How it will all play out, for better or for worse, is beyond anyone's guess. But in the meantime I will wonder if this

Ukrainian revolution, the Maidan revolution, might not end up setting a very unique precedent for all future revolutions moving forward: namely, be careful what you wish for, and don't count your chickens before they hatch. It is indeed a treasure trove of academic trendsetting. It just seems to be a situation no one in the West wants to recognize.

To Live and Die in Donetsk

JUNE 13, 2014

Not that anyone would notice, but there is a disturbing and quite frankly depressing reality taking place in Eastern Ukraine. While it is true the conflict that rages has been largely downplayed now and shoved off the media spotlight in the West, whatever coverage does emerge tends to be giving a relative free pass to Ukrainian police forces, special operation forces, and the military as they seek to reinstitute control over their national territory. At first glance this does not sound particularly offensive: after all, a country should have the right to protect its sovereignty and ensure that various groups do not arbitrarily try to secede. But a deeper glance reveals that the way you do this in the modern era is by killing people. And unfortunately, these casualties cannot be universally declared as enemy combatants or unlawful separatists, despite authorities in Kiev wishing to push that very scenario to their own people and outward to the rest of us in the West. There have been many civilian casualties in Eastern Ukraine over the past two months. These people simply had the unfortunate circumstance of being born and living in Eastern Ukraine while having no connection whatsoever to politics in Kiev or geopolitics in Moscow or foreign-policy strategy in Washington. The silence regarding the sad circumstances of the civil unrest in Ukraine is laden with blatant hypocrisy and the rationalization of killing.

It should be recalled that when the prospect of violence breaking out in Eastern Ukraine was a major media issue in the West, approximately three months ago, the protests and indignation and opposition were voiced primarily under the context of expecting that violence to come from Russian military forces invading the country. It was the assumption that the only way authorities in Kiev would take to arms and resort to violence was if the Russians made it inevitable with their own attacks. This is clearly *not* what has happened in Eastern Ukraine. Russia did not invade. Whatever Russian intelligence or special operation forces happen to be in Eastern Ukraine at the moment, they are decidedly and some might say surprisingly inactive. Collecting data? Reporting back to Moscow? Absolutely. But actively being the sole forces responsible for fomenting violence and civil unrest within Eastern Ukraine? Absolutely not. Just as the authorities in Kiev misplayed their hand after the Maidan revolution, assuming all parties across the world would universally praise and support their removal of the president, they badly analyzed the situation on the ground in Eastern Ukraine.

In several media interviews I gave in the United States following the referendum in Crimea, I warned that the greatest possible danger in Ukraine would be civil groups in major Eastern Ukrainian cities looking to Crimea as a model to emulate and at the Crimean referendum as a precedent to follow. The reason I said back then that this was the greatest danger was because it seemed to me that the relatively dull and boring aftermath in Crimea would clearly instigate local opposition groups in Eastern Ukraine to follow suit. After all, why can't these cities and regions have the same advantages and privileges that the people in Crimea just apparently earned for themselves with no violence or damage done to their region? Not only was this potential copycat effect obvious, in my opinion, but the consequence was equally so: authorities in Kiev would have to act against these maneuvers; otherwise they would be basically saying to the eastern half of the country that it would be perfectly acceptable to disintegrate. My challenge in those media interviews was for the authorities in Kyiv: Could they outmaneuver these opposition forces in Eastern Ukraine without resorting to violence and bloodshed? Failing to do so seemed to be an open invitation for the Russian military to actually come in order to protect the lives of ethnic Russians. This was the irony of Eastern Ukraine: no one in the West took the Russian entreaties seriously when it was said the lives of ethnic Russians needed to be protected in Crimea. How ironic, then, if it turned out that Russian forces would end up needing to invade Eastern Ukraine because ethnic Russians were in fact being killed with impunity.

But that is not what has happened. People have died in Eastern Ukraine. They continue to die in Eastern Ukraine. They die largely because of one side's forces. But those forces are not Russian. And here in the West there is basically silence. There is no indignation. There is no wringing of hands. There is no rending of garments. Apparently, the killing of people in Eastern Ukraine is only disturbing to the West if it happens at the hands of the Russian military rather than at the hands of Ukrainian forces. Yes, it is true that civilians always die in war and that civil unrest often results, historically speaking, with many civilians being killed in the crossfire between opposition groups and loyalists. I am not naïve of these basic facts in the history of war. But what is sadly disappointing is to see so many countries that were lined up to make sure conflict did not erupt in Eastern Ukraine when it was thought said conflict would come from the Russians basically turn the other cheek and turn their media cameras away from the bloodshed and the slaughter of these very same people simply because the flag doing the killing is yellow and blue instead of white, blue, and red. I doubt that the people of Eastern Ukraine feel that it is an atrocity to die by a Russian bullet but an acceptable loss to die by a Ukrainian one. Unfortunately, it seems that certain governmental and media groups in the West have made that very conclusion. Therefore, we see the quiet continuation of violence in the name of sovereignty and territorial integrity. To live and die in Donetsk is indeed a cynical web of global geopolitics.

Saving Lives or Saving Face?

Sanctions, Russia, and the West

JULY 16, 2014

New sanctions were levied against Russia on July 16 by both the United States and the European Union. America has taken the lead in explaining the sanctions, claiming continued unrest in Eastern Ukraine is primarily because of tacit Russian support behind the scenes. This new round is a bit broader than the original sanctions from a few months back that tried a new tactic of strategically targeting individuals. Basically, it was one of the first examples of a state trying to make Putin's personal friends hate him (which of course had little to no impact on Russian foreign policy, and if it had, to be completely honest, I would have been spectacularly unimpressed at the lack of resolve on the part of the Russian government). These sanctions—which target strategic industrial firms involving energy, banking, and arms manufacturing—are meant to signal the West's resolve to make Russia stop supporting what it calls "pro-Russian insurgents." Obama himself commented that he hoped this sent the message to Russia that actions have consequences. In this case, support of rebels in Ukraine will be directly responsible for supposedly weakening the Russian economy and intensifying diplomatic isolation. To all of this President Putin's reaction can be summed up in one word: YAWWWWWWWWWWN.

Indeed, the diplomatic tête-à-tête that has gone on between the West and Russia over the past few months over Ukraine should lead any non-emotionally invested observer to wonder: If sanctions come down in a forest, do they make any noise? So far the answer seems to be a resounding *no*. Original sanctions were meaningless. These sanctions supposedly have more teeth, but what triggered them? What did Russia do in particular that suddenly made the West feel it was essential to launch new action?

The Pentagon announced that Russian troops were building up along the border. Of course, for those of us who have followed this conflict for the past half year, we have heard this accusation at least half a dozen times. Sometimes there has been evidence to partially support the claim. Sometimes the claim has seemed utterly baseless. But what has been universally consistent across all of the accusations of Russian troop buildup along the border of Ukraine in 2014 has been one single thing: *no Russian troops have moved into Eastern Ukraine or launched any major military offensives*. Even intelligence and diplomatic agencies in the West have been unable to find evidence of this, so it seems that Russia was punished today for, well, for having its soldiers hang out on its own sovereign territory. Sanctions based on possible mental intent, let's call them, which leads me to wonder if these sanctions are based not on what Russia is doing but on what the West really, truly, desperately, breathlessly, deep-down-inside-it-just-can't-stand-it-anymore *wishes* Russia would do.

I wrote just a couple of months ago that Russia's best strategic foreign-policy move after the events in Crimea would be to *not* take the bait of getting bogged down in the internal chaos and instability of Eastern Ukraine. Not only did I not see any major strategic, economic, or political advantage in such a maneuver, there was a decided surprise victory in *not* doing anything: with the West expecting a Russian incursion at any moment (some might even say posturing to incite it), not giving the West its narrow-minded foreign-policy assumption about Russian objectives would in and of itself cause such consternation and confusion that at the very least it would provide countless hours of humor and amusement to all who sit in the Kremlin and at the most give it a position of diplomatic leverage and strength. This is, for all intents and purposes, exactly what Russia has done.

What has been disappointing is to see countless political actors and diplomatic agencies in the West fail to capitalize on Russia's relative restraint to create new opportunities for discussions, negotiations, and settlement agreements. Instead Russia's nonincursion has almost been relegated to the Twilight Zone, where Western leaders will first admit no one can find significant numbers of Russian troops inside of Eastern Ukraine but then still say everything going on inside of Ukraine is Russia's fault. Even today's analysis of the situation on the ground, which seems to show pro-Russian rebel forces weakening, causes concern in the West that they will try to hunker down for "extended urban warfare." The irony of course is that the forces in Eastern Ukraine so far responsible for hitting civilian buildings, incurring civilian casualties, and pursuing actions that closely resemble urban warfare have been the formal military and police agents of Ukraine and not the pro-Russian separatists. Nevertheless, given the aforementioned trend, if conflict in the east of the country becomes a protracted and nasty street-to-street, building-to-building infestation of violence, it seems likely Russia will be found responsible for it, even if its troops are still just "building up at the border" but causing very little excitement besides smoking cigarettes and drinking the occasional vodka shot.

I have always been quick to point out that conflicts are never clean. There are rarely if ever pure heroes or villains, and every side in a war clearly has its own agendas and interests and will do for the most part whatever it can to see those objectives achieved. War has always been this way, and it is highly unlikely that war will start being something different any time soon. But this internal unrest across Ukraine has been a rather frustrating event, at least for those few of us in the West who feel in our foreign-policy heart of hearts that Russia and the United States line up better as allies rather than adversaries. The new leadership in Ukraine has not been able to stop the unrest, and it has certainly not made people excited about the country's future. The European Union has been even less impressive at creating peace, and quite frankly its initiatives pre- and post-Maidan have arguably caused more chaos and instability than calm and tranquility. The United States has clearly been frustrated by these two facts and has not been able to come up with something innovative or progressive that might create a new road to stop the violence.

And this is what leads to the frustration: faced by these extended cases of political failure and diplomatic impotence, the players seem to have not boldly striven for new ideas and novel initiatives but rather have fallen back to the tried-and-true tactic of conjuring a bogeyman. Clearly, that bogeyman is Russia, as it is both convenient and easy. Alas, it is also lame and somewhat pathetic, because this tactic is not about stopping war but rather about finding blame. As Bob Corker, the top Republican on the Senate Foreign Relations Committee, said today: "While the delay in imposing real costs on Russia has been damaging to US credibility, today's announcement by the administration is definitely a step in the right direction."

Today's sanctions are not so much about saving lives as they are about saving face. This is not about sanctioning conflict but about salvaging credibility. Unfortunately, this has hardly ever stopped a war. But, even more unfortunately, it has often started a new one.

This Little Piggy Won't Be Missed

JULY 25, 2014

One of the odd things inevitably lost in the mire and labyrinth of complex high politics is how often executive leaders purposely and subtly prolong conflict, confusion, and corruption because to minimize it or to make progress against it will signal the start of actually assessing the effectiveness and power of their own leadership. This seemed to be what Ukraine was experiencing under the guidance of Arseniy Yatsenyuk as prime minister. Now that he has resigned, let us make sure his leadership is not inaccurately assessed and evaluated. Ukraine can do better.

It is easy to forget, since it was never highly emphasized in Western media to begin with (a special exception goes to Forbes.com, which has always looked skeptically and critically at Yatsenyuk, even before he was elevated to his present primary leadership position), but Ukraine's prime minister was a rather uninspiring and noninnovative thinker, whether that be politically or economically. His appeal to Western power brokers was his ability to be pliable, to be worked, to be a "company guy." Of course, the company in question for this discussion was the European Union, not the sovereign national interests of Ukraine.

And that seemed to cause major problems for the new Ukraine: the only thing it discussed was whether or not it would follow EU interests or American interests or Russian interests. Its own leader was not apparently striving to carve out and determine what might be truly *Ukrainian* interests and then figure out how those interact and coordinate with the interests of others. This is the high politics formula of foreign affairs and has been so for over a thousand years. Not engaging this formula properly basically means the leader of Ukraine was simply trying to decide which power group to be a vassal state for. This is disappointing, but perhaps not unexpected.

Yatsenyuk was not simply a technocrat (and we all know there has never been a new or innovative idea, *ever*, from such types), he was a relatively little-regarded technocrat in his own country just six months ago. At the beginning of the year he trailed in local popularity to figures such as the boxer Vitali Klitschko and the rather wild nationalist leader Oleh Tyahnybok. This is not an exactly inspiring pedigree to pin your political future to as a country. But what Yatsenyuk had was the interest of the European Union and the United States. Again, not because he was particularly awe-inspiring or truly seemed to stand out amongst all possible choices for a better and stable Ukraine: he was the candidate who was most willing to maintain a staunch opposition to whatever maneuvers or initiatives came out of Russia while also not having many independent ideas of his own. And that revealed itself to be one of the major stumbling blocks to closing the chapter on the Ukrainian conflict.

So what did Yatsenyuk leadership actually translate to? Basically, economic austerity and political frigidity toward Russia. That's it. That's all it was. On the economic side I would be hard pressed to find any objective financial observer to say Ukraine's best bet is to look admiringly at what Greece did to itself while trying to follow EU austerity plans and rules. And yet Yatsenyuk's ideas didn't evolve much beyond that position. On the political side I would be hard pressed to find any truly objective foreign affairs advisor who would think ignoring Russia or dismissively pushing away any and all attempts at negotiations and peace talks that came from Moscow is sane and rational. But that is what Yatsenyuk did and continued to do repeatedly, because this was what the European Union wanted, and he had hitched his wagon exclusively to it.

In America there is an old term that applies to such behavior: pigheadedness. It is something that goes beyond merely stubborn or obstinate. It carries a tinge of irrationality and intimates that such a person can and does do things that may even be detrimental to their own interests, just for the sake of remaining an obstacle or barrier to some other side or group. This is how I would characterize Yatsenyuk's leadership: it didn't really follow reality, or observe cold, calculated logic, or seem arranged for Ukraine's best interests. But it *did* stand in the way of working with Russia as a partner where both sides accepted that they had some mutual interests and some conflicting interests. That is why countries come to the negotiating table. That is the fuel of foreign affairs. There is no reason to sit down if everyone already agrees, nor is there a point in sitting down if all someone intends to do is stubbornly repeat individual positions with no give and flexibility. This is why Eastern Ukraine still sits in such discomfort today: the prime minister had no interest working with the side willing to sit down (Russia) while staying "true" to the interests of the "partner" (the European Union) that has no intention whatsoever of getting more deeply involved in the impasse. The obstinacy of Yatsenyuk's leadership has resulted in the emptiness and despair of prolonged and impotent conflict where the victims, in this case the people of Eastern Ukraine, are abandoned in real terms even while their country's leadership endlessly drones on. Welcome to the vision of a pigheaded technocrat.

It will be interesting to see what will come of this trend now that Yatsenyuk has resigned. For in the end surely this trend must be broken. Hopefully it will not be done with reintensified military conflict and more senseless civilian deaths. And while I have no doubt that Yatsenyuk's hope was that he could create a more active and financially preemptive European Union "coming to his rescue," I am more inclined to think that Ukraine's more realistic best bet would be to accept the reality of disbalanced power and actually try to interact with Russia so that it can achieve a sense of peaceful stability and finally be able to truly govern itself and strive to pull itself out of this political and economic morass.

Then again, maybe the cold, harsh light of media scrutiny on how Ukraine is being truly governed is exactly what any of the possible new leaders are afraid of most.

Putin

Cleaning Up an American Mess

OCTOBER 6, 2015

The recent appearance of Russian President Vladimir Putin before the United Nations was a must-see for any Western analyst who wants a deeper access to Russian global affairs thinking. The traditional mistake made, by Americans most certainly, is to dismiss Russian argument as nothing but crying over spilt geostrategic milk: in short, since Russia lost the Cold War and lost its beloved communist system, it cannot stop whining about the victor. While there is no doubt that there have been some examples of resentment by the Russian government over its fall from grace off of the bipolar world stage, it would be reckless and unwise to permanently paint Russian diplomacy with the bitterness brush. American political recklessness can indeed be found just as much, if not more than, examples of Russian diplomatic petulance.

Indeed, some of the more memorable quotes from Putin's speech are in fact ideas he has spoken openly about for the past decade:

> After the end of the Cold War, a single center of domination emerged in the world, and then those who found themselves at the top of the pyramid were tempted to think they were strong and exceptional, they knew better.

> An aggressive foreign interference has resulted in a brazen destruction of national institutions. . . . Instead of the

> triumph of democracy and progress, we got violence, poverty and social disaster. Nobody cares a bit about human rights, including the right to life.
>
> We are all different, and we should respect that. No one has to conform to a single development model that someone has once and for all recognized as the right one.

The problem in all of this, of course, is that the United States will adamantly defend its good intentions in each and every case of foreign intervention and/or pursuit of its national interests on the global stage. Ironically, Russia has been the only country to date that accepted the American right to behave in this manner *but only if that right was granted as a universal reality of global affairs and power disbalance*. And that is where the United States and the Russian Federation have always wildly disagreed. I have written many times before, much to the chagrin of my American colleagues, that on this one point at least logic and consistency side more heavily with Russia's argument. Anyone who studies international relations knows well the internal philosophical dilemma between politics as they are versus politics as they ought to be. Think of it as Locke and Rousseau fighting against Hobbes and Machiavelli. Russia openly and unabashedly accepts global affairs as being the exclusive, realist domain of Hobbes and Machiavelli: life is brutish, nasty, and short, and the preservation of power is not moral or immoral but rather an amoral pursuit that is simply about capability and effective strategy. Before you think that means America sits squarely on the side of Locke and Rousseau, on the side of freedom and civil liberty, think again: America has always been equally ready to recognize the nastiness of foreign affairs and the deviousness that is sometimes required to get a mission accomplished. But America is just about the only country on earth that can recognize that reality while simultaneously proclaiming itself and its own behaviors as somehow above such realist ends-justifying-the-means gamesmanship.

Welcome to what drives the Russian diplomat absolutely insane with incredulous frustration. Russia (and to a lesser extent China) has always dismissed this inconsistency. In fact, some might argue Russia has been somewhat gleeful in pointing this hypocrisy out. This was exactly what was happening this past week at the United Nations with Putin's speech. The Russian president basically stood back from the podium, symbolically spread his arms out wide, and, with a Cheshire-cat grin, declared to the world watching: "So, America, are you happy now? Are we ready to get serious about cleaning up these messes now?" While most of America has been critiquing the Russian presence in Syria as just a cheaply veiled attempt to keep Assad in power while supposedly trying to do damage to DAESH, Russia looks on bemusedly and says, "Ah, yeah, exactly. What's your point?" After all, it was over three years ago that Russia publicly said the removal of Assad from Damascus might not be all that America was cracking it up to be: the rebel alliance seemed to be a fractured and disorganized band of miscreants. While some were true rebels aiming to topple a decrepit regime with the democratic experiment that had been washing over the Middle East in general with the Arab Spring, there were plenty of others who were crossing secretly over the border from Turkey looking to help radical Islamists fill what could be an expected power vacuum.

Russia will always be worried about radical Islamists on its southern flank. The fact that this happened to be taking place in a country whose leader was politically aligned with Moscow just made the decision-making calculus simpler. Thus, when America lobs an accusation that Russia isn't fighting DAESH but supporting Assad, Russia with complete sincerity responds that it is openly and unashamedly doing *both*. The only country in the world more afraid of or against the spread of radical Islam than the United States is Russia. It also does not have a problem with countries determining and preserving whatever system of power central authority can maintain (see quote above). No, Russia does not believe this principle results in the most free, most open, and most democratic societies emerging. But it does believe this principle keeps the global stage far more stable. American contradictory experiments in tampering (where it believes that it is exceptional to all other countries but that its exceptional system and beliefs should be exported everywhere else) is what rocks global equilibrium to Russia. China has always believed in this reality as well. But it is Russia that has taken on the unique responsibility to call the United States out for it. Again and again and again.

What some might think is that Russia's protests are a diatribe against American arrogance or Russia striving to resist American "moral imperialism." I think this is an overstatement. I don't believe Russia worries about such things. It may state things to that effect for the mere drama and "media sexiness" of calling America out. But the real reason Russia stands against the posturing of American exceptionalism is that it sincerely believes it leaves nothing but a mess behind. The worry is not that America is taking over the world (anyone who looks at Iraq, Afghanistan, and now Syria understands that American intervention doesn't result in any immediate and positive American interests), even if Russia thinks America might *want t*o take over the world, fantasy-style. No. The problem is that America never truly actively commits but rather "half-commits" to its interests. This is what results in the chaos. Russia entering Syria and actively conducting air raids on various DAESH and rebel positions is simply Putin saying, "*This* is our priority, and so we will act. Because we have the power to do so, and therefore it is our right." Russia believes America acted upon this same right with all of its adventures overseas. What's good for the American goose will always be seen as also just fine for the Russian gander. At the very least, there is something refreshing about a country stating where it stands and then acting exactly in accordance with that position, rightly or wrongly. And for anyone who knows Russia and Russian history, this aspect, of charging forward whether it is undeniably proper and correct or irrefutably brash and impatient, is wonderfully consistent with the Russian foreign-policy character.

Hypocrisy, Crisis, Catharsis

IGOR IVANOV JULY 7, 2015

A stronger EU-Russia partnership now looks like a pipe dream, reflects former foreign minister Igor Ivanov. On the plus side he sees less hypocrisy on both sides and outlines five steps toward repairing the relationship. Interestingly, those five steps are still crucial and yet still not anywhere close to being implemented even today.

Relations between Russia and the European Union are in deep crisis—perhaps the most serious crisis since the end of the Cold War. As the Russian Federation's former foreign minister, I particularly regret this bleak state of affairs, as along with my European counterparts I myself invested much time and effort in building a stronger Russia-EU partnership, with all its political, social, economic, and humanitarian dimensions.

Many of our past plans and hopes now look like pipe dreams that are remote and seemingly irrelevant to today's grim realities. I am sure that many in Europe share my frustrations and concerns, although there is little sense in just being disappointed and pessimistic. We should instead analyze the mistakes and blunders of the past in order to reveal the opportunities of the future.

The most graphic manifestation of the deep gap that has emerged between Brussels and Moscow is, of course, the situation in and around Ukraine. We can debate endlessly about who is to blame for this situation and whether it could have been avoided. Both Russia and the European Union have, in my view, contributed to the escalation of Ukrainian problems and so both should bear their fair share of responsibility for the unfortunate developments in that country since autumn 2013. As I see it, though, Ukraine has not been the main cause of the Russia-EU crisis. Rather, it has been a product of the more fundamental rifts that have emerged between Moscow and Brussels over the last few years. In short, the Russia-EU partnership has not worked out in the way that had been anticipated some ten to fifteen years ago.

So, the question must be, what went wrong? Unless we look back into our past, we cannot realistically plan our future. Twelve years ago, we agreed at the 2003 Russia-EU summit in Saint Petersburg to proceed with the so-called "four spaces" in our cooperation. I was personally involved in drafting these four spaces and I still believe that it was a very important achievement in the relationship. Later, these four spaces were to be complemented by the EU-Russia Roadmaps supposed to define specific goals, schedules, and benchmarks in each of the spaces.

Since then, we have not made a lot of progress. In many ways, we have lost ground and not gained it. We failed to sign a new EU-Russia partnership agreement to replace the old one that expired long ago. We couldn't move to a visa-free regime between Russia and the Schengen zone and were unable to reconcile our differences on the European Union's "third energy package." Even on less controversial matters like research cooperation, environmental protection, and transportation, our progress was modest, to put it mildly.

That said, I would not want to downplay the efforts of the committed men and women in both the European Union and in Russia who did much to bring cooperation to a new level. Yet the overall balance sheet isn't impressive. It is true that our economic cooperation continued to grow until 2014, as did the scale of EU companies' investments in Russia and the number of joint ventures. But the relationship's institutional framework failed to catch up with these new economic realities, so the gap between businessmen and politicians grew wider and wider, then turned into an abyss during the crisis over Ukraine.

Why didn't we succeed in using the last fifteen years to their full extent? Why could the private sector on both sides not lobby for a new level of political partnership between Russia and the European Union? One of the most common explanations is that on both sides politicians were distracted by such other priorities and events as the global economic crisis of 2008–9, the conflict in the Caucasus, complications in the eurozone, the relentless rise of China, the Arab Spring, the US-EU transatlantic trade and investment negotiations (TTIP), and so on. There may be some truth in this explanation, but what does that prove? It only tells us that for both the European Union and Russia, their mutual relations seemed of secondary importance and could therefore easily be shelved or even sacrificed for the sake of more central and more urgent needs.

The Ukrainian crisis has thus become a very explicit manifestation of the fragility of our relations. Both sides pursued their own policies toward Ukraine without any coordination, or at least consultations, with one another. The question of the "European choice" for Ukraine was raised only in the old "zero sum game" logic of the Cold War. I am myself convinced that with the necessary efforts on both sides we could have avoided the Ukrainian tragedy—at any rate in the dramatic form it has finally taken.

Rather than emphasizing the differences in our approaches and blaming each other, we should have looked for what unites us in this extraordinary situation. Above all, neither the European Union nor Russia has anything to gain from Ukraine becoming a failed state in the center of the European continent. On the contrary, such a development would create a whole range of fundamental threats and challenges to everybody in Europe, not to mention the countless tragedies and suffering it means for the Ukrainian people. It will now be much more difficult to restore the relationship between Russia and Europe than it was only a year ago, but we have no alternative to limiting the damage and moving ahead.

A lot has been said about the European institutional deficit that was clearly demonstrated by the Ukrainian crisis. And it's certainly true that the many European and Euro-Atlantic organizations and mechanisms that were specifically designed to prevent or to resolve crises failed to do so—with the qualified exception of OSCE, the Organization for Security and Co-operation in Europe. Instead, the crisis gave birth to new forms of international cooperation like the so-called Normandy process. This new format may look extremely fragile and shaky, but it at least demonstrates our common ability to make tangible progress under even the most difficult circumstances.

Where, then, should we go from here? In my opinion, five urgent steps are needed if we are to start repairing the badly damaged EU-Russia relationship.

First, we must prevent any further escalation of the military conflict in the center of Europe. The Minsk agreements have to be implemented in full by all the sides without any exceptions or procrastinations. All violations of the agreements by rebels in the east or by the Kiev authorities should be brought to light and properly investigated without resort to bias or double standards.

Second, we have to enhance and broaden the Normandy format. Aside from sporadic meetings at the very top or at foreign ministers' level, we need a permanent high-level contact group in Kiev that will work on a day-to-day basis with the parties to the conflict. It is critically important that the United States should be included in the contact group to avoid any misunderstandings or failures of communication across the Atlantic.

Third, Russia and the West should refrain from hostile and inflammatory rhetoric that fuels public mistrust and hatred. The vicious spiral of today's propaganda war has to be stopped and reversed—at least at the official level—if we do not want to turn the current crisis into a long-term confrontation that will divide our common continent for years, if not decades, to come.

Fourth, both sides have to invest political energy and capital in rescuing what can still be saved from the best days of EU-Russia cooperation. So far as is possible, we should maintain our joint projects on education and research, in culture and civil society, environmental protection, and climate change. We should try to preserve our successful trans-border cooperation, contacts between Russian and European regions, and between "twinned" cities. These are the seeds of the future renaissance of the EU-Russia relationship.

Fifth, the time has clearly come to explore opportunities for closer and more intensive contacts between the European Union and the Eurasian Economic Union (EEU). The EU has little to lose by reaching out to this neighboring integration project, while in terms of influencing the emerging EEU's standards, mechanisms, procedures, and modes of operation, the rewards could be handsome.

I don't want to imply that we should be getting back to "business as usual" by ignoring the deep political divisions between Moscow and Brussels. That approach wouldn't work even if both sides were prepared to stick by it. But one of the positive side effects of this crisis is that there is today less hypocrisy and political correctness between Moscow and Brussels. Unless we learn the lessons of this crisis, mistrust, instability, and losses in both East and West will continue to multiply.

First published by the Europe's World summer 2015 edition under the title "The Tough Lessons of the EU-Russia Crisis."

PART III

DIPLOMACY, ECONOMICS, AND FOREIGN POLICY

The United States and the Problem of Being a Geopolitical Prom Queen

MARCH 6, 2014

I have some bad news for the United States. Russia doesn't listen to America. Unfortunately, I have worse news: contrary to what many specialists, analysts, and commentators across the transatlantic community may think, it is not because Russia is trying to rekindle the Cold War or desperately grasping at whatever remnants of old Soviet power it used to have. No, I'm afraid Russia doesn't listen to America because of the unfortunate tendency of the United States to act like a geopolitical prom queen.

In the past it has warned Russia about how it acted with Chechnya, China, Venezuela, Iran, and Syria but ultimately done nothing. It is now warning Russia that "there will be costs" if it acts inappropriately in Crimea and onward with greater Ukraine. One might forgive Russia if it reacts to such warnings with a giant foreign-policy yawn.

Let us look briefly at Ukraine. Yanukovych was a thug. But he was a thug popularly elected in his own country. He was elected via means that were clearly not free or fair and rife with corruption. But despite "official American protest" about these corrupt elections, they still went through without any major interference. The main consequence of this acquiescence was a reign of corrupt negligence full of largesse, abuse, and misrule. Which despite "official American protest," again, also went on uninterrupted until his own people forced him out. In short, one doesn't see the boy who cried wolf when looking critically at American foreign-policy posturing; it sees the petulant prom queen who cannot understand why people will not follow her rule and who seems surprised that her crown does not translate into instantaneous and actual obedience.

America doesn't stand on the geopolitical high ground, either, if it wishes to critically assess Russia hosting/harboring Yanukovych. Cozying up at one time or another with questionable leaders because they happen to look favorably upon your own global positions and foreign-policy interests? Hello, (place any number of developing corrupt nations from Latin America, Africa, Middle East, and South Asia here).

None of this is meant to say America shouldn't be critical of Russian motivations or Russian interests. In many areas the two countries are pure rivals, let alone the long, intense history of competition between them. I am simply critical of the foreign-policy hubris America so often exhibits. I offer this not as a plea for diplomatic humility or being a better global partner: on the contrary, I simply fear the presumptuousness of American posturing comes off in such a way that makes the United States look silly rather than intimidating. That is the real problem. Talking the talk without ever walking the walk with Russia serves no purpose other than to undermine your own self-perception of impressiveness. To wit: American commentators need to stop crowing about the Ukrainian situation being an example of "Russian exceptionalism." There is a humiliating irony being dangerously missed when they speak of such things. The only other country in the world with a richer, deeper, and more pronounced sense of exceptionalism is the United States. And the Russians know it. American sides criticizing Russia for exceptionalism falls on such a deaf ear in Moscow it cannot be overemphasized. For Russia, that is like the great white telling the bull shark not to be so aggressive in the water.

Russia's coming actions within, around, and about Ukraine will no doubt be self-serving, in pursuit of its own priorities, and with only a modicum of consideration, at best, as to what is in the long-term interests of Ukraine. More pertinently, it will no doubt couch those actions with declarations of constitutionality, stability, normalization, and international assistance. And in doing so Russia, in its own mind and with some foreign-policy evidence, will be acting just as the United States has countless times in countless arenas over countless years. This is the true nature of *real foreign-policy* power: to do as you please while getting everyone else to drag their feet and ultimately do nothing. Such old-school, realist *power* has not left the global stage, despite all the good intentions to create greater adherence to international law and build actual foundations for global governance.

It is incorrect to say Russia is invading Ukraine. Its strategy was never "rush and overwhelm." To be frank, it was "sit and squat." The aftermath of a revolution is a time when many states would feel almost obligated to engage the instability, real or perceived, in order to safeguard their strategic interests or further enhance areas of strategic import that need improving. Russia doesn't want Ukraine. Russia wants control of Crimea (whether that means Crimea seceding into Russian Federation territory or just de facto controlling the territory doesn't really matter to Russian foreign-policy/military strategists). Crimea's importance to Russia as its sole warm-water port means it has been and always will be a strategically crucial area for Russia. It just saw the opportunity arise because of what happened in Kiev. So their plan is to sit, squat, stay, and see if anyone on the global stage will make enough ruckus to force them to leave. Right now, even money is on no.

America really cannot stand when Russia acts as if it still has a right to behave in a heavy-handed and self-interested manner on the global stage. What the United States must come to realize is that Russia envisions such action as simply staying on the dance floor and following the rules of the dance already in place. It does not grant the United States exclusivity for acting in accordance with its own state interests on the global stage. No doubt this irritates the United States. But until those warnings actually come with something other than "promises of stern consequences," it is highly doubtful there will be any behavioral modification. Please remember, America, that the prom queen in the end isn't really a queen after all, and on the global dance floor there is always more than one self-professed belle of the ball.

Putin and the West

To Dance or Not to Dance?

MARCH 31, 2014

These are the days of garment rending. Obama's recent trip to Europe to shore up greater resolve and commitment for strengthening sanctions and isolating (or is it shaming?) Russia after the Crimea annexation (or is it secession?) was fairly uneventful. The fact of the matter is no one in Europe seems to be all that eager to truly push violent confrontation with Russia as long as Russia doesn't seem intent on trying to obtain other new pieces of territory. Of course, no one in Western Europe approves of how things went down in Crimea. But despite constant bleating in the West about Russia's greater aspirations to violate sovereignty and its alleged desires to reinvigorate old Russian visions of imperial grandeur, the empirical reality in Crimea is that things were, well, rather dull: the Russians came, they saw, they sat down and refused to leave. That pretty much describes the affair in a nutshell. And so far, nothing else has happened.

An uninvolved but curious reader in the West would think that last statement is utterly farcical. On any particular day you can read dozens of articles and opinion pieces attesting to military movements here and troop and materiel organization there that can only possibly mean one thing: preparation for a massive Russian incursion into a whole host of different areas, most notably the eastern half of Ukraine. There are very few American reporters venturing an alternative viewpoint (the accomplished Jim Maceda of NBC

News is one of the few). Think tanks and academic institutes are not doing much better. The powerful and extremely influential Foreign Policy has clearly drunk the Russian imperial Kool-Aid, putting out no less than a dozen articles in the past month veritably guaranteeing the dictatorial intentions of Vladimir Putin (the most recent one coming just three days ago, offering ten reasons why "no one should believe Putin when he says he is not going to invade Eastern Ukraine"). And this is what prompts my rather presumptuous opinion as to what President Vladimir Putin can do: namely, just keep laughing, and, for goodness' sake, don't make Foreign Policy look right.

The issue at hand right now is that too many powerful decision makers in the West feel a bit bamboozled and outplayed. They feel, rightly or wrongly, as if they have ended up with proverbial egg on their faces, and they don't like it. Even worse, they cannot stand the possibility that this game of chicken ended after only one round with no opportunity to regain the upper hand. Thus, it really isn't about how horrible it was for Russia to "annex" Crimea (with Crimean consent) and do it basically without any violence. What is most horrible to these rather dull thinkers still stuck in and/or pining for the return of a Cold War environment full of purpose and dire circumstances is that they won't get the chance to beat Russia back or deliver a diplomatic defeat of the same intensity that they feel they just received themselves. Thus, this situation cannot be just about Crimea. Russia must not be satisfied with this as the endgame. There simply must be another shoe to drop or chess piece to be moved. Because . . . well . . . just because: because Russians aren't supposed to be diplomatically agile and astute. And they most certainly cannot be strategically deft and subtle. At least, not when they are compared to their counterparts in the West, who think Russians are rash; Russians are emotional; Russians are capricious; Russians are sneaky; and quite frankly, Russians are a bit daft. All of these things they can be, because all of these things suit the players at the other end of the chessboard. And for this very simple and seemingly minor reason alone, Russia is far better off letting Crimea be its one and only move on the board. What victory could be better than checkmate *and* confounding your opponents, who had previously thought they had completely understood your psyche, methods, objectives, and purpose? Eastern Ukraine is nothing compared to that value.

And so, if I were President Putin, I would not make a move. I would allow Crimeans to continue to voice their satisfaction with their own political status. I would stoically receive news of sanctions with little fanfare or drumbeating of my own. And, as they say, I would watch everyone else sweat as they desperately sit and hope for a sign of aggression and invasion only to ultimately have their hopes dashed. I say this not because I am secretly rooting for Russia over my own America or applaud anything transpiring in Ukraine. I say this because the world will *not* be a better place if America and Russia renew a rivalry based on old hatreds and stale misperceptions. If there is going to be a rivalry, let it be one not reminiscent of the fear and panic most of the world suffered from for fifty years. Let it be *Game of Thrones* and not *The Walking Dead*. Most of all I do not want to see Russia affirm a few critical decision makers in the West so eagerly and earnestly hoping for a return to stereotypes.

In the world of intelligence studies, we are taught to analyze situations amorally, apolitically, and unemotionally. This is not because we do not have a rooting interest or a personal preference but because only cold and callous perception leads to accurate and astute analysis. And accurate and astute analysis, lacking in emotional drama and macho bravado, has a higher possibility of finding resolution instead of pushing exacerbation. And so, for Russia, now is the time to do nothing. Do nothing, and, quite frankly, you win. Do something to affirm the shrill harpies craving another chance to "face the Russian enemy," and we all lose. Honestly, times will be much more interesting if all sides on the board have to recognize a new side to an old foe. I would prefer to live in interesting times, not violent ones.

The American Failure behind "Grand Strategic Cultures" and Modern Conflict

NOVEMBER 2, 2014

This work is about how a specific conceptualization of culture in intelligence studies, among scholars at first but subsequently practitioners as well, has taken on too powerful a role, one that has become too restrictive in its impact on thinking about other intelligence communities, especially non-Western ones. This restriction brings about unintentional cognitive closure that damages intelligence analysis. My argument leans heavily in many ways on the fine work of Desch in security studies, who cogently brought to light over fifteen years ago how ultrapopular cultural theories were best utilized as supplements to traditional realist approaches and were not in fact capable of supplanting or replacing realist explanations entirely. Intelligence studies today needs a similar intellectual intervention as it has almost unknowingly advanced in the post–Cold War era on the coattails of security studies but has largely failed to apply some needed corrective measures that discipline enforced on itself when it came to cultural approaches over the past two and a half decades.

In the early literature within intelligence studies there were two traditions of culture that, while affiliated with each other, were still quite distinct. The more accurate version, in my opinion, dealt with intelligence culture more in the manner of organizational culture, with its commensurate, almost corporate-like elaborations. A second, broader version coexisted alongside this, tied more intimately with the concept of a country's strategic culture grandly defined. This version stated intelligence cultures would be fairly accurate mimics or mirrors of the grander strategic national culture. Every country's strategic culture would be inevitably unique, tied within a complex web of language, history, local custom, religion, ethnicity, etc. In its time as a discipline, intelligence studies has shifted from the quieter, more humble, and quite frankly more accurate and accessible conceptualization of organizational culture to the grander one that is inherently more mysterious: semiknowable at best. This is of course rather ironic given that the nation most responsible for this push is the state with by far the largest, most organizationally micromanaged intelligence community and is almost always victim to the accusation by other nations of having no true, definable culture at all *not* dependent upon innate, business-corporate concepts.

The semimystical conceptualization of intelligence culture has important consequences: it can actually cause scholars and practitioners to get bogged down searching for "intrinsic essences" of a grand strategic culture when all they should rightly focus on is how national security priorities can suddenly or surprisingly change and evolve, forcing intelligence communities to alter and adapt their organizational culture and subsequent priorities and foci. It is very much like the corporate mind-set. In fact, intelligence communities by training and objective strive to be pragmatic and noncultural. For some reason, intelligence studies over time has transformed this innate pragmatic struggle and made it more about problems within a state's unique grand strategic culture, whatever it may happen to be. This not only oversteps the mark in terms of how we should be pursuing our research in intelligence studies, it does not accurately reflect reality as it encourages scholars to ignore important modern minutiae that would otherwise be emphasized in a system focusing on corporate organizational culture instead. I find a connection with this process to the cognitive closure discussed brilliantly by Hatlebrekke. Indeed, I am basically arguing here that overadherence or overemphasis on this grand strategic cultural approach to intelligence evaluation often induces its own cognitive closure among scholars and practitioners, thus leading to inaccurate analyses and conclusions.

Intelligence communities by hook or by crook seek optimal information for gaining optimal insight over a dynamic, evolving issue range. This is especially so for non-Western intelligence communities, which often have to deal with political instability, an absence of the rule of law, and no real clarity as to the rules of engagement between government and intelligence. Thus, this work is both a rebuke against how the concept of grand strategic culture has evolved to dominate the research thinking of intelligence studies scholars and a plea to consciously return to the less grand but more accurate tradition of corporate organizational culture as a primary causal pathway to determine modern non-Western intelligence community behavior and priority making.

Let's take two very distinct quick-glance cases to illustrate all of this high-minded theory: the rise of radical Islam in the 1990s and the conflict in Eastern Ukraine today. There are *tons* of scholarly, diplomatic, and journalistic confirmations since the 1990s testifying to the fact that the United States always had ample opportunity to understand the threat Osama bin Laden and Al-Qaeda could represent to the country. While this intelligence failure has been examined from numerous sides that deal with communication gaps, bureaucratic infighting, and turf wars, what has been largely ignored is the fact that the national myopia on the part of America can be largely explained by its overreliance on this grand strategic cultural approach of intelligence, which simply dictated to the entire country in the 1990s that America was impervious to any external terrorist threat. If it had jettisoned this approach and instead focused on the more corporate organizational cultural approach, then all of the aforementioned information could have gained greater focus and relevance.

The conflict in Ukraine today is still massively misconstrued in the West. Once again, it is the overreliance on grand strategic culture that pushes the problem. This approach leaves an analyst with no choice but to begin from a foundation that assumes Russian aggression, Russian aspiration for reestablishing empire (whatever that actually means is never defined, of course), and Russian desire to interfere in the affairs of its neighbors. All of these approaches are overblown and sometimes purposely misconstrued for the agendas of other parties. When utilizing an organizational cultural approach for intelligence, however, one is forced to look more carefully at the economic, political, and military agreements and deals that were *already in place and meant to be enforced* when the Maidan revolution took place and forced the Ukrainian president to flee. Focusing on the aftermath of that removal and the consequences to those microrealities goes much further in explaining how the conflict has proceeded across Eastern Ukraine. The failure of the West to understand this or to know how to engage the conflict so as to be a positive source for resolution rather than a hindrance to all parties is still stronger evidence of how the grand strategic cultural approach forces analysts to think in limited, stereotypical, and highly polarizing ways, let alone the fact that accuracy is reduced as a consequence.

Since it is useless to close the scholarly barn door after the intellectual cows have escaped, the proposal here is to adopt the term "condition" to take the place of the organizational concept of culture and allow the grand strategic concept of culture to maintain its naming rights. To understand intelligence communities—their beliefs, priorities, and operational goals in the modern day—one need not be a prophet of a country's particular and parochial grand strategic culture. One simply needs to focus on the strategic and dynamic intelligence conditions that engage, create friction, and produce change—sometimes slowly, sometimes quickly—within the community in question. This call for a similar "Deschian" intellectual intervention that took place within security studies more than fifteen years ago also offers intelligence studies a chance to properly differentiate itself as a discipline from its big brother and thus further solidify its place within the pantheon of intellectualism.

Bears and Byzantium

How America Misreads Russian Grand Strategy

NOVEMBER 26, 2014

Common complaints within intelligence studies about the examination of foreign intelligence communities, especially those not residing in the West, run the gamut from being too historically driven to being completely ahistorical and thus nothing more than a simple organizational review of facts and details to being too often inevitably compared against a standard framework that uses either the United States or the United Kingdom as the backdrop. While these analyses are all important, they have failed to look at how the competing conceptualizations of culture within the discipline engender entirely different approaches and therefore radically different conclusions about how we view and evaluate said communities. Below is a "case glance" of the phenomenon utilizing the Russian Federation. Perhaps most interesting and fairly unexpected is how, in terms of security affairs, American understanding about Russia seems to be hurt more analytically by grand strategic culture and is almost never analyzed from a perspective that emphasizes contemporary reality, purpose-based objectives, and actual organizational functionality.

RUSSIAN FEDERATION

Despite every effort by officials within the Russian Federation since the end of the Cold War to implement a new foreign-policy strategy and to instigate new relations based on ideas of multipolarity and balanced global power, most American analyses of Russia cannot seem to get past characterizing every Russian maneuver and interest in a grand strategic cultural way. When this is done, Russia is inevitably seen as aspiring to new "great power" status or attempting to reconstitute Soviet glory or is subconsciously beholden to an autocratic instinct that dates even further back, to the czars or even back to Byzantium.

This type of cognitive closure is detrimental to American intelligence and diplomacy because it is purposefully limiting the potential frames of engagement between the two sides. In many ways the United States, both in terms of its scholarship and diplomatic efforts, has blindly created self-fulfilling prophecies when it comes to the Russian Federation because of a repeated inability to see past its own reliance on grand strategic culture as the chief defining point for understanding Russians. This type of thinking is what led outstanding scholars like Samuel Huntington as early as 1993 to make statements like, "If, as the Russians stop behaving like Marxists, they reject liberal democracy and *begin behaving like Russians* but not like Westerners, the relations between Russia and the West could again become distant and conflictual." In the same vein, scholars seem to think the modern day has no real relevance to understanding Russian foreign policy and intelligence/national security prioritization. This incredulous overreliance on ancient culture, where scholars and practitioners alike believe the roots of all Russian decisions in 2014 require an understanding of the Russian soul from five hundred or even a thousand years before, leads American analysts down a rabbit hole of quasi-mysticism and vague truisms. This is why so many Russian intelligence officials scoff at American analysis, whether it is from the ivory tower or Foggy Bottom.

> Of the organization of the Soviet and subsequent Russian state we can draw no specific indication of Byzantine bureaucratic organization, but *in spirit* the way the Soviets organized their government for security purposes is still quite Russian. . . . What is being argued here is that the way the Byzantines managed their security and intelligence was a function of the political culture of the state, the same political culture that was inherited later by the Kievan and then Russian state, and which has served the Soviet and subsequent post-Soviet Russian state.[1]

The above has been singled out, for it is truly an exemplar of the kind of analysis that passes for grand strategic culture when examining Russia. Not only are the arguments nonscientific, they are ultimately spurious: these analyses are not trying to ascertain the true motivations of contemporary Russian intelligence decisions. Rather they are trying to make sure Russia stays within the frame that already exists. This is cognitive closure at its worst: where the question "Why do they do what they do?" transforms instead into "What kind of Russia do we want, and how do we make sure it becomes that and that alone?" Grand strategic cultural thinking on Russian intelligence reveals relatively little about modern Russian thinking for American analysts, but it reveals a wealth of information on American thinking for Russian analysts.

An emphasis on grand strategic culture will actually make for better reading, as you will inevitably be taken down a road of

1 K. C. Gustafson, "Echo of Empires: Russia's Inheritance of Byzantine Security Culture," *Journal of Slavic Military Culture* 23 (2010), 591.

the most interesting and intense historical and cultural impacts, possibly going back thousands of years. Organizational cultural conditions will instead leave you diving into budget concerns, internal turf wars over specific issue areas, and the changing dynamics of microsubjects that might not even make the paper, let alone a history text. But those conditions are the things that reveal the most about the contemporary prioritizing of intelligence communities, much more so than fascinating turns down history lane. More importantly, there seems to be a disconnect in our discipline where the more important security/intelligence countries are dominated by grand strategic cultural analyses. Perhaps that is a reason we seem to make so little headway in better understanding those impactful intelligence communities like Russia.

America v. Russia

Bringing a Knife to a Foreign-Policy Gunfight

JULY 7, 2015

In some ways the United States has played a very strange, self-injurious game since 1991 when it comes to Russia. On the one hand, it expects that the former rival accept a new stage after the dissolution of the Soviet Union in which there are no more fundamental ideological battles and that DEMOCRACY, in big capital letters, is the clear and undisputed victor.

Accepting this outcome means that, as the greatest champion of democracy, the United States is implicitly supposed to be considered the world's only superpower, the hegemon with no rivals. On the other hand, while expecting Russia to acquiesce to this state of affairs, America still tends to see Russia as scheming to relive Soviet glory days and interacts with Russia only on its own terms and in that distrustful light. Given this general backdrop, it is a bit disingenuous for those of us feted as "Russian experts" to question why Russian-American relations have been such disjointed, bipolar affairs for the past generation.

What remains fascinating and frustrating, however, is the continued Cold War residue that refuses to leave the stage when it comes to how the United States and Russian Federation deal with each other. Too often the instinctive academic and diplomatic figures in the West place responsibility for poor relations exclusively on the Russian side. While Russia undoubtedly plays a major role (it does indeed take two to tango), there is an inexplicable absence of focus on the culpability of the United States in fostering this negative interaction. Foreign policy is difficult enough, let alone when sides refuse to recognize geopolitical reality.

This situation only worsens when you get to the specifics. Since 1991 there have been three major situations with direct Russian military involvement that gained intensive scrutiny from the United States: Chechnya, South Ossetia, and Crimea / Eastern Ukraine. In Chechnya, Russia was often privately outraged that many in the United States characterized that conflict as a battle for independence by an oppressed minority rather than a war against radical religious extremists engaging in terrorism. In South Ossetia, Russia was outraged once more when it was accused of invading another country when it felt it was justifiably responding with strength to unrest and instability threatening its own North Ossetia (which resulted in Russian peacekeepers being killed, according to the United Nations) and sending an appropriate force message to Georgia to stop exacerbating the situation between North and South. In Crimea / Eastern Ukraine, Russia is bluntly pursuing its own foreign-policy interests during a time of political turmoil in a region that was once its own (Crimea was given to Ukraine in the 1950s with an air of diplomatic indifference, as the expected eternal nature of the Soviet Union made the "gift" irrelevant—i.e., Moscow would always control it from afar), while listening to the West say it is trying to ultimately occupy all of Ukraine and possibly beyond.

In each case, when you look back over numerous media, academic, and diplomatic sources, the word "imperialism" factors prominently: Russia's motivations in each case were not based on national security interests but were instead founded on its inevitable need to regain an old Soviet nature. This Cold War residue even made the categorization and scope of the conflicts themselves a source of political discord: in the West, Chechnya often became "Southern Russia," South Ossetia became "Georgia," and Crimea has now become "Ukraine." In other words, time and again Russia preferred keeping situations more case-specific and minimalized, while the United States (in Russia's opinion at least) effectively re-characterized the situations so that they seemed more far reaching and tyrannical in terms of danger and concern.

No doubt even more galling to Russia has been the need to answer such criticism while the United States has pursued decidedly more aggressive maneuvers on a global scale without interference and relatively minor criticism. Russia did not interfere when campaigns were launched in Afghanistan and Iraq. Russia did not interfere with maneuvers in Libya and Yemen. What Russia bristles at is when America characterizes its own maneuvers as somehow being something "above" basic foreign-policy priorities and national security objectives while everything the Russian Federation does in much the same light is declared neoimperialist or in violation of international law.

Make note: this is not any lame or manic anti-American diatribe. Russia is not anti-American. Russia is simply first and foremost pro-Russian, just as it expects and assumes America to be first and foremost pro-American. And here is the tricky part: on this issue, in the eyes of most of the world when speaking privately, Russia is right. America is the only country that indefatigably explains its positions as being about something more than just purely American interests. But the United States needs to understand that this sermon is being delivered from a pulpit more and more often to an empty congregation: no one except America believes this diplomatic propaganda.

Surveying allies and adversaries alike reveals nothing but dismissive smirks about the idea that American global maneuvers are based on higher moral principles rather than on what best positions American national interests. Again, remember the subtlety: such dismissiveness is not anger about America trying to leverage its power for maximum output. It is rather irritation at how often America tries to judge and prevent other states from doing the exact same thing on the regional and/or global stage. Other countries might not like how Russia expresses its power but they accept those maneuvers, for better or worse, as the way the geopolitical game still works on the modern global stage of differentiated power capacity. As long as the United States continues to delude itself on this basic fundamental aspect of global affairs—envisioning itself as the great preserver of international principles while supposedly never acting opportunistically or self-servingly—then it will continue to blow a mighty wind on situations like Crimea while accomplishing nothing.

Indeed, Russians have complained about the essence of this American diplomatic grandstanding for decades, in earnest since 9/11, when they believed America would be joining them in the global fight against radical Islamist extremism only to be inexplicably (to them) rebuffed. America has long held pride in the fact that it can and does project its global power independently when it wants to. It has never, however, responded positively whenever any other nation tries to do the same, whether it is Iran, China, Saudi Arabia, Venezuela, or Russia. And for those who think it is all right to constrain such nations, keep in mind that France, Germany, Israel, and India have all complained at times of the same thing. There is nothing wrong with trying to manage your power brand so that it comes across as something nobler and more righteous than pure nationalist desire. But when the United States seems to complain about other countries not buying in and wanting the same rights to enact their political will as America, then it underserves its own true global power by seeming a bit petulant and unsubtle. Such complaints, unfortunately, explain why Russia has been so successful in maintaining geopolitical sympathizers outside of Western Europe: other countries see the United States as bringing a knife to a foreign-policy gunfight when it says Russia should be constrained and/or punished for doing the very same maneuvers as America while Russia simply asks for a level playing field on the global stage.

Blowback Diplomacy

How the United States Was Locked Out of the Caspian

LAURA GARRIDO OCTOBER 22, 2015

It has been almost one year since the IV Caspian Summit in Astrakhan, Russia, where the presidents of the five Caspian states signed a political declaration that denied any foreign military presence in the Caspian Sea. This means that possible future deployment of NATO forces in the area will not be allowed. According to Russian President Vladimir Putin, this declaration "sets out a fundamental principle for guaranteeing stability and security, namely, that only the Caspian littoral states have the right to have their armed forces present on the Caspian." While this is a threat to the United States, the decision may not have been as much of a shock. It may have been US policies that pushed this decision to the forefront.

Looking back to the collapse of the Soviet Union, the United States was careful not to make it seem as though it was siding with the new states in their efforts to achieve independence from Russia. This was important because the United States did not want to give the impression that a "cordon sanitaire" was being created around Russia in order to isolate it from Europe. The new states and Russia were given the opportunity to create arrangements amongst themselves that were acceptable to both sides. The United States was to basically stay out of it. This policy was a way to allow the United States to slowly and strategically become involved in these new states in the years following the collapse of the Soviet Union without bothering or irritating or worrying Russia.

After giving the newly independent states some time, the United States became increasingly active in its diplomatic efforts in the region. It started out with official visits, first by the leaders of the region to the United States: President Islam Karimov of Uzbekistan visited the White House in 1996; President Eduard Shevardnadze of Georgia, President Heidar Aliyev of Azerbaijan, President Nursultan Nazarbayev of Kazakhstan in 1997; and President Saparmurat Niyazov of Turkmenistan in 1998. These visits were then followed by US Secretary of State Madeleine Albright touring the region in 2000.

To add to this, in possibly one of the most significant US policy decisions in the Caspian region, the Clinton administration appointed a "special envoy," or a special interagency working group, which focused on Caspian policy. This was interesting because so much focus was placed on this remote region, even though there was no significant trade relationship between the Caspian littorals and the United States, no real threat of major war, and no immediate threat to regional or international peace and stability. The United States military also began to pay attention to the region. Many training sessions and programs were conducted in the area and between 1992 and 1999. The United States also provided the Caspian area with nearly $1.9 billion under the Freedom Support Act to promote democratization, market reforms, health care, and housing.

However, not all good deeds go unpunished. While supporting the region, the United States also addressed the importance of Central Asia and the Caucasus. In an address before the Senate Appropriations Committee's Foreign Operations Subcommittee, Secretary of State Madeleine Albright noted that it was of national interest to support states in the Caspian Basin because they were strategically located and energy-rich. This may have been a mistake, planting a seed of suspicion in Russia about US motives in the area, which could have led long-term to the decision to lock them out of the region militarily in last year's summit.

Thus, the very policy that was meant to help the United States gain the littoral states' trust and future access to the Caspian's resources and strategic location may have backfired. The United States invested so much time, money, and energy working to build the navies and strengthen the military in Turkmenistan, Azerbaijan, and Kazakhstan. However, all of that training and the arms supplied were ultimately manipulated by Russia and Iran, as they cajoled the states into believing that they could protect their interests themselves without more direct foreign military aid and involvement. The littoral states bought into the idea that their bolstered militaries, along with Russia and Iran's supplemental, pledged military support, would be enough to protect themselves. It seems apparent that the idea of needing protection from Russia and Iran in the future was not considered. This concept is something loudly crowed about in the West, but these decisions show it is not shared by the "lesser" Caspian littorals.

Another policy of the United States that may have contributed to this lockout decision was the imposition of sanctions on Russia and Iran. Russia not only has soft-power influence throughout the region, many of the littoral states are fearful of a belligerent Iran. The United States imposed sanctions on Russia in response to the annexation of Crimea and subsequent involvement in the war in Ukraine. The sanctions have caused severe economic harm to Russia, causing food prices to soar, the exchange rate to weaken, inflation to increase, and incomes to decrease. The United States also imposed further sanctions on Iran due to its illicit nuclear activities. Like in Russia, the sanctions severely affected Iran's economy, causing incredibly high inflation, unemployment, and food prices. Thus, Russia and Iran's distrust and anger toward the United States, along with their own national security interests, fueled their actions to push the littoral states to agree with the lockout.

The decision to block foreign militaries from the Caspian Sea is a threat to the strategic interests of America and, to a lesser extent, the European Union. Potentially, it could have negative repercussions on energy security. By removing any Western military influence in the region, Russia will be able to maintain the regional hegemony it considers its natural birthright. In addition to that, Iran will be able to ensure greater strategic flexibility moving forward with the JCPOA nuclear accord.

It is now clear that there were policy decisions made by the United States that negatively affected its relationship with Russia and Iran and fueled the push for the military lockout. The American discussion of the strategic location and energy wealth of the Caspian Basin undoubtedly caused an air of doubt by the "greater" Caspian littorals and clearly motivated them to improve their relations with Kazakhstan, Azerbaijan, and Turkmenistan enough so that those three could legitimately believe in the wisdom and efficacy of relying on their own regional securitization. In short, the biggest decision that came from the IV Caspian Summit was the product of a gradual process of "blowback diplomacy," where the United States was forced to reap a bitter harvest from its earlier sowing season.

Chessboard Strategy

Russia and UN Resolution 2117

ZR SEPTEMBER 23, 2015

The Russian government has made great leaps since the collapse of the Soviet Union, "moving from a globally isolated, centrally planned economy toward a more market-based and globally integrated economy." The privatization of most industry was a large boost to its economy. However, two notable sectors were kept under government control: the energy and defense-related sectors. The purpose of this brief paper is to examine the current actions of Russian approaches to influence the transnational weapons market throughout the Caucasus, Central Asia, and the Middle East. This will be accomplished through critically analyzing Russia's actions associated with UN Resolution 2117, where it abstained from voting and honored instead an arms-sale plan with Iran, shipping a modern-day missile-defense system, and a recent sale to Iraq that provided fighter jets for the fight against DAESH.

In 2013, the United Nations, "expressing grave concern that the illicit transfer, destabilizing accumulation, and misuse of small arms and light weapons continued to cause significant loss of life around the world," felt a need to remind governments of their obligation to comply fully and effectively with council-mandated arms embargos. By a vote of fourteen in favor to none against, with one abstention—the Russian Federation—the Council adopted Resolution 2117. It was the first-ever resolution dedicated exclusively to the issue of small arms and light weapons. The ensuing debate marked the first time in five years that the fifteen-member body had taken up the issue, which had been previously deleted from its agenda.

The choice of Russian council members to abstain from this vote was an interesting move politically. A vote to abstain meant that Russian officials could avoid criticism for a negative vote but also kept them from being obligated to follow the treaty that prohibited sales of light weapons, something from which Russia greatly benefits. One such transaction, though not small-arms in nature, revolves around Russia's plans with Iran on the S-300 air-defense system. According to US officials, "Russia is moving ahead with plans to sell Iran a sophisticated missile defense system that could undercut Washington's ability to challenge Tehran's airspace." This system, identified as the S-300, would result in a rather concrete air-defense system for Iran which would mean that "US or Israeli warplanes likely couldn't sneak into Iranian airspace if they wanted to bomb Iran's possible nuclear facilities." Additionally, the S-300 could provide an early warning for the Iranians against any attempt to launch preemptive strikes and afford them time to shore up other defenses.

Iran had already fronted Russia the money for the weapons system, nearly $800 million, but there were some nondelivery disputes. In January 2015, official Russian media reported that the two sides had settled their differences after Moscow agreed to provide older Tor surface-to-air missiles with an unspecified date of delivery. Iran's state media also reported a settlement, but without providing details. At around the same time, reports emerged also that Russia and Iran were again discussing either the S-300 system or a newer system, the Antey-2500. This Russian-Iran weapons deal gives Russia a staunch foothold in an already anti-Western nation and affords additional options for future transactions. Another interesting fact: the transaction is not in disagreement with any current international prohibitions because the weapons system is defensive in nature. Additionally, Secretary of State John Kerry raised US concerns with the Russians directly after Iranian Revolutionary Guard Commander Qasem Soleimani recently traveled to Moscow, a probable sign that the S-300 deal and future deals were back on the table and being finalized. Iran is not the only country garnering weapons sales from Russia, however. Iraq is also benefiting from Russia's proactive capitalist strategies in the weapons market.

In 2014 and 2015 the Iraqi government struggled to rebuild its tactical air force. The Middle East government worked closely with the United States in an effort to purchase F-16 fighters; however, the United States was not the only seller in the region. Due to an urgent need for close-air support and growing delays in the US government's provision of thirty-six F-16s, the Iraq government turned to Russia and Belarus to purchase used fighter jets. Iraq Prime Minister Nouri al-Maliki chastised the United States' slow ways. The delay in sales allowed Maliki to turn to other sources for purchase and exacerbated an apparent bitterness within the Iraqi government, as it believed that it should not have just bought US jets, but also British, French, and Russian ones to provide air support and prevent the fall of Mosul. The jet purchase followed desperate requests by Maliki to combat DAESH. The fact that Russia was able to swoop in and provide assets to a struggling government not only created another revenue stream for Russia, but it also showed Iraq that Russia can be a proven ally within the region and fostered greater doubts about substantive American support for the regime.

The Russian government has taken great steps to influence the transnational weapons market throughout the Caucasus, Central Asia, and the Middle East. In light of Russia's actions, its abstention vote on UN Resolution 2117 was an ingenious diplomatic move. Russia is able to pursue its own legitimate national security interests (only the United States prioritizes the fight against radical Islam as adamantly as Russia), bolster an important economic market that bypasses the severe sanctions levied against it, and foster cooperative engagement in a geopolitically crucial region within which the United States wishes to remain dominant. While America clearly has criticized Russia for abstaining from the Resolution 2117 vote, it is a perfect example of how conflicted and complex global affairs tend to be. Although America sees Russia's abstention in purely black-and-white terms, there are many other significant players on the global stage that do not see it so clearly. In this convoluted fog of multiple interpretations, Russia so far has proven to be the more adept chess grandmaster.

Playing Chess, Not Checkers

Russian Responses to US Hegemony in Kind

LOGAN WILDE MAY 26, 2016

Few would argue that Russia's recent display of military assertiveness, in both its hybrid confrontation in Ukraine and recent intervention in Syria, is antithetical to its proposed self-image as a regional power. This is largely the basis of Emil Aslan Souleimanov's article explaining how Russia is using the threat of the Islamic State to attempt to reinstate political-military hegemony throughout the former Soviet states. But Souleimanov missed the broader aspect of Vladimir Putin's true motivations in the Middle East and throughout the Caucasus: countering perceived US and NATO hegemony in the region and beyond.

The 2008 skirmish in Georgia marked the first use of Russian military power to engage an independent post-Soviet state since the fall of the USSR. The weak reaction by the United States only highlighted the efficacy of the strategy, which came to be known as the Medvedev Doctrine, where the Russian president proclaimed that "protecting the lives and dignity of our citizens, wherever they may be, is an unquestionable priority for our country. Our foreign policy decisions will be based on this need. We will also protect the interests of our business community abroad. It should be clear to all that we will respond to any aggressive acts committed against us" (Friedman, 2008). This ambitious military strategy rested on the reality that Russia was suffering from an economic downturn due to low oil prices and the political threat of NATO expansion to its borders. It is not a coincidence that Russia's involvement in Georgia and Ukraine symbolically coincided with each country's stated intent to join the NATO Membership Action Plan.

Souleimanov gets into Russia's consistent effort to link the United States to any political or military objective it deems worthy of pursuing: besides the obvious connections to NATO, the Russian media (heavily controlled by the government as to message) assumes that "the Islamic State is a US project to redraw the political map of the Middle East, or that it is used by Washington to either boost America's supremacy in this part of the world or destabilize Russia's Muslim-dominated areas in the North Caucasus, as well as Russia's sphere of influence in Central Asia" (Souleimanov, 2015). Paradoxically, this link also requires that Putin necessarily downplay the immediate threat that the Islamic state poses to Russia, which Souleimanov correctly points out. Instead, Putin speculates that North Caucasian fighters participating in the Syrian war will return to their homeland and continue the fight on native Russian soil against Russians. This is one of his primary reasons for military intervention in Syria.

Members of Russia's political and intellectual elite are now arguing that the Islamic state could in fact pose an immediate threat to Russia's political and military interests in the central Asian region. This narrative helps to justify Russia's strong military presence in the region, itself a response to a substantial US military deployment in Afghanistan. Russian analysts point to "Tajikistan, Turkmenistan, Uzbekistan, and Kyrgyzstan as the region's most vulnerable states in the event of a concentrated attack perpetrated by ISIS or its local allies" (Souleimanov, 2015). Although Souleimanov correctly identifies that this is actually an unlikely threat, he does not do enough to explain this conclusion. All of these states are at least semiauthoritarian and while they do not have large militaries, they do rely on Soviet-style military agreements. They also have substantial police forces that are trained to identify and respond to any insurgent or terrorist crises, while regularly employing torture and extralegal tactics to silence opposition (Human Rights Watch, 2016). In other words, this region is fundamentally hostile to an influx of Islamic state members. Unlike in war-torn Yemen or Syria, the states in this region have absolute control over their respective populations and therefore represent a significant barrier for most jihadist groups. This at least partly explains why home-grown Islamist groups have been fairly weak throughout central Asia for the past generation.

Souleimanov also suggests that Russia may be complicit in allowing its citizens to travel to Syria to fight alongside jihadists. There is little reason for Russian police to prevent these individuals from leaving. In addition to Souleimanov's explanation that Russian authorities are counting on many of these individuals being killed in combat while in Syria, they also serve to further destabilize—and therefore undermine—US intentions in Syria itself. It was also these same individuals that gave Russia the initial justification to enter into Syria, keeping in line with its doctrine to "protect its citizens." Partnering with Assad was merely another strategic maneuver to display Russia's independence from US goals in the region, despite both the United States and Russia having a similar objective of defeating the Islamic state. As Russia withdraws from Syria it will remain focused on tracking the Russian-born jihadists that are intent on returning to their homeland to continue their fight once the Syrian battlefield has grown stale.

Russia's declining political and economic influence throughout the region has forced its hand in its attempt to establish itself as a regional power comparable to China or India. Unfortunately, as Souleimanov points out, the "Central Asian elites have grown increasingly suspicious of Moscow's expansionism, its hybrid warfare in eastern Ukraine, and its rhetoric of protecting Russians abroad" (2015). This presents a problem for Russia, which has few potential solid partners beyond its former Soviet states. Embarrassingly, the only parties that officially recognized Russia's claim to Ossetia and Abkhazia in 2008 were Hamas and Nicaragua—not even the central Asian states were willing to ally with Russia on such an openly anti-NATO maneuver (Matthews, 2008). The most palpable example of Russia's focus on military strategy is its use to maintain its influence in the Arctic region, an area that is bound to see vastly increased economic activity as the region begins to melt and reveals access points to vast reserves of hydrocarbons (Mitchell, 2014). This level of military quasi-aggressiveness on the international stage is unique to Russia. Even China's military posture to preserve its influence in the South China Sea is not nearly as robust (Rizzo et al., 2016).

Without the economic clout of China or the political standing of India, Moscow is forced to rely on modernizing and utilizing its military as a means to counter Western influence. With Syria as a showcase, Russia has taken its first step in establishing itself as a dominant military force once more that is capable of defending the region from Western—or as the Russian populace understands it, Islamic state—influence. But Russia must establish a foreign policy that does more than attempt to undermine US and NATO activity in the region if it hopes to truthfully achieve the level of regional influence that China and India enjoy. After all, it is China's trade with the United States and India's strong political ties with Washington that have allowed them to grow. Russia must embrace a similar strategy if it wishes to compete in a similar fashion on the international stage. It may have a legitimate strategic reason for all of its military posturing, but ultimately its biggest global successes and most powerful regional influence will be in showing how well it is able to partner with others as opposed to going it alone.

Russia and Africa

More Than Economics

KESTER KENN KLOMEGAH SEPTEMBER 17, 2016

A lack of focus and lack of interest are hindering what could be a beneficial economic and political relationship between Russia and the African continent. Russia today does not have a concrete policy agenda for Africa and offers much less to the continent now than it did during the Soviet era, at least according to Irina Filatova, professor emeritus at the University of KwaZulu-Natal in South Africa and a professor at the National Research University at the Higher School of Economics in Moscow.

"Russia is interested in developing economic relations with Africa, but does not have much to offer," Filatova said. "And what it does have to offer, it does not quite know how to. There are some good projects there on the continent."

Although South Africa is now part of the BRICS grouping, this partnership is more about global political relations than connecting Russia with Africa. "This is, as we know, an ideology aimed at changing the world economic (and political) order," said Filatova, discussing BRICS. "Any other strategic partnership between Africa and Russia does not exist, and is impossible because of Russia's negligible economic ties with the continent." BRICS does not fulfill the need for a "platform for Russia-Africa dialogue," in the words of Lesley Masters, a senior researcher at the Institute for Global Dialogue in South Africa. "African engagement with Russia has been difficult, especially in building up economic ties. Relations need to be more visible and opened up to promote greater exchanges across sectors between Africa and Russia. There is not enough understanding in Africa regarding Russia," Masters said.

From Russia's perspective, there are important geo-political implications for working with Africa. The continent's fifty-four states represent a key voting bloc within the structures of global governance. Nevertheless, Russia's soft power efforts in the region have been limited thus far. Dr. Shaabani Nzori, an expert in Russian-African relations, says that Russian president Vladimir Putin and his foreign policy team are pragmatic, and so African leaders interested in working with them should take a very business-like approach.

"Our (African) leaders must formulate exactly what they want and what to expect from Russia, what they are ready to offer in exchange and spell this out very clearly without any bonhomie," said Nzori in an interview. "With regard to African mineral resources and Russia's intended role in their exploration and exploitation, we need to be principled and not let Russians determine the agenda on how these our resources ought to be exploited and managed," he said. So far, Nzori continued, African authorities have failed to use mineral assets as trump cards to negotiate better terms when going into contracts with foreigners, not only in exploiting and managing the minerals deposits themselves but also in using them to achieve inroads into other spheres of economic, technical, and technological cooperation. For example, obtaining access to Russia's technology and prowess in nuclear power generation or asset-swapping for ownership stakes in Russian enterprises.

Dr. Bashir Obasekola, from the Russian chapter of the Nigerians In Diaspora Organization Europe (NIDOE-Russia), a nonprofit social organization based in Moscow, said that many people still expect to see a very robust Russian policy implemented in Africa, despite the fact that China has outpaced Russia significantly in African engagement in recent years. "Some attempts were made by Medvedev to change the trend," Obasekola said. "He even appointed a special envoy on African affairs, Mikhail Margelov, to bring in new ideas to Russian-African relations. On his part he organized a business forum in Addis Ababa, visited southern and eastern African countries drumming about Russian investment, but with little results. Nevertheless, the potentials of Russian-African relations are still yet to be maximized."

In June 2009, Medvedev paid an official visit to Nigeria, during which six bilateral agreements were signed aimed at boosting the strategic partnership between the two countries. When Medvedev returned from his African trip, Russia's then-president declared that such a visit should have been made sooner, but that it was not too late for Russia to play a role on the continent. Summing up his trip, he noted frankly that Russia was "almost too late" in engaging with Africa. Medvedev remarked that work with Russia's partners in Africa should have been started earlier. Africa is waiting for Russian support. "Our policies here will be very friendly, but at the same time pragmatic," Medvedev said, noting that the Soviet Union "always held very friendly positions with regard to African countries, helping them win independence." But despite such ties—particularly with countries such as Namibia and Angola—Moscow's influence has waned since the fall of the Soviet Union, as countries turned to the United States and Asian states such as China and India. The interest of major international players in Africa is actively discussed on the continent and during his visit, Medvedev declared: "We should be also involved."

Ana Cristina Alves, a senior researcher from Global Powers and Africa at the South African Institute of International Affairs and lecturer from the Witwatersrand University in Johannesburg, South Africa, thinks that there is a lot of potential for trade and economic cooperation to improve in the medium-long term, but doesn't think Africa is a priority for Moscow right now.

"The impression I have is that Russia's engagement in Africa is being mostly conducted by private Russian interests to explore mineral resources without any support from their Russian government," Alves said. "People talk about China, India and Brazil in Africa—Russia hardly make it into the academic discussions here."

From the Russian perspective, the challenges of doing business in Africa may outweigh the potential benefits. Andrei Petrov, founder of New African Initiative (NAI), a nonprofit organization that seeks to change negative perceptions about Russia and help Russian investors in Africa, said that the major problem Russian companies face in their investments abroad is the absence of a system for obtaining financing from the government and commercial institutions.

Next to that is related to political risks of investing in North Africa. Due to political events in Libya, for instance, Russian Railways lost many projects, including the construction of the Bengazi-Sirt railway at a total cost of $2.7 billion. Petrov added that it's very difficult to compete with China, which is very dynamic and active on the continent and has low-cost financing in sufficient amounts for nearly all investment projects planned for Africa. In his assessment, Rex Essenowo, an independent economic analyst based in Moscow, said that Medvedev was more focused on Russia-African economic policies during his four years in office than

Vladimir Putin had been in his previous eight, and businessmen and political leaders on both sides are now waiting to see if Putin will continue Medevedev's engagement or not. Putin visited only South Africa and Morocco during his eight years as president from 2000 to 2008.

Essenowo said that the emergence of the BRICS regional bloc presents a good platform to renew trade and economic relations with Africa, but added a caveat. "Let me quickly point out that South Africa is still far away from being the flag bearer in determining African economic policies and integration with Russia, if you take into consideration the potentials that Africa and Russia has," Essenowo said. "We are not lacking the resources to boost the relationship, but the will power has always been put on hold or totally ignored." Essenowo also pointed out that there are many meetings at the bilateral and regional levels between Russia and the United States, the European Union, and Southeast Asian nations, but there has yet to be a single high-level Russian-African summit. Essenowo believes that there is still a chance to revive Russia's relationship with Africa if African nations also resolve to work together to focus on improving the Russian-African relationship.

Russia and the United States

An Alliance in the Making

LUIS DURANI MARCH 28, 2016

In the last decade, Russia, under the leadership of Vladimir Putin, has regained some of its standing. The combination of high energy prices and authoritarian leadership has allowed Russia to secure a stronger position on the global stage while boosting Putin's popularity at home. Despite the US-Russia relationship reset early in the Obama administration, the two nations once again find themselves on opposing sides due to conflicting interests in the Middle East and Eastern Europe. Despite being at odds, the United States and Russia will form an alliance, albeit nominal, in the next few decades due to two factors: regional dynamics in Siberia as well as the rise of Chinese regional hegemony.

Russia is the largest nation in the world, divided up into eleven time zones. Politically the Russian government divides the country into eighty-five federal administrative units, geographically Russia is bifurcated by the Ural Mountains, with one-quarter of Russia in Europe and three-quarters in Asia. European Russia is known for Moscow and Saint Petersburg, while Asian Russia is known for the freezing prison tundra of Siberia. Due to its harsh climate, the Siberian region is sparsely populated. Yet what it lacks in people, it more than makes up for in natural resources. Beneath the veneer of subzero snow lie abundant resources of gold, diamonds, minerals, gas, and oil. Asian Russia is where European Russia derives its ability to project power. The nearly three-thousand-mile border between China and Russia was effectively closed for most of the Cold War due to China's rapprochement with the United States under Richard Nixon. After the fall of the Soviet Union, the border opened up and Sino-Russo exchanges took off. Ever since the opening of the border, the fear of a Chinese "invasion" of Siberia has been present in the minds of many Russians. Even though the border is accepted by both sides, there are certain elements within the Chinese government that do not recognize it. They believe it is a product of the Century of Humiliation, where a great European power forced China to cede its territory due to its weakness at the time. The Russian-Chinese border was established by the Peking Convention in 1860, where a stronger Russia essentially demarcated a line on a map and obliged a weaker China to recognize it.

Aside from the conspiratorial apprehensions, the facts on the ground also dictate a similar pattern. While China's burgeoning 1.4 billion people are occupying a relatively smaller land mass, Russia has a population of 140 million people. The numbers become even more ominous around the border area of the Siberian region. The Russians have about 6 million people versus the almost 90 million Chinese. With the borders open since the end of the Cold War, there has been a large cultural and financial osmosis from the Chinese side to Siberia. The Chinese have flooded the area in investments, workers, and trade, and there have been marriages between citizens on both sides. With such exchanges, Beijing feels closer than Moscow to locals, both symbolically and literally.

Recently, China decided to lease a large portion of Siberia from Russia in order to develop agriculture on the large swath of land. The land was leased for forty-nine years in exchange for annuities as well as regional investments. Many in Russia have decried the deal and point to the similarities between the United States and Russia deal almost 150 years ago that became known as Seward's Folly. The deal resulted in the United States purchasing Alaska from Russia for mere cents per acre. While Russia has not sold but only leased the land, many in Russia believe this is one of the final steps before a full reclamation process by the Chinese. The territory contains what China so desperately seeks, energy sources as well as raw materials. With the land leased, the region is officially immersed in everything Chinese except the redrawing of the border. With the Chinese side of the border being so densely populated and the Russian side sparsely, a Chinese "invasion" looks almost inevitable. To justify such actions, China just might ironically employ the Putin Doctrine to "help" ethnic Chinese wherever they may be in the world if they are being oppressed by issuing passports for those in the region that are willing to accept them. Once they are deemed Chinese citizens, the Chinese army can move in to defend them and secure the Siberian region as well. This tactic would be similar to the Russian justification in Abkhazia and South Ossetia or Crimea.

Even though the premise seems far-fetched in today's geo-political context, nothing is impossible, as history has shown. Today, Putin, in a bid to outdo the United States and the West, has looked to China as an ally to rival what they view as the Western domination of global affairs. With the Russo-Chinese alliance being stronger than ever, the plausibility of such a scenario seems nonexistent. However, as with anything in politics, time changes all. When the Soviet Union found a fellow comrade nation across its border with a similar communist disposition, the United States saw a potential alliance that could have threatened it in the long run. But as Machiavelli pointed out, no nation wants a stronger neighbor than itself. Thus, in 1972, Nixon traveled to China to null their alliance with the Soviets and bring the Chinese into the American sphere. In the end, the Chinese saw a greater benefit by allying themselves, albeit nominally, with the Americans who were an ocean away than a stronger neighbor across the border, despite professing their commitment to the same ideology.

As China grows stronger, economically and militarily, and reaches the status of a regional hegemon, Russia will have two daunting challenges come to light: a stronger neighbor as well as a more populous one that can flood one of its very vital regions. In order to prevent such a disaster, the Russians will need to ally themselves with the United States, similar to the way Mao's China did with Nixon. This eventual Russian-US rapprochement is not something out of a Tom Clancy novel or wildly unbelievable. Despite their antagonistic stances toward each other currently, the Russians and Americans will potentially become allies one day to help contain a growing China.

PART IV

SYRIA, SANCTIONS, AND EXTREMISM

Old American Punishment, New Russian Strength

The Strange World of Unintended Consequences

DECEMBER 21, 2014

On December 18, President Vladimir Putin gave his traditional end-of-year holiday speech. Think of it as a Russian version of the American State of the Union address always given by our president. In it Putin expressed dismay and concern at the manner in which Russia's "Western partners" were behaving, even going so far as to declare Western intentions as being purposely aimed at controlling Russian national resources and leaving Russia a de facto vassal state. He vividly used the analogy of a chained bear, with Western powers looking to declaw and defang Russian power so as to make it compliant and impotent. There was even a dramatic use of old-school symbolism in this expansive three-hour speech. The made-for-TV event was accompanied by such strong Russian images as the Sochi Olympics and Putin petting a baby tiger and greeting Russian cosmonauts. The traditional reaction of American power to such open displays of bravado, defiance, and strength is usually one of disdain and dismissal. In most cases it is fairly harmless to disregard such macho acts. But in this case I believe there are certain signals within the speech that indicate America would do well to pay closer attention and not simply think these are the desperate actions of a man pushed to his wits' end by sanctions that are having the desired effect on Russia.

America needs to disabuse itself of the notion that the sanctions are causing a precipitous decline in the popularity of Putin. It is not uncommon today to find numerous media accounts in the West testifying to this very issue, with many supposed Western experts on Russian politics declaring predictions about when, not if, Putin will finally be ousted by a dissatisfied populace. Most survey polling data in Russia today—and no, not all of these polling facilities are simple sycophants of the Russian government—have President Putin hovering as high as 80 percent approval during these difficult times, marked most powerfully by the decline of the Russian ruble. In America, where economic problems immediately and automatically translate into dismal popularity ratings for its politicians, it is easy to see where such assumptions come from. Inexplicably, we in the West seem to ignore the fact that it is relatively easy to characterize and position the decline of the ruble as a direct consequence of Western interference in the Russian economy, i.e., a result of Western sanctions against Russia. Putin for his part took a relatively stable and steady approach to the ruble crisis, saying he did not approve the Central Bank overreacting and burning through Russia's hard-earned cash reserves and that slow, progressive countermeasures would be enacted that would see the return of a healthy ruble over the course of the next two years.

Perhaps most intriguing of all was the fact that Putin actually claimed that sanctions had only a 25 to 30 percent causal value in the fall of the ruble. Much more important was Russia's continued dependence on oil and natural gas, thereby making it especially vulnerable to fluctuations in the world market. Again, most in America will laugh this off. Surely this is just posturing by a delusional president. However, more astute and objective thinkers will agree that this reasoning is not only politically wise but quite possibly economically accurate. The sanctions pushed by the West throughout 2014 have been unfortunately combined with a precipitous lowering in world oil and gas prices. What this has done is potentially pushed Russia to come to a very harsh but valuable conclusion. In the past, Russia has always been rather cavalier about being a natural-resources-dependent country. Given its vast reserves and untapped potential it is not entirely illogical to see where such hubris came from. But the year 2014, looking deeper within Putin's speech, may end up being a watershed, turning-point year for the Russian Federation. Putin emphasized that it is necessary and indeed essential that Russia strengthen its domestic economy and domestic sources of economic production so as to not be as vulnerable and dependent upon a world market that is too often connected to the priorities and interests of the United States. If Russia truly does make inroads to enact measures that might achieve this goal long term, then the entire nature of the Russian-American global relationship could change fundamentally.

So here we sit, once again looking at a Cold War–like detente between Russia and America, with the latter side utterly confident that its maneuvers and actions will have the desired deterrent effect on the former, bringing it to heel and making it more compliant with Western interests. But what we might be seeing instead is the impetus for creating a new Russian strategy for an economic future that will engender greater political power and more global independence. America right now sits in a position of strength, convinced it has Russia on the ropes and backed into a corner. Anyone who has even the slightest familiarity with Russian history knows that it has been just such occurrences in the past in which the Russian state has usually acted in a completely unanticipated and antithetical way. Acting against the expectations of foreigners is almost a national pastime for Russia. I do not believe the current situation in Russia is going to result in the ousting of President Putin, in the collapse of the Russian economy, or even in something as symbolically simple as Russia capitulating to Western demands on Ukraine. I find it much more likely that the events of 2014 will make the more nuanced thinkers and more profound strategic analysts in Russia devise an alternative path toward a future that will make it less vulnerable and less dependent on what it considers to be the whims of Western strategy. The recent massive economic cooperation agreement signed with China easily fits into this perspective.

So it might end up painfully surprising for the United States if its actions, done very much in the style of the Cold War, create motivations in Russia that really were not there beforehand. The greatest irony in all of this might be seeing old American punishment creating new Russian strength. Most disturbing of all, while this irony could create a more level global playing field between Russia and America, I fear this equality would not create a stronger cooperative partnership between the two countries.

An Anti-Theory of Sanctions

Why an Iranian New Deal Was Necessary

DIANNE VALDEZ AUGUST 26, 2015

While the debate over the wisdom of concluding the Iran nuclear deal continues, this article takes a slightly more involved, intellectual approach to explain why an alternative to the long-standing sanctions was likely inevitable. This is especially the case if there is a sincere desire to see Iran incorporated long-term into the global community and not simply continue to punish it as a pariah into political perpetuity. Several conceptual and theoretical explanations have been used to highlight key indicators that counteract the effectiveness of sanctions within the Middle East and how the spread of certain ideologies and social practices have impacted the success of international mediations. This microcosm analysis of the various social variables, mostly stemming from historical and political events, supports the need to judge more harshly the long-term efficacy of sanctions. It provides an analysis concerning weapons proliferation within Iran and will question the overall potential success of sanctions against such targeted states.

In an effort to provide a clearer scope of imposing sanctions against independent states, it is required to assess the overall political stratagem. According to many political theorists, the application of sanctions against various states has become the most popular alternative to military force that may otherwise lead to war. Past war efforts, however, have provided a misguided concept of the efficacy of sanctions, implying that a one-size-fits-all approach will produce identical results. “Sanctions—either bilateral, in conjunction with informal coalitions of like-minded countries, or through international organizations like the United Nations—have long been a staple of US foreign policy. Their appeal is obvious: sanctions provide an intermediate step between normal negotiations and outright hostilities in our attempts to a) alter the behavior of foreign states or even b) force the removal of their governments. There is a voluminous and disputatious literature on the effectiveness of sanctions.” Put another way, the overpopularity of sanctions as a policy refuge demonstrates a lack of awareness within the international political spectrum, implying that all political arenas are the same and general applications can bring about similar change. This is simply false.

Unfortunately, it was not until the recent failures of multiple Western-imposed sanctioning projects that security theorists began to see key variables that have contributed to the lack of effectiveness within such measures. Such factors have included: the targeted state’s form of government, levels of state patriotism, and unilateral control. To begin with, assessing the form of government of the subjected state has proven crucial in generating success of applying sanctions. “Because of different institutional incentives, economically punishing sanctions are less likely to succeed against a nondemocratic target than against a democratic target. Sanctions increase rents. This benefits nondemocratic leaders more than democratic ones. Also, nondemocratic leaders have smaller winning coalitions, so their core constituents suffer less from sanctions than democratic leaders.” This certainly was the case with Iran, and other targeted states with authoritarian-led regimes, in that democratic societies are human rights driven and tend to focus on the overall well-being of their societies. Democratic states in general maintain multiple parties. Majority-led parties can then petition their views by vote, which can in turn push sanction compliance. On the other hand, authoritarian-led regimes like Iran lack this outlet, resulting in the authority of the government being the only and final determination of sanction negotiations, regardless of differing views, isolation, or general populace suffering.

In terms of considering state nationalism and the successful outcomes of sanctions, research has proven that applying sanctions to countries with strong nationalist perspectives will most likely fail. This mitigating context is widely seen throughout countries with strong anti-Western perspectives and can definitely be applied to the case of Iran. "Nationalism is as strong among Iranians as it is among Americans. And it is easy to imagine a similar 'rally round the flag' effect were the United States to face foreign pressure aimed at altering our policies. It is one of the curiosities of our foreign policy that Americans often assume that foreigners will act in ways that we ourselves never would." As seen with Iran, the original premise of instituting sanctions was to negatively impact the country's economy, hoping to turn the people against its own government. The reality is that the Iranian state, along with many other authoritarian countries, maintains strong anti-Western perspectives that often engender a counterreaction to sanctioning efforts. Such countries often effectively lay blame on Western leaders for increasing levels of poverty that then contribute to the growth of stronger nationalist perspectives and thus increase the long-term resistance against Western sanctions.

Multilateralism, also explained as the concept of international control, has been identified as a contributing variable to the overall effectiveness of state-centered sanctions. Due to many economic interdictions often involving the international cooperation of surrounding states, individual compliance by other countries is required. Multilateralism, according to Ruggie's definition, "requires that states sacrifice substantial levels of flexibility in decision-making and resist short-term personal temptations in favor of long-term universal benefits." As Martin explains it, "effectively, international cooperation is often described as a product of national self-interest in an increasingly interdependent world." Thus, multilateralism holds that independent states must not only be aware of their individual contributions but also that they sacrifice the possible individual benefits of pursuing their own interests. This is quite indicative of one of the ways the Iranian case went wrong, as some nations contributed to Iran's resistance simply by not dismissing their own international personal benefits in order to ensure sanctioning success.

The form of government, levels of nationalism, and multilateralism are all factors to be considered when looking at the potential success (or lack thereof) of sanctions on a nation as a general phenomenon. The presence of these elements, as well as their intertwining relationships, can often undermine the overall efficacy of employing sanctions to coerce change within a subjected state like Iran. In "Thinking Strategically about Sanctions," the author Olivier Schmitt discussed the onset of factors in deciding to introduce sanctions against a country. This especially considered the overall environment of the subjected state and how that might produce primal behaviors that would ultimately lead to future violent conflict. "And once the process is launched, studies of potential radicalization of the actors are needed. I am not here talking about a 'path-dependency' phenomenon. Rather, using the 'rise to the extremes' theory, I suggest that the beginning of sanctions imposition can have a radicalizing effect on the targeted country." Therefore, prior to enforcing sanctions on a state as poorly positioned to respond to them as Iran, someone should have acknowledged its negative position independently and how sanctions could lead to undesirable results and further disastrous outcomes.

After reviewing the conceptual shortcomings of instituting sanctions and assessing theoretical flaws, it is clear for many reasons that UN-led sanctions were arguably always going to fail majorly in pushing Iran to cease its nuclear enrichment program or soften its general anti-Western stances. In spite of multiple efforts at coercion by the United States and facing heavy declines in Iran's economy, the nuclear enrichment program not only continued to exist, but the authority of the theocratic regime was able to fairly easily handle the largest public resistance against it back in 2009, the Green Revolution. It was arguably always imperative to the future of international security that policymakers and diplomats alike begin to consider alternative approaches to deterring Iran's nuclear weapons capabilities. These alternatives would have to be something not exclusively based on punishment and isolation but rather inclusiveness and mutual accountability and responsibility. For these reasons, the new Iranian deal, far from perfect and despite Western misgivings about it, marks progress when it is compared to the old long-standing sanction regime.

SPILT MILK

The Unintended Consequences of Russian Sanctions

VLADISLAV LERMONTOV OCTOBER 7, 2015

In the United States, the Office of Economic Sanctions Policy and Implementation (SPI) holds responsibility for the development and implementation of international sanctions. A key factor in the development of effective international sanction policy and support is the cooperation of various internal organizations.

The SPI focuses on providing guidance to the Department of Treasury and Commerce and continuously works with Congress for the purpose of drafting legislation in order to achieve policy goals in foreign areas. Many of the developed sanction policies focus on placing the largest amount of harm on a targeted state, while simultaneously minimizing the amount of economic harm to the United States and/or neighboring states. Economic sanctions are also enforced in a manner where a threatened state will be rewarded for good behavior through the removal of certain aspects over time. Effective enforcement of international sanctions also relies on joint cooperation with the Office of Foreign Assets Control Department of the Treasury, Bureau of Industry and Security Department of Commerce, and the President's Export Control Reform Initiative. But as we shall see, these carefully laid rules have not worked well in the Russian case.

Economic sanctions involve several financial initiatives, such as annual appropriation bills. Over the years, sanctions have become a very popular first-action initiative in foreign policy maneuvers.

Post–Cold War, there have been an increasing number of sanction impositions on foreign nations. Between 1993 and 1997 alone there were sixty-one US laws and executive orders enacted against thirty-five countries. According to the Institute for International Economic Sanctions, US sanction enforcement cost the United States between 15 and 19 billion USD in 1995 alone. Just such sanctions have been imposed on Russia today due to the recent activities occurring in Ukraine. While initially effective, the potential for major economic turmoil to neighboring countries is very real due to the important role that Russia plays in the regional economic system and beyond.

How much sanction imposition is too much? Imposing economic sanctions on nations that are heavily involved in trade, import, and export could have serious ramifications to surrounding areas, resulting in more harm to not only the neighboring countries but the global system as well. Affected states or nations could in turn punish sanction-supporting entities by cutting off valuable supplies, resulting in a downward economic spiral. Economic sanctions by the United States and the European Union onto the Russian government have resulted in this kind of collateral damage and intentional retaliatory actions. One of the smaller but vital consequences has been Europe facing one of its largest dairy farmer economic crises in the last decade. Swedish farmers who need the cost of milk to remain at roughly 3.6 and 3.7 krona in order to survive are put in crisis by the current milk cost of 2.65 krona. This could lead to the bankruptcy of a large portion of the 4,200 private dairy farmers that currently exist there. Such negative effects, seemingly insignificant, can and will spill into various other industries and create a negative cascade effect on the everyday lives of ordinary citizens across many countries.

The impact of economic sanctions on Russia has had a very far reach. The dairy crisis seen in Sweden is also felt in Eastern and central Europe. Massive quantities of dairy products that before went to Russia now need a new home due to the inability to export products there. Germany has lost 12,600 tons of cheese, equivalent to 1.26 million dollars, due to sanctions against Russia. For those who hold a close economic relationship with Russian trade, such as the Baltic states, sanction enforcement can have long-term ramifications leading to great economic stress and internal turmoil. Current global policy does not offer side support to offset the harm being done to nations peripherally connected to target nations under sanction enforcement.

The continuous enforcement of economic sanctions on Russia will lead to not only short-term ramifications but long-term economic strains on the Russian economy for years to come. Russia is suffering from inflation, foreign capital is continuing to flow out of Russia, and its 2 trillion dollar economy is beginning to stall. The bans imposed by the United States and the European Union on transactions with Russian companies such as VTB Group, OAO Novatek, OAO Rosneft, and OAO Gazprombank have created a great deal of financial stress on the people of Russia, not just Russian oligarchs. According to a report from Bloomberg Business, construction volume has fallen by 8.1 percent, while retail sales have dropped over 8.2 percent. Again, there is a great risk that sanction enforcement could lead these harmful effects spilling over to neighboring nations. Therefore, the US has tried to ensure that existing contracts between states would be honored in order to limit the potential for additional foreign economic strain in the short-term.

The most crucial long-term ramification from sanctions on Russia, however, is the negative impact it will have on disconnecting Russia from the global economy. Over the last several years the integration of the Russian economy brought 140 million new Russian players onto the global market, creating a financial boom that began to finally create a legitimate Russian middle class. Now that economic integration has been threatened, the potential of seeing that middle class disintegrate beyond recovery is very real. It is ironic that the United States, the leader in pushing Russia into the global economy and wanting consolidated democracy to take root there, has single-handedly also created a counter-force that could risk those priorities. It is a clear example of when short-term national security concerns trump and compromise long-term ones.

Nevertheless, the United States is not short on allies when considering further sanction extensions. Russia's inability to create and hold a ceasefire in Eastern Ukraine is said to be undermining international diplomacy. It is clear both the United States and the European Union consider that failure to be purposeful. Allies and adversaries do not have to be government entities alone, however. The general public can play an equally important role. According to a poll done by American news corporation CNN, 59 percent of people approve of economic sanctions imposed on Russia. While public support is crucial for international policy enforcement at first, long-term economic spillover due to strict sanctions can cause a shift in approval ratings over time. Import and export trade limitations with Russia will continue to have a negative impact on Europe and the United States. The longer this plays out, the more likely international support may wane.

While the overall impact of sanction enforcement on Russia could lead to more international instability and disruption, it seems to be having minimal impact on Vladimir Putin and his agenda at home. While economic sanctions have been a nuisance on the Russian government, it is the people of Russia that seem to be paying the largest price. Traditionally, this is exactly when those imposing the sanctions hope for internal pressures to enact change within the target nation. But in Russia the opposite has actually occurred: able to effectively and compellingly show the decline in everyday standards of living coinciding perfectly with the imposition of foreign sanctions, Putin has actually seen his home approval rating recover and increase to levels never before seen. In this case, it seems something as small as spilt milk has a diplomatic and geopolitical ripple effect far more significant than the United States and the European Union ever thought possible.

An Entanglement of Enemies

What Russia's Presence in Syria Truly Reveals

NOVEMBER 8, 2015

Over the years America has made little progress in Iraq and Syria, something Russia is determined to change, apparently. The Obama administration maintains that a lasting political solution requires Mr. Assad's departure, but facing Russian military involvement, Iranian ground troops, Hezbollah military units, many armed jihadist groups, and the world's worst humanitarian crisis, the United States is facing a very convoluted and unclear situation that it seems unable to overcome on its own. NATO is concerned with the recent Russian creation of an A2/AD zone (anti-access / area denial system) in Syria. This anti-access / area denial strategy could severely hinder the ability of the Western alliance to use its military assets in Syria. Moscow's military moves in the Middle East and its geopolitical positioning around the globe strive to embarrass America's image as a reliable and confident player when it comes to geopolitics and fighting terror. For the most part, this is just Russia employing a "turnabout is fair play" principle, after what it feels is American harassment of Russia on many fronts. What is clear, after a subtle analysis of the consequences of Russia's entrance into Syria, is an entanglement of enemies that might signal much more chaos before any substantive coordination.

The new US strategy against DAESH in Syria will be backed by special operations forces in Erbil, Northern Iraq, and is meant to be strengthened by cooperation with the Iraqi military in retaking key cities, with expanded security assistance by Jordan and Lebanon. This was done to counter the sudden Russian military expansion into the region. Iraqi Shiite politicians were calling for Russians to conduct airstrikes against DAESH in Iraq as well. Following intensive talks between Iraqi and US officials, the chairman of the Joint Chiefs of Staff, Marine General Joseph Dunford, said the Iraqi government had promised it would not request any Russian airstrikes or military support for operations against DAESH. The United States is trying to engage in very demanding diplomatic talks, which include the foreign ministers of Russia and Iran, firm supporters of Assad, and nations such as Saudi Arabia and Turkey, which are opposed to the Syrian Assad regime. Of course, it would have been better if these diplomatic talks took place earlier with more intensity, because it is hard to overestimate just how difficult getting all of these disparate players to cooperate at the negotiating table is.

The complexity of these current diplomatic talks is evident by the fact that are still no agreements to establish areas of collaboration in various air campaigns or even to share intelligence and target information in Syria. The lack of military and diplomatic cooperation between Russia and the United States is pushing both sides to resort to Cold War–style tactics of proxy war. In addition, Russian cooperation in the region with Iran could create future tension with Saudi Arabia, Turkey, Qatar, the UAE, and Kuwait. The United States is walking a fine line by attempting to court multiple sides while ensuring certain relationships do not escalate into something much worse. Indeed, it is proving quite difficult to wage war when "allies" do not agree on the enemy.

Before Russia's entrance, America's Persian Gulf allies wanted to fight the Syrian government but refused to attack radical

Islamist groups. Turkey was against the Syrian regime and DAESH, but in reality it wanted to fight and weaken the Kurds, which so far have been one of the few good American allies and effective fighters against DAESH. Another US ally, Israel, is cautiously observing the landscape and seems to be ready to act if any threat materializes against its interests. But other than that, Israel seems intent on remaining outside the fight. In all this it is fair to describe the fight against DAESH not so much as a coalition but as a competing potpourri: it is more chaos than coordination. Then Russia arrived with a lean but clear objective to assist its old Arab ally, Assad, while restoring its national prestige in the Middle East. Russia has received full endorsement to stay in the region from both Syria and Iran. A third party, Iraq, is considering the same. US diplomats are facing the very difficult task of appeasing many different allies whose demands seem nonnegotiable and incompatible.

Asking Russia to stop its air campaign would play into the propaganda that the United States is not interested in defeating DAESH if someone else does it. If Russia is allowed to weaken DAESH in Syria and Iraq, then that would be a major blow for the United States. If the United States chooses to follow Turkey's example of arming certain militant groups, then the risk is that it could find itself with a group of jihadists who are impossible to control at the end of the conflict. This is the original criticism Russia made against the United States back when the first opposition groups fought against Assad. Another choice is to join Russia in its fight, but that will make the United States look like it is endorsing a leader it has accused of dictatorship and oppression. America simply seems incapable of cooperating openly with Russia, even with the terror fight.

Are there any real options for this conflict in terms of diplomatic negotiations and concessions? Realistic electoral transition in Syria cannot take place without advanced talks and a lasting ceasefire, in addition to international observers. Only the combined pressure from Russia and the United States can realistically force those conditions on Syria. Russia can use massive debt to pressure Syria to comply and to promise economic relief once Assad is replaced. The alternative for Moscow is to indefinitely support the Syrian regime and military. That could be something economically unpalatable to Putin. In a show of goodwill, Europe and the United States could suspend their sanctions against Russia and encourage Turkey to remind Russia of its plans to expand trade there from $32 billion to $100 billion in the next five years. The European Union can assure the Russians that they will support cutting the weapons flow to jihadist groups throughout the area that often include Chechens. Reassurance from the European Union and Turkey about stopping the weapons flow would make Russia feel better about militant groups such as Jaish Al-Muhajireen and Jaish Al Fatah, in addition to DAESH, which all include Chechen fighters. Russia is worried that hardened Chechen jihadists will always return from Middle East battlefields to southern Russia and launch terrorist attacks against Russian citizens, something that has already played out in the past with both the Afghanistan and Iraq conflicts.

These diplomatic discussions could potentially bring some militants and government representatives into direct negotiations, which Geneva talks have always failed to accomplish. To this end, aid could be provided only to non-Salafist militants who promise a protection of religious minorities. The role of YPG (Kurdish People's Protection Unit) will have to be carefully negotiated with Turkey. In short, there are far more questions than answers involving far more players than most Western media reports seem to realize. This entanglement of enemies is far more complex than a simple reduction to Cold War proxies. Indeed, the world should be afraid when we look longingly at the prospect of Cold War proxy conflicts as an improvement over the current state of affairs.

The Russia-OPEC-America Nexus

Reimagining the Great Oil Game

BRIAN HUGHES — AUGUST 17, 2015

The geopolitical implications to the sudden fall in oil prices have had broad-reaching ramifications for a number of very powerful countries. Two of those countries, Russia and Saudi Arabia, are the most important energy commodity exporters in the world. The other, the United States, is the single most crucial oil importer in the world. The possibility of Russian fatalism awakening is very real as the country faces tightening sanctions, severely under-priced oil exports, and rapid inflation as military spending has increased. Similarly, Saudi Arabia's diminishing currency reserves and its military adventurism in Yemen have many questioning how the economy can diversify to stabilize the budget. In the United States, shale companies have largely been cannibalized to consolidate power across fewer but larger corporations. At a time when the world is increasingly looking at alternative energies to lower pollution and greenhouse gases, oil industries have drastically lowered prices to the detriment of budgets and investors. The question that looms among these oil producers: who will blink first?

The Organization of Petroleum Exporting Countries (OPEC), controlling over 40 percent of the global crude oil production, curiously refused to cut production while oil prices were plummeting last summer, further exacerbating the price fall. OPEC stated that the decision was not politically based and that prices were simply returning to "normal." OPEC's decision to force prices lower in the wake of the worldwide glut confounded oil market pundits. Many looked to shale oil for a formidable explanation. Producing over five million barrels a day, the US shale oil revolution has revitalized the local economies of North Dakota and Texas, while little regulation has allowed companies to produce at prodigious rates. This has lowered US oil imports and softened the influence of OPEC producers on US foreign policy.

While the US shale oil industry only accounts for roughly 6 percent of the global oil market, OPEC's decreasing reach into the US market may have initiated the production glut. OPEC may have wanted to deliver a severe blow to the shale oil companies, who operate with smaller margins than traditional producers, but the simple reality is that OPEC was too late to react. Shale oil production increased after the drastic price collapse last year and has only recently shown signs of stagnation. However, consolidations have kept the industry alive. Large shale oil companies have repeatedly bought previously thriving small shale companies for pennies on the dollar as possible bankruptcies have loomed. This consolidation of the shale industry has provided more oil fields for future exploration to companies that have the capital to wait until prices again rise.

But the most intriguing geopolitical connection to the oil price collapse is the Western sanction regime on Russia. As inflation hit the Russian economy and protracted recession weighed on Russian morale, OPEC ramped up production. Because Russia has (as of May 2015) also produced more oil since the end of the Soviet era, interestingly, this economic stand-off brought the two biggest oil-producing countries (Saudi Arabia and Russia) to the bargaining table. Russia is now considering closer ties to OPEC. Since the formation of OPEC, it has never allied with Russia—the alliance would drastically increase OPEC's global power in determining oil prices. In any event, OPEC has never really trusted Russia and an alliance may only form out of dire necessity, and it would surely be something the United States would staunchly oppose.

As Iran will likely demand greater regional power responsibility as the lifting of sanctions occur in coming months, Saudi Arabia will find its close Western ties strained. Thus, a closer OPEC relationship with Russia would be a geopolitical conundrum for the Western world as the Middle East once again faces possible political destabilization. Witnessing the difficulties of Russian natural gas dependency in recent conflicts in Ukraine, Georgia, and Estonia, an OPEC-Russian alliance would control nearly half of the world's oil, with Russia becoming the likely leading producer. This could echo the 1973 oil embargo, a time when OPEC controlled 53 percent of the world's oil and subsequently handicapped Western economies. With Russia continually looking for ways to damage Western economies and strengthen its own geopolitical position, more Russian energy control would be deplorable to the West.

Additionally, cooperating with Russia would further strain interrelations with Western powers and would be a difficult political gamble for Saudi Arabia. As Western economies are projected to continually dwarf that of Russia for the foreseeable future, and with an apparent divide between the United States and Saudi Arabia regarding Iran, any further strain would leave Saudi Arabia's Western relations questionable. However, as China becomes the world's major oil importer, Saudi Arabia has monopolized the Chinese market and increased Chinese sales 37 percent in the last year, while every other country lost market share. However, Russia is unlikely to agree with any OPEC policy of lowered production while Saudi Arabia continually strives for dominance in the coveted Chinese market. While market competition has surely decreased oil prices, oil remains the most geopolitically significant commodity in the world by all measures. In this environment of little policy clarification and OPEC's failure to halt shale oil production, Russia has faced the harshest conditions of all oil-producing countries. Although Russia would benefit from an end to shale oil, its economy was already facing difficult projections. Vladimir Putin has had to balance his military adventurism with economic difficulties, exacerbated by the oil glut. So it might seem that Russia would be aligned with Saudi Arabia in wanting to damage the US shale oil industry (and, at the same time, US oil giants, like Exxon). Saudi Arabia and Russia have deftly managed budgets, low debt (a meager 2 percent and 18 percent respectively), and strong nationalism. While they would serve each other better as partners in OPEC, the United States cannot allow it, and Saudi Arabia is, as of now, most unlikely to make that gamble, while Russia has more to lose than Saudi Arabia.

All countries involved have much to gain and, similarly, much to lose by way of oil. The United States will be the last to consider any kind of radical action in the oil market as low prices serve the White House's policy for the moment. Russia has little history of giving in to foreign pressures and most likely will adapt to lower oil prices. Saudi Arabia, as the leader of OPEC, will most likely act first to balance its budget. While this will leave Russia to increase oil production if OPEC lowers theirs, it may be the only workable political solution. As of now, however, production remains high as all sides stare down each other and decide which direction is the best direction to take. For the first time in a long time, because of so many diverse geopolitical maneuvers happening at one time amongst the world's energy producers and consumers, the future of the status quo may indeed be very uncertain.

Russia Wants to Use CSTO in Syria

URAN BOBOBEKOV JUNE 27, 2017

For an expansion of a military-political influence in the Middle East, Moscow wishes to use in Syria members of the Collective Security Treaty Organization (CSTO), which is a rather amorphous military block. On June 22, 2017, the chairman of the Defense Committee of the State Duma of Russia, former commander of the Airborne Forces, Colonel-General Vladimir Shamanov, said that Russia was negotiating with Kyrgyzstan and Kazakhstan to send troops to Syria to monitor the military situation. According to the former general, this issue is being worked out with the political and military leadership of the two central Asian states, but the action has not yet been taken. This statement indicates that Russian President Mr. Vladimir Putin is trying to expand the allied governments' composition that could support Moscow's military actions in Syria. Today in the Middle East, only Iran is a staunch ally of Russia, which plays a key role in supporting the political regime of Mr. al-Assad Bashar. It bears reminding that on the side of the progovernment forces of Syria, the elite Iranian Revolutionary Guards Corps, the pro-Lebanese Lebanese Hezbollah movement, and the progovernment militia Shabiha are all fighting under the slogan of fighting ISIS. Russian aviation covers the ground operations of these allies from the air. The Syrian Observatory for Human Rights more than once accused the Russian military of bombing not only the ISIS-controlled territories but also the territories controlled by moderate Sunni armed opposition.

During the fourth international meeting on the settlement of the situation in Syria, which was organized by Moscow, representatives of the guarantor countries in Syria (Russia, Iran, Turkey) signed a memorandum on the creation of four zones of de-escalation in Syria in May. These four zones included:

1) Idlib province and certain parts of the neighboring provinces (Latakia, Hama, and Aleppo provinces);
2) Certain parts in the north of the Homs province;
3) Eastern Ghouta; and
4) Certain parts of southern Syria (Deraa and Al-Quneitra provinces).

The memorandum also provided for sending the military guarantor countries to de-escalation zones to monitor the ceasefire regime. After that, Ankara, Moscow, and Tehran confirmed that they were ready to send their military observers to Syria. According to preliminary data, Turkish military observers would be deployed in the province of Idlib, and observers from Iran and Russia would be in the region of Damascus.

Following the results of these inter-Syrian talks in Astana, the Russian president's special representative for Syria, Alexander Lavrentiev, said that participation of military observers and other countries is possible, but only on the basis of consensus and with the consent of all three guarantor countries. Iran and Turkey immediately agreed with Moscow's strong offer to expand the number of observer states.

On June 22, the representative of the president of Turkey, Mr. Kalın İbrahim, publicly announced that Russia proposed to deploy military observers from Kazakhstan and Kyrgyzstan in the de-escalation zones in Syria. The Turkish side expects that this issue will be included for discussion in the agenda of the fifth international meeting on the settlement of the inter-Syrian conflict, which will also be held in Astana. This shows that Russia is trying to strengthen its position in the Middle East through two former protectorates of Moscow. Kazakhstan and Kyrgyzstan consider Russia their strategic partner. During a recent meeting with Mr. Putin, Kyrgyz president Mr. Atambayev noted that he did not think about the future of his country without Russia. However, officials in Bishkek and Astana don't hurry to confirm words of the Russian and Turkish high-ranking officials. Atambayev has noted "to send troops to Syria, first, the unanimous decision of all members of the CSTO is necessary; secondly, the resolution of the UN is necessary; thirdly, the parliament of the country has to agree; fourthly, if such question arises, Kyrgyzstan has to direct nonactive armed forces, meaning persons interested from among professional soldiers, and officers who could accumulate experience there and earn money."

The Ministry of Foreign Affairs of Kazakhstan also issued an official statement: "Astana is not negotiating with anybody to send servicemen of Kazakhstan to Syria. The question of how the security and effectiveness of the four zones of de-escalation in Syria will be ensured is currently in the competence of the guarantor countries of the Astana process, which will discuss these and other issues during the next meeting on July 4 and 5 in the capital of Kazakhstan." In Astana's opinion, a crucially important condition for sending Kazakh peacekeepers to any hot spot in the world is the existence of a resolution and the mandate of the UN Security Council.

Thus, Kazakhstan and Kyrgyzstan refer to the issue of sending their troops to Syria very carefully. But we should expect that Russia will try to achieve its goal within the Collective Rapid Reaction Force (CRRF) of the CSTO. Today, the CSTO CRRF includes the Ninety-Eighth Guards Airborne Division and the Thirty-First Guards Air Assault Brigade of Russia, the Thirty-Seventh Air Assault Brigade and the Operational Battalion of Kazakhstan, and one battalion each from Armenia, Tajikistan, and Kyrgyzstan. At the time of its creation in 2009, the CRRF numbered twenty thousand troops.

However, Moscow's desire to obtain the military support of two CIS member states in the Middle East is a difficult task. First, the authorities of Kyrgyzstan and Kazakhstan understand perfectly well that sending their troops to Syria and the possible death of servicemen in a "foreign war" can become more difficult for their own internal political situations.

Second, if the two countries intend to send troops to Syria, they will have to get permission from the national parliaments, which is extremely unlikely, especially for Kyrgyzstan, in the run-up to the presidential elections in October 2017. Any such action may lead to the failure of a candidate from a progovernment party. Kyrgyzstan and Kazakhstan do not want to dirty themselves politically with the blood of their soldiers in Syria.

Third, the religious factor plays an important role in this issue. It is known that Russia supports the Alawite Bashar Assad, who belongs to the Shiite branch of Islam, while the armed opposition represents Sunnis. The Kazakhs and Kyrgyz are Sunnis, and the religious leaders of the two countries repeatedly expressed their discontent with Russia's military expansion into Syria. If Kazakhstan and Kyrgyzstan send troops to support Assad, their authorities may lose the electoral support of Muslim believers.

Fourth, because of Western economic sanctions against Moscow, which is the main trade and economic partner of Kyrgyzstan and Kazakhstan, the economy of both countries has been seriously affected. In the context of the economic crisis, for Astana and Bishkek, sending troops to Syria will place an additional burden on the state budget which they cannot afford.

So, in conclusion, it should be noted that Moscow's desire to enlist the support of its military policy in Syria from Kazakhstan and Kyrgyzstan is a PR campaign directed primarily to the West. Politicians of Western countries and the media have repeatedly blamed Mr. Putin for deploying the Russian military on the side of Assad's army in the Syrian civil war. By inviting his "Central Asian vassals" to his side, the Russian emperor Putin wants to give the world a clear and unambiguous message that Russia is still a force to be reckoned with. The further development of events will show whether Russia is able to create an international alliance in opposition to the US-led anti-terrorist coalition in the Middle East, or whether the authorities of Kazakhstan and Kyrgyzstan are able to pass this test of strength of their state independence.

False Promise

How the Turkish-Russian Dilemma Unmasks NATO

EVAN THOMSEN NOVEMBER 27, 2015

There is no shortage of security threats to the NATO alliance: a resurgent and militarily active Russia; the territorial and global jihadist threat of DAESH; and the movements of over four million refugees. Now, more than ever, would seem a time where solidarity of purpose and the coordination of logistical and security efforts would serve as a useful mechanism for minimum basic security. While NATO could hardly be described as a model of solidarity or efficiency before, the outlook of NATO has dramatically changed after the November 24 downing of a Russian Su-24 warplane, and its very purpose for existing may be now called into question.

While the data is insufficient at this point, the narrative is developing predictably. Turkish President Erdogan said that the Russian warplane violated Turkish airspace and that it failed to respect ten warnings from the Turkish military. Ultimately, "Turkey is a country whose warnings should be taken seriously and listened to. Don't test Turkey's patience. Try to win its friendship." Erdogan doubled down by highlighting the estimated two million Syrian refugees in Turkey—a burden that far outpaces any commitment by other NATO member states. These are nothing short of targeted threats and are intended to resonate more within the NATO alliance than act as a hedge against Russia's military activity on or within Turkish borders.

Russia's reaction has been equally predictable. President Putin has quickly adopted a harsher tone, not only highlighting the consequences of this action on Russian-Turkish relations but directly calling this "a stab in the back by the terrorists' accomplices." The board is set, the die cast, and the pieces moving. The next steps are now what crucially matter. In this sense, it is easy to see why some are questioning how this is not the start of WWIII. We are witnessing a nearly global response to a series of metaconflicts that have seen tens of thousands of lives lost and millions displaced. Meanwhile, global and regional powers are now openly brandishing military, economic, and political tools, bound in seemingly contradictory relationships as everyone has a web of shared/conflicting interests. Forces are gradually being amassed, reminiscent of a situation preparatory to war, and now the traditional security dilemma could be starting to unfold. The only ingredient missing is a modern-day Ferdinand-Princip moment.

It would be overly pessimistic to say that this is a foregone conclusion. Similarly, it would be foolishly naive to say that the current state of affairs in the Syrian-DAESH conflict is not a potential tinderbox that could unravel the world's strongest military alliance. Unfortunately, the varied and inconsistent reactions by NATO member states are doing little to prevent the pessimistic narrative from becoming reality. The brief moment of opportunity and unity of purpose between the United States, Russia, and France in light of DAESH's global strikes in Paris seem to have been as substantively robust as internet selfies transposed with the French flag on Facebook. The Turkish strike, which could technically be called a strike by NATO against Russia, has effectively sublimated any global sentiment for transcending traditional rivalries.

While the message from NATO Secretary General Jens Stoltenberg was clear ("we stand in solidarity with Turkey and support the territorial integrity of our NATO ally"), the responses from leaders of other NATO member states have been less clear. The responses have been a mix of passively enumerating international law, a call for calm and de-escalation, and confusion, given the many reports citing that the Russian aircraft was only in Turkish airspace for thirty seconds. This last claim, which comes out of an early report from the United States, gives credence to Putin's charge that this attack from Turkey was far from reactionary but premeditated. How, ultimately, can the NATO alliance move forward given the disparate reactions to the events of November 24, their competing goals in the two-front challenge of Syria-DAESH and Russia, and the increasingly emotional political discourse heavily laden with nationalistic overtones?

It is important to put the NATO alliance into context. It is a military alliance intended to provide mutual security and protection against external threats. This function was a strategic priority of the highest order. The history of NATO was rather simple in this regard: it was designed to be a bulwark against the Soviet Union in a bipolar world with interstate security threats expected to be fought in conventional theatres. Twenty-five years on, a lot has changed in the global political and security landscape. And while NATO has not adapted, one cannot be overly critical: NATO, in effect, served its purpose. If its purpose now is to support and extend ad infinitum the status quo of "Pax Americana," then its aims are aspirational and its structure is subordinated to interests based upon values (or dogma) rather than security.

It is at this point where we ought to be reminded of another set of European values—the specific and changing interests of the state. To paraphrase the famous quote from Henry Templeton: "I say that it is a narrow policy to suppose that this country or that is to be marked out as the eternal ally or the perpetual enemy of [insert country]. We have no eternal allies and we have no perpetual enemies. Our interests are eternal and perpetual and those interests it is our duty to follow." NATO is not a single sovereign state, and it is no longer singularly charged to defend the collective interests of Europe against the no-longer-existent Soviet Union. Security threats and interests change, as do individual state strategies toward pursuing those interests and defending against diverse threats. NATO, in its current structure, no longer adequately addresses the security challenges to its member states nor serves as a convening body to unite a set of similar interests among diverse parties. This alliance is in tatters and basically has been for twenty-five years. The Turkish strike on the Russian aircraft was not the straw that broke the camel's back, therefore, but simply the removal of a blindfold that has long needed to be removed.

More Bear Than Eagle

Russia Taking Advantage of an American Vacuum

NENAD DRCA MARCH 25, 2016

It is evident that the United States cannot fight DAESH as if there is no complex war raging in Syria. Considering the conditions on the ground, the US administration must address not only how to degrade and destroy DAESH, but how US policy can help restore stability across the Syrian state. It must do both by being diplomatically active in engaging all major actors in play in the region. For America, Russia and Iran cannot be allowed to set diplomatic precedence in Syria and Iraq and be the leaders. The United States must formulate integrated strategy that would involve Washington in any major diplomatic discussions regarding potential political solutions. So far this is not the case. This new approach will require expanded engagement with the Syrian players, both domestic and foreign, in order to improve possibilities for change.

Without inclusion of the Russian side, Russia will be more likely to undermine Western plans and potentially drag America into protracted and chaotic proxy war. Once it was clear that Syrian leader Assad would not step down easily, US policy did not adapt nor did policymakers create a viable alternative strategy to achieve its goals. It is apparent that Syria is becoming a geopolitical Chernobyl, spreading violence and fanaticism across the region. Once DAESH is eliminated, any new strategy must aim to achieve an immediate drop in violence by coordinating a ceasefire across all sides. The difficulty is going to be determining the political price for the elimination of DAESH.

American political and military lethargy in Syria should be viewed as a result of having no compelling strategy that could push for deeper effective involvement. This must no longer be the case, as the United States must work towards curbing further spillover of the Syrian crisis, which has brought refugee mayhem to Europe. Now US allies in Europe must contend with the massive potential threat emerging. The United States and European Union should use a combination of assertive military initiatives and broad diplomatic approaches to establish communication with all major regional actors. The United States must pressure Saudi Arabia, Qatar, and Turkey to halt financial and weapons assistance to their groups of choice within Iraq and Syria. Both the European Union and the United States can use an integrated strategy that includes arms embargos, economic sanctions and airstrikes.

Keeping Russian pride in mind, cooperation is possible by working parallel, coordinated air strikes and other operations for maximum effect against DAESH. In April, Foreign Minister Lavrov called radical Islamist violence "the main threat" to Russia today. Jihadists who live in Russia's North Caucasus have switched their allegiance to DAESH and declared their regions part of the DAESH provincial network. Russia is worried that the Syrian Assad regime could be replaced by a worse Islamist extremist force. The collapse of governments in Libya and Iraq has been used by Russia to affirm such concerns. The United States should use this shared fear to motivate Russia and the European Union to work together. This is an opportunity to develop a new diplomatic path and establish new beneficial connections to Russia and come out as a cohesive positive influence in the area. But so far this has frustratingly not happened.

Former deputy director of the CIA Michael Morell said that any strategy should probably include working with Syrian President Bashar Assad and Russia. Proxy war with Russia will not help America, and it will not decimate terrorist groups that are more important in the immediate-term. The priority for all involved sides right now must be the absolute destruction of DAESH and its allies. DAESH has clearly achieved capacity to strike the European Union, and it has the same plans for the United States. The question of whether President Assad needs to go can be tackled in a post-DAESH world.

The fight against radical Islam is something that the European Union, Russia, and even China support. There is a potential to use this international sentiment to start working on new diplomatic relationships. While some countries can help militarily, many more can help financially by providing supplies or impeding DAESH financial networks. After multiple brutal terror attacks in France and now Brussels, the European Union is out of time and must act as soon as possible on new ideas. Meanwhile, the United States must stop appearing hamstrung by the continued lack of valid partners on the ground in Syria, whether diplomatically or militarily. Too much time and resources are wasted and it is only adding to the image of the United States being indecisive and even impotent.

Continued diplomatic dialogue should present realistic and achievable goals that many countries find attractive. At the moment most countries want DAESH to be eliminated. But the United States should not allow Russia to continue to lead the way in military and diplomatic action. It should be a primary part of all regional, high-level negotiations, which at the moment it is not. The current rigid and recalcitrant American strategy should be abandoned. The Middle East must understand that America will be the part of any solution no matter what. That is something Iran should be reminded of due to its recent political and military assertions.

At the moment, the European Union lacks cohesive leadership that can mandate decisions and act in a timely manner. Following the recent attacks in Paris and Brussels, it remains to be seen if NATO can react according to its accord of mutual protection. If it doesn't, then some of America's prime European partners might start looking more toward Russia. For example, British Prime Minister Cameron is open to compromises on the future of Syrian President Assad in return for Russian help targeting DAESH. French President Hollande will travel to Washington and Moscow to discuss ways of increasing international cooperation in the fight against DAESH. The United States must act to avoid losing the leadership position to Russia in this fight. Putin is more than willing to exploit the void left by Washington in Syria and Iraq. France and the United Kingdom cannot single-handedly defeat DAESH. They are now painfully aware that they both need foreign assistance. So what remains to be seen is, Who is going to step up to that desperate need in real terms: America or Russia? Disturbingly, so far in real terms, the answer seems to be more bear than eagle.

Russia Self-Trapped in Abkhazia and South Ossetia?

RAHIM RAHIMOV OCTOBER 20, 2016

Abkhazia and South Ossetia, the two Russian-backed breakaway regions of Georgia, were recognized by Russia as independent states following the Russia-Georgia war of August 2008 in a hasty and emotional move. This state recognition must be reviewed in the light of the annexation of Crimea and the two brutal and bloody wars Russia has fought against its own breakaway region Chechnya.

The Russian perspectives on Abkhazia and South Ossetia are inevitably made more complicated and awkward due to Russia's positions in Syria, Chechnya, and Crimea. Since the international community sees Russia as being aggressive and intrusive in those previous situations, it is unlikely it will give any serious consideration to the independence desires of Abkhazia and South Ossetia. The two regions are, in essence, getting punished for their association with Russian support. To justify its annexation of Crimea and its recognition of Abkhazia and South Ossetia, Russian leaders have repeatedly and publicly stated that Kosovo declared independence and was recognized by Western nations. Russia's own recognition of secessionist regimes in the post-Soviet space like Abkhazia and South Ossetia may well trigger a new wave of nationalist movements like the past Chechen initiatives by the force of the same logic.

Russia doesn't seem to have a valid answer to counter that possibility. Although Crimea's secession from Ukraine may be regarded as encouragement for Chechens, Crimea's annexation by Russia sends a crystal-clear and strong message: you may secede from other states but not Russia; you may be annexed to none but Russia. The question of secession and independence may be raised not only by Chechnya but also by other Muslim regions of "multi-national and multi-faith" Russia. Such a scenario may end in fatal effects on Russia's national security and territorial integrity because the independence of a Russian autonomous republic could become a precedent for other Russian regions to follow. A vital nuance to understanding the situation is that Georgia had made moves toward Euro-Atlantic integration, which could have meant a US or NATO military presence on Russia's borders in the near future. During the Chechen wars, Russia repeatedly blamed Georgia for being used by Chechen rebels. Any third-party military presence in Georgia is perceived by Moscow as a direct threat to its own national security. This perception is amplified by assumptions that such a presence could result in more opportunities for secessionists in Russia's North Caucasus. Therefore, secessionist conflicts in Abkhazia and South Ossetia are like a diplomatic buffer gift for Russia to prevent such scenarios from happening elsewhere.

Russia looks at the future of Abkhazia and South Ossetia through the prism of national security. Therefore, it is very likely that Russia will aim for annexation of Abkhazia and South Ossetia at some point in the future in a way that is similar to their recent Crimean annexation. What would that scenario mean for Abkhazia and South Ossetia? These breakaway regions seceded from Georgia to supposedly become independent, not part of or dependent on Russia. They might have been better off within Georgia rather than within Russia. Better to be in a stronger position within small Georgia rather than in giant Russia and just one of numerous autonomous republics. They could find themselves in a humble position, lost in the Russian federal shuffle.

However, apart from political aspects, practicalities of the Abkhazian or South Ossetian independence look troubled. North Ossetia was already within Russia. Perhaps one day North Ossetia and South Ossetia would like to be united. No doubt, Russia will not allow them to unite as a nation independent of Russia. So, the best possibility for their reunification lies within the borders of Russia. The populations of Abkhazia and South Ossetia are around 240,000 and 60,000, respectively. These tiny populations are not homogenously Abkhazian or Ossetian. The demographic compositions are ethnically and religiously very diverse. Abkhazians and South Ossetians often sound furious with Georgian nationalism and obsessed with promoting their own ethnic, linguistic, and cultural identity. All well and good. But Abkhazia and South Ossetia are both inhabited by other ethnicities like Russians, Ukrainians, Georgians, Armenians, Jews, Turks, and more. Which cultural identity do these states wish to take for themselves?

But there is additional domestic opposition to unification within Russia, in particular in Abkhazia. Russia doesn't seem to be attractive to Abkhazia. As a result of the Russian military campaigns in Chechnya, the number of Chechen civilian casualties is estimated around 200,000-300,000, which roughly equates to the total population of Abkhazia and South Ossetia. Additionally, Russia's record of democracy, rule of law, human rights, freedom of speech, and the rights and powers of autonomous republics is troubled. All these factors help to explain why ordinary populations as well as elites in both Abkhazia and South Ossetia would oppose unification with Russia or at least would be very divided on the issue. Yet, conversely, these regions are also heavily dependent on subsidies from Moscow and they have become more isolated from the international community after the Russian-Georgian war of August 2008.

As Robert Strausz-Hupe famously said, "a nation must think before it acts." Russia should have thought before acting with regard to the recognition of the breakaway regions of Georgia. A consequence of that hasty and emotional decision is that Russia is confronted by a terrible dilemma either to let Abkhazia and South Ossetia go on as independent states or to annex them. Neither works very well from the Russian perspective. The annexation could have bitter consequences: on one hand, it could trigger opposition from Abkhazia and South Ossetia, and on the other hand, it could cause another wave of international sanctions against Russia, aggravating Russia's already damaged international reputation, and even more importantly, contribute to depicting Russia as aggressive and hostile on the neighboring post-Soviet states. To put it differently, Russia looks like it trapped itself with its decisions about Abkhazia and South Ossetia.

World War Z

Why Russia Fights DAESH Zealots

DECEMBER 1, 2015

America has made little progress in Iraq and Syria, something Russia is determined to change, apparently. The Obama administration maintains that a lasting political solution requires Assad's departure, but facing Russian military involvement, Iranian ground troops, Hezbollah military units, many armed jihadist groups, and the world's worst humanitarian crisis, the United States confronts a convoluted situation that it seems unable to solve on its own. In light of these prodigious challenges, louder voices are demanding that the United States basically leave the Syrian mess to the Russians and let it be an Afghanistan Redux. More careful consideration, however, reveals that this analysis of the situation is misplaced and faulty.

This camp's basic logic rests on how full-spectrum talks would demand the bringing together of so many sworn enemy groups (internal and external) that herding cats would prove more feasible. But there is also sinister realpolitik going along with these arguments: namely, that America should not counter Russian involvement but rather sit back and enjoy watching Russia get sucked into a conflict that might be the only real chance to significantly weaken Putin.

While no one should be surprised to hear that major global powers consider their own interests when becoming involved in the conflicts of other states, there is something disturbingly naïve about the above-mentioned arguments: Western commentators have too often brazenly declared across the Middle East and post-Soviet space Machiavellian strategies in public while still hoping the nobler yet quieter motivations of freedom enhancement were believed. Alas, they are not. Consequently, it does America no good to hang back from Syria while Russia does all the dirty work, hoping the Russian Federation receives a devastating blow to its global power as President Obama talks eloquently about Syrian democracy. The only thing this does in real terms is create an environment of diplomatic insincerity that does far more damage long term to American legitimacy than the possible advantages of a weakened Russian state. On the ground, Russia's reputation would still be rewarded for making the effort while America and the European Union would look rather craven and manipulative.

These are not, however, the most serious errors in strategy. The premise that Russia might get sucked into a Syrian quagmire just as America has in Iraq and Afghanistan misses one very elementary but profound point: Russia is *not* in Syria to establish freedom and democracy for the Syrian people. Rather, it just wants to return the region to a more recognizable status quo where the preferred regime is in place and the potential of radical Islamism seeping into Russia's southern flanks is markedly reduced. This is what makes the often-heard Western criticism about Russian air strikes hitting not just DAESH strongholds but also well-known rebel areas somewhat odd: Russia has never wavered on its principal position that the key foreign-policy element to be handled in Syria is fighting terrorism. Russia was never interested in seeing the now-stagnant Arab Spring reach Damascus. And while it has also freely stated that there is no formal state love or personal preference for keeping Assad in power, Russia *does* demand that whatever regime is in place needs to be as committed to preventing radical Islamist groups from operating as Assad was.

This was always a sharp point of contention for Russia since the early days of the anti-Assad uprising. Russia never felt comfortable with the boast that the United States knew who actually made up the various rebel groups and was equally certain that America was recklessly funding and arming people that could either be replaced by radical Islamists or be co-opted by them. Given that the rise of DAESH in the region is at least partially seen in Russia as a consequence of American strategy gone awry in Iraq and Syria, Russia's skepticism cannot be so easily dismissed. Under such political chaos, Russia was quite happy with throwing its support behind Assad, no matter how heinous his own authoritarian rule might be. While it may have been unfortunately true that everyday Syrians would be hurt by a continued Assad tyranny, the Russian Ministry of Foreign Affairs felt that would at least be an internal Syrian affair and not immediately destabilizing to the global community. The same could not be said for the resulting chaos if the Assad regime fell to a hodgepodge of amorphous rebel groups mixed with jihadists who dreamt of apocalyptic caliphate fantasies.

This is the strange reality often missed in the West: Russia's passion about eliminating radical jihadists is as fervent as American claims for promoting democracy. Thus, there is not really a Russian political goal in Syria that mirrors the American one. Russia does not need a strong Assad or a competent Assad regime: it simply wants a return to the previous status quo where it had close ties to the governing regional powers and carte blanche permission to eliminate Islamic jihadists seen as legitimate threats. Therefore the criticism that Russia's strategy is doomed to fail because there really are not any groups to bring to the table to forge a pluralistic Syria is hollow. The reality is that Russia is not in the region to be the personal guarantor of such a goal. This level of optimal fantasy diplomacy is what Russia usually criticizes the United States for and believes brings more problems than solutions. Ultimately, Russia only wants to make sure its larger regional interests remain intact and, concurrently, no jihadist groups have the ability to spread beyond the region and attack its people.

If America had its "Vietnam syndrome" for at least a generation—where getting stuck in a complex and horrifically violent conflict dramatically influenced its foreign policy and military thinking—it is fair to say Russia has had its own "Chechen syndrome," which for the same amount of time has influenced Russian strategic conflict thinking in much the same way. It has always drawn a direct line between the Chechen wars of the 1990s to 9/11 to the Taliban to the Madrid train attacks to the Boston Marathon bombing to the Sharm el Sheik civilian airliner crash to the Beirut-Paris-Kenya attacks. For Russia this has always been a single elongated fight meant to unite the modern world in a death match against zealots. It has always openly declared that this needs to be tackled by all sides and all countries, whether formally allies or adversaries. This is why it has been so utterly frustrated with the United States: the one obvious partner that should share its distaste for such violent religious zealotry has always steadfastly refused to engage in real counterterrorist partnership with it. What is Russia to assume about gamesmanship and strategy when it gets criticized for air-strike targeting but is rebuffed by the United States when asking for specific targets to hit or locations to avoid? How should the general public react to criticism of Russian motives as new voices begin to recognize the comprehensiveness of Russian strikes and that its air campaign might be working?

So when people like Simpson criticize the conflict in Syria as a dilemma with no military endpoint because it is and can only be a fight to the death, they are unknowingly acknowledging the Russian argument that has been in play all along. This is exactly why Syria could end up a swamp that Russians are willing to get dirty in. When framed in the language of millenarian religious struggle harkening back to the vile barbarism of the Chechen wars, Russians on the whole are willing to fight if it might mean there will be no Paris tragedies in Moscow or Saint Petersburg. For Russia, this is not a battle about political systems or economic markets or global positioning (which is what it always accuses American adventurism of being about) but rather a war over the very lifeblood of modern society.

So caution should be urged when critics claim impending Russian doom in Syria and an inevitable political quagmire. Syria is no Afghanistan Redux: Russia is not trying to ideologically claim the territory for itself in a move of proxy prestige. Its goals are actually far more attainable and far more easily aligned with popular attitudes at home. It is not necessarily striving for a perfect political solution that the whole world can get behind in order to claim personal victory: these are the lofty and often unrealistic foreign-policy goals with which America pushes itself into a corner. Russia, in the end, can claim victory if there is a local regime in Damascus partial to its interests and it continues to have the opportunity to kill jihadists at will there. In the Russian diplomatic mind-set this matters because it means relevance on the world stage while having to worry less about creeping Koranic quasi-insurgencies across its own major cities.

Two things are certain as the battle rages on in Syria: assumptions about American foreign-policy superiority need to be taken with a grain of salt, as there is as much rational geostrategic self-interest in America's positions as there is with Russia's. And when it comes to the fight against groups like DAESH, Russia has been rather uniquely candid about its purposes and goals, all while hoping America and the West would be willing to join in. Even if that never happens and the West continues to refuse such a partnership, it might not want to hold its diplomatic breath waiting for the demise of Russia in the quagmire. Reports on the inevitability of Russia's slow Syrian death may just prove to be greatly exaggerated.

In the end, the mistake the Western world has made for nearly two decades is that it has drawn up civilizational lines based on geography, political ideology, state/religious boundaries, and even economic strategies. These lines have allowed the world to divide itself into ever-smaller camps, making the civilian undersides of societies ever easier and more susceptible to extremist bloodshed and horror. In this battle Russia feels it should not be seen as the West against the rest or white against color or the Global North against the Global South. It is about the modern world fighting the zealot world. Until leaders in the West embrace this reality and begin to smash their own self-imposed boundaries of nationalism, statehood, and geostrategy, they will constantly be putting themselves in a limited and exposed position against a radicalized enemy. And scenes like the ones played out in France, Lebanon, and Kenya will only continue. Hope at the moment does not seem bright: already less than two weeks after the Paris attacks and increased pressure from world leaders to consider cooperating in the fight against terrorist zealots, Turkey downed a Russian jet fighter that it claimed did not respond to "warnings about crossing into Turkish airspace." Worse still, initial reports are that the two pilots successfully ejected from the fighter, only to be shot at while floating to the ground via parachute. Incidents like this, in the face of a greater common enemy, means the modern world is not taking the zealot world as seriously as it needs to. It means that World War Z will continue to be lost.

For an explanation as to what DAESH actually stands for and where it comes from linguistically (while also being provided a compelling reason why the global community needs to shift off of the terms ISIS and ISIL and IS and exclusively use the preferred Arabic acronym DAESH), please see the Mirror *article "What Does Daesh Mean? ISIS 'Threatens to Cut Out the Tongues' of Anyone Using This Word" by Nicola Oakley and Suchandrika Chakrabarti.*

PART V

EDUCATION, MEDIA, AND ANALYSIS

Cold War Triumphalism and Chicken-and-Egg Dilemmas

FEBRUARY 5, 2015

There is a decided chicken-and-egg question when it comes to trying to unravel Russian-American relations. The general pessimism and pejorative characterizations that come from the US Congress clearly have a negative influence on Putin's strident bravado and dismissive arrogance to the United States. What is perplexing is how this dilemma, which implies that it is difficult to figure out which truly came first, never seems to be an actual problem for American politicians: the Russian corrupt and violent chicken *always* comes before the calm and diplomatic American egg.

Of course Russia feels equally strongly that the American oppressive and interfering egg came well before the Russian self-defense chicken. It refuses to accept sole blame for all of the bombastic rhetoric. In this particular case reality better supports the Russian side: it is more accurate to describe Putin's hostility toward America as one far more deeply rooted in frustration. But instead, America characterizes Russia as having an unstable mania that is obsessed with remaining a great Derzhava (powerful state) and will not recognize its culpability in creating its own future political cataclysm.

The failure of America to move past the crowing Cold War triumphalism has produced a decided negative impact on Russian-American relations that precludes a new era from developing. It is as if Russia is being criticized that it simply does not know its place or will not accept its role, both of which, of course, are decided by America and are not open to negotiation. Prominent thinkers and players like John McCain, Charles Krauthammer, Ariel Cohen, Hillary Clinton, George Will, Alexander Motyl, and Fiona Hill are quick to damn "Russian provocations" (such as the Chechen conflict, the Crimean annexation, the intimidation of Russian journalists, and oil/gas gamesmanship with the European Union) as moving the country toward becoming a de facto "fascist" state. In reality no such explicit initiatives can be found backing up such radical accusations. More calm analyses find that Russia is simply not accepting being told what to do on the world stage, and that general position (operating in its own interests for its own interests) is so incredibly basic and elementary for all nations it is perplexing how much kvetching happens in America when Russia does it.

This is especially true when one considers that Russia feels, with some validation, that it has been incredibly nonconfrontational with the United States on many issues since the end of the Cold War that have not necessarily been aligned with its own national interests. As a result, it is not uncommon to find Russian political players quite adamant that the United States "owes" it for accepting moves that could have easily exploded into formal conflict between the two sides after the Cold War.

Americans at times can play too fast and loose with semantics. As long as the United States does not actively try to create political discord in a country like Russia, it thinks it cannot possibly be seen as a source of such discord with controversial communiqués about political unrest and civil disobedience. There are simply no Russian actors that would agree with that interpretation. They instead see US communiqués as subtle but nonetheless direct attempts to massage and influence the political environment inside their country. Russians to this day point to Georgia, to Ukraine, to the countries of the Arab Spring, and to Syria and believe the buildup to the unrest was either directly orchestrated by the United States or at least subtly fostered by America. To Russians, there is no difference, while to Americans it is unthinkably false to say that encouragement equates to orchestration. And while on some global stages it would be an exaggeration to place a large portion of the blame for outbreaks of unrest upon America, it would be naïve to think that open American support and encouragement, at least through formal media declarations and diplomatic speeches, did not have an impact on increasing the intensity and duration of domestic protest. The difference for most Americans is that they see countries like Libya, Syria, Egypt, etc., as *needing* governmental change. But you have to forgive the Kremlin if it does not agree that it is on par with despotic, theocratic Islamist regimes. Similar rhetoric from the US government regarding both is what allows Russia to take statements from Washington about bilateral cooperation and substantive partnership and see nothing but animosity, mistrust, and manipulation.

There is no doubt Russia has accepted that the end of the Cold War signaled a decided shift in the balance of power. It did not, however, allow that change to mean that it now had to be permanently relegated to the status of nation-state also-ran. And quite frankly, too many voices in American institutions of power, both governmentally and academically, have taken that premise as an unquestioned reality and as the expected diplomatic path Russia should place itself on. This is why the more strident voices in Russia are so quick to use the word "appeasement" when describing what they think America wants Russia to do and be. As long as the two nations continue to engage each other with this attitudinal chasm, then the relationship will likely continue to be dogged by vast differences of opinion, massively divergent interpretations, and seemingly contradictory positions on nearly every issue. If we do not move beyond Cold War triumphalism and flawed chicken-and-egg dilemmas, then Russia and America will continue to create chaos for each other where there should be cooperation.

Keeping Russia the Enemy

Congressional Attitudes and Biased Expertise

MAY 20, 2015

America seems reluctant to accept the fairly benign fact that countries do not like to be dictated to and thus is missing opportunities to create new dialogue. Understanding this is particularly helpful in explaining the United States' poor relationship with Russia at the moment. But the United States goes beyond dictating to Russia; its so-called expert analysts seem to view Russian politics through a deliberately darkened lens with a perpetually negative and pejorative outlook.

The recent exit of Alexander Sytnik as a senior fellow from the Russian Institute for Strategic Research is a prime example of this problem. Upon his exit early in 2015, Reshetnikov unleashed a torrent of information that, while interesting, really does not amount to more than just gossip and hearsay. Worse, American media and political analysts adopted it almost wholly as fact rather than as one perspective from a source motivated to talk badly about Russia:

> The Russian analyst's scathing remarks about the country's leadership and about the community of government experts *confirm* that the concept of Russian supremacy has a strong hold on the Russian leadership. These supremacist views are not limited to the post-Soviet space, where "only ethnic Russians are capable of creating statehood." The West is also seen as decadent and somewhat spiritually inferior to

> the Russians. The spread of such views in Russia, especially among the country's leaders, precludes easy and quick solutions to the Ukrainian crisis, but rather suggests a relatively lengthy period of tensions between Russia and the West, even if Russian strongman Vladimir Putin were, for some reason, to step down.[1]

The tendency here is to use personal opinion as *confirmation of fact* when it could be easily rejected as biased material. The only confirmation taking place is the affirming of preconceived ideas and a particular agenda that undermines any new attitudinal environment developing between Russia and the United States.

It is easy to find "research" proclaiming Russian goals that have never been formulated or addressing Putin objectives that have never been stated. This is not to say that Russia is incapable of having ulterior motives or secret agendas. Truly, every country to one degree or another has them. The criticism here is that there is a propensity in the Russian analytical sphere to presume such agendas and then cherry-pick information to affirm those assumptions. In pure methodological terms, selection bias is rife within the community that analyzes Russia, leaving those analyses decidedly weak.

While much hope was initially placed on the so-called Obama reset in American relations with Russia in 2008, the reality is that enthusiasm quickly faded, and the Democratic Party's attitudes

1 Valery Dzutsati, "Analyst Provides Insider View of Russian Government Think Tank," *Eurasia Daily Monitor* 12, no. 11, https://jamestown.org/program/analyst-provides-insider-view-of-russian-government-think-tank/.

toward Russia subsequently became as squarely pessimistic and adversarial as traditional Republican Party views. Indeed, in today's environment of divided government, having a problem with Russia seems to be one of the few happy consensus points in Washington. The only problem, of course, is that consensus is built more upon partisan posturing, each side trying to one-up the other in order to earn foreign-policy merit points.

There are voices that decry a picture being painted that combines inaccuracy with heightened rhetoric while purposely ignoring mitigating contexts and less negative observations. However, those voices are extremely rare and at the moment easily drowned out by the drumbeat of Russian derision. Until more unbiased, reasoned voices grow louder or strive to become more prominent public figures in Washington, it seems there is little hope for an improvement in relations between the United States and Russia based on actual events in the real world. Image and attitude, unfortunately, seem to carry greater weight.

Unbiased Media, Biased Agendas

How to Make a Russian Demon

JUNE 18, 2015

A little over one year ago, the world was given a foundational lesson in how an impartial press can unknowingly construct a partial opinion. The consequences of that lesson are still being heard today, and much to the detriment of the Russian Federation.

March 16, 2014, marked the day when the people of Crimea went to the voting booths to decide whether they would be part of Ukraine or part of Russia. While the referendum was no doubt important to people living in Crimea, I for one remained highly skeptical that the results would actually be the ultimate arbiter on the territorial decisions made about Crimea. The outside players, namely Ukraine, Russia, the United States, NATO, and the European Union, were simply too big and too influential to let this small peninsula play an independent role far beyond that of the geopolitical football that it represented. I felt deeply for the people of Crimea, but the bitter reality and perhaps even more bitter truth was that high politics on the global stage are still enacted in such a blunt manner. Unfortunately, this type of cynical maneuvering has been going on for literally thousands of years and will likely not end with the current crisis between Russia and the West over Ukraine. We have seen it in potential American military initiatives today involving the Baltics and recent egregiously reckless comments made by US representative to the UN Samantha Power about Russia and Ukraine.

Ending crises such as the one in Crimea is not only the work of governments, diplomats, and militaries. Reporters play a crucial role as well. While Western journalists as a whole tend to be a conscientious lot, simply pursuing an interesting story and often putting themselves in harm's way in order to get it, the Cold War residue that remains between the United States and Russia has put a grimy film over more than just political actors. It often affects the way in which stories are told, the lens through which "impartial observers" focus their attention. Unfortunately, this usually happens at a subconscious level, resulting in news stories that were meant to be "fair, free, and impartial'" that instead have decidedly biased perspectives snaking their way from reporter to reader.

For an illustration on this unconscious bias, look no further than the first reporting on referendum day from the highly respected and august news organization Reuters. It reported how "thousands of Russian troops have taken control of the Black Sea peninsula and Crimea's pro-Russian leaders have sought to ensure the vote is tilted in Moscow's favor. That, along with an ethnic Russian majority, is expected to result in a comfortable 'yes' vote to leave Ukraine." These are actually two very different perspectives conflated into a single position. On the one hand, readers were given the distinct understanding that the referendum was basically rigged, commandeered by Crimean leaders, who were nothing but sycophants to the Kremlin. But the very next sentence also accurately mentioned that Crimea was majority ethnic Russian, which should have indicated to a reader that a free and fair referendum might end up producing the very result the reporters told us could not be genuine. So which was it? Was Crimea manipulated by local leaders and the Russian military, or was its majority Russian population voting its free and voluntary will? By writing the piece so that the suspicious manipulation theory was conflated with the demographically true statistic, a reader was either left confused or pushed into thinking the referendum itself was irrelevant and that Russia was rather, well, evil.

The piece further reported, "The majority of Crimea's 1.5 million electorate support leaving Ukraine and becoming part of Russia, citing expectations of better pay and the prospect of joining a country capable of asserting itself on the world stage. But others see the referendum as nothing more than a geopolitical land grab by the Kremlin. . . . Ethnic Tatars, Sunni Muslims of Turkic origin who make up 12 percent of Crimea's population, said they would boycott the referendum, despite promises by the authorities to give them financial aid and proper land rights." Again, this deftly presented evidence in a manner that delegitimized the ethnic Russian majority by highlighting a small minority group, ethnic Tatars, and how it would boycott the referendum. This is playing a bit fast and loose with the complex ethnic makeup of the former Soviet Union, portraying a picture that is not entirely accurate: ethnic Tatars have a long and rich history within the Russian Federation. One of the most powerful ethnic republics and richest regions in Russia today is Tatarstan. The idea that ethnic Tatars in Crimea were protesting the referendum because they were somehow worried or fearful of being part of Russia was simply fallacious. It was much more likely, given the present environment of political turmoil and open discussions about autonomy and self-rule (let us not forget that Crimea was itself a semiautonomous region within Ukraine under the Ukrainian Constitution), that the ethnic Tatars saw what Crimean leaders were doing and hoped to also earn their own piece of newly acquired political and economic power. Rejecting the Crimean offer of financial aid and proper land rights meant they weren't arguing about principle anymore but just how big their piece of the pie would be. All of this background and subtle nuance would have made readers more informed and impressed with how complex and multilayered the Crimean situation is. Instead, they were left with a picture that had Crimean authority mere puppets on Kremlin strings and oppressed minorities politically stomped over by Russian jackboots.

The Reuters piece continued to explain the situation, stating "the protests began when Yanukovich turned his back on a trade deal with the European Union and opted for a credit and cheap oil deal worth billions of dollars with Ukraine's former Soviet overlord, Russia." I have written on this issue in the past, and it continues to perplex me how the above transaction is only portrayed in Western media as Yanukovich simply being in the back pocket of Moscow. Entering into greater trade cooperation with the European Union, paving the way for closer relations, also means ultimately answering to European Union financial demands. Perhaps we could ask Greece, Italy, or Portugal how that goes at times. Not all paths to the European Union are paved with gold, especially given the cyclical and topsy-turvy nature of the global economy. Considering this, why did Western media portray acceptance for a credit, oil, and gas deal worth "billions of dollars" for Ukraine right now as being akin to a Faustian bargain made with a "Soviet overlord"? What was the impact on uninformed readers who did not know that the Russian credit deal basically meant Russia forgave a massive amount of oil and gas debt owed by Ukraine? If a country was truly looking to be an "evil overlord," might it not be far easier to simply call in its chips without remorse rather than offer deals that eliminate debt with no repayment?

Finally, the Reuters piece reported, "Voters have two options to choose from—but both imply Russian control of the peninsula. On the surface, the second choice appears to offer the prospect of Crimea remaining with Ukraine. However, the 1992 constitution which it cites foresees giving the region effective independence within Ukraine, but with the right to determine its own path and choose relations with whom it wants—including with Russia."

The problem apparent in the Reuters piece and others like it is not that the journalists that produce them are unprofessional or have some anti-Russian personal agenda. I have no personal knowledge of the journalists who wrote the above Reuters piece, and I am sure they take their profession with the utmost seriousness and have high personal standards of integrity. The problem, as I have mentioned, is a pervasive, subconscious Cold War residue that has a major influence on how uninformed readers around the world learn about the situation in Crimea and Russia's subsequent larger image even today.

For example, the 1992 constitution the Reuters piece mentions is the *Ukrainian* Constitution, not the Russian. It does indeed grant the Crimean region effective independence within Ukraine and the right to determine its own path and relations with whomever it wants. Ukraine wrote those words in the immediate glowing aftermath of Soviet dissolution, when, quite frankly, most in the West felt the true political and economic prosperity path shone brightest for Ukraine and not Russia. Many seem to have forgotten this, but any simple source search back to the time period will reveal massive Western enthusiasm for Ukraine's prospects, while Russia was deemed too large, too ethnically diverse, and too dependent on decrepit and degraded Soviet infrastructure. It is easy to grant "autonomy'" when authorities feel confident a region will never act upon it. But now, a generation after the fall of the Soviet Union, no one makes comparisons anymore between Ukraine and Russia where Ukraine is the golden child and Russia the basket case. So yes, it was quite true that the constitution recklessly gave Crimea the opportunity to pursue the very path it was pursuing a year ago. But the hands that wrote that problematic constitution were Ukrainian, not Russian. This reality was not revealed to readers. Instead, they were fed an opposite impression of the referendum as being not only illegitimate but manipulatively engineered by Russia and forced on the local people.

Russia, no doubt, was not guiltless. No state is in complex geopolitics. It absolutely took advantage of the turmoil and instability of the Maidan revolution in Kiev. But it took advantage of this opportunity by maneuvering with a small peninsula that had always been militarily important to and, quite frankly, politically and culturally aligned with Russia. Was this maneuver nice? No, it was not. But was it geopolitically strategic? Yes, it most certainly was. Which thought process do you think matters most to states on the global stage, the former or the latter?

What I wish to see more of is reporting that testifies to this inherent nature of geopolitics and the admission that most states—no, all states—will be strategic before they choose to be nice. Be warned: this won't make for light or fun reading, per se. But it would make for more informed and more accurate reading than the quasi-impartial pieces that clearly push a psychological caricature of one particular side to readers who do not have the background to know what is fact and what is farce. The consequence, of course, is the creation of a Russian demon that is not entirely accurate and most certainly does not serve anyone's enlightenment or the amelioration of conflict. There are enough real demons in the political world without the free media creating more absentmindedly.

Russia's Right to Revive

HASAN EHTISHAM & USMAN ALI KHAN NOVEMBER 8, 2016

Russian involvement in the Levant, which began on September 30, 2015, is very important in the context of the Kremlin focusing on its Southern flank, particularly the Middle East. The Russian current rapprochement over Middle East policy is a manifestation of how Moscow can catch the West by surprise. In the current scenario of disorder in the region, Moscow can be appreciated as a systematic force attempting to find a peaceful solution to conflicts in the Middle East. In our understanding, Russia is following a duplex strategy with two phases to revive its role across the pan-Asian continent. In the first phase, Moscow is focusing on central Asia and the Middle East, as these regions are in direct contact with it geographically. In the second phase, Russia has to focus on south and Southeast Asia, where the pattern of alliances has already been shifted.

The first phase has already begun and can be observed by Russian involvement in the Syrian civil war. Under the leadership of Vladimir Putin since 2000, Moscow has become a reemerging power at both the regional and global level. Though its position may not be where it was at the peak of the Cold War, it is immensely influential nonetheless across the global stage. Reemerging as a strong power, Putin has focused Russia's policy in the Middle East by taking bold military steps against the anti-Assad intervention in Syria. This has reemphasized Russia's Middle Eastern ties and caught many by surprise. Arab allies, however, still remember the days when they used to cooperate with the USSR regarding infrastructure, industry, training, and weapons.

Russia is yet again trying to reach out to Middle Eastern markets, especially those related to defense industries. After the effective air operations against DAESH (ISIL/ISIS) in Syria, Moscow is willing to preserve its position as a major arms exporter to the region. According to Nikolay Kozhanov of Chatham House, Russia is not only concentrating on trade benefits but also engaged in exerting geopolitical influence across the Middle East. The decision taken by Putin to intervene in Syria's civil war has given an impression that Russia is there to ultimately replace the dominant outside power (the United States). Interestingly, Russia's diplomatic maneuvers to place itself at the center Middle East's civil war crisis have received notable results, such as the prevention of the collapse of Assad's regime, which seemed imminent a year ago. As said by Salim al-Jabouri, the speaker of the Iraqi parliament and the country's leading Sunni politician, "Russia sent a message to the Middle East with its direct intervention in Syria: we are more serious in settling the region's problems than the Americans are." Meanwhile, Turkey is blaming the United States for facilitating the recent failed coup attempt. Ankara is reassessing its foreign policy objectives. If Russia and Turkey can reach a deal in this situation, then it will be checkmate to the United States and rebels in Syria.

So far, the first phase of Russia's duplex strategy is producing the desired results for Moscow. But the most imperative phase is yet to begin, in which Russia will have to reconsider its slant concerning south Asia. In this region, the United States has already overextended its interests, creating a de facto alliance between Russia and China against American policy. The United States wants sidekicks in the region to pursue its interests, and India is offering her services. Meanwhile, Washington is constantly disengaging from Pakistan, opening up a number of areas where Moscow can cooperate with Islamabad to redefine the alliance structure in South Asia. The Russian team is holding talks with Pakistan on the sale of military hardware, and both countries are conducting their first-ever joint military drills. But the two countries have no urgency and are for now mostly in cautious mode. Thus, Russian diplomacy is moving into a higher gear as it tries to build a policy that establishes traction from the Middle East to Southeast Asia. If it is successful, then it will have a new sense of global power and would have likely nudged the United States out of its current place of prominence in these two regions.

Censorship or Saving Grace?

Academic Scholarship and Intelligence Vetting

OCTOBER 23, 2015

A new article by the *Moscow Times* revealed a mixed reaction to supposed FSB vetting of academic scholarship. The *Times*, which has largely become a holding repository of intense criticism of the Russian government (and no, the irony of a media organization sharply critical of the government for infringing on media freedom has apparently not sunk in yet in Moscow), is clearly siding high on the indignation side of this issue: for the most part the article is a not-so-thinly-veiled accusation of Russian intelligence services trying to basically return the country's academic community to a Soviet-era intellectual censorship system. And while it is true there are examples of Russian academics unfortunately being subjected to investigation and even arrest, there are aspects to this story that are irresponsible and propagandistic.

The past is no help to the Russian Federation in this case. Older-generation academics indeed remember all too well a time when literally all academic scholarship had to be approved by the KGB. The article that the *Moscow Times* took from the prestigious journal *Nature* highlighted how scientists today need to seek permission from their home university's First Department, an entity that supposedly exists in all Russian universities and is meant to be "closely associated" with the FSB. It is at this point that even the *Times* article gets a bit confusing. Administration officials in the powerful Moscow State University admit that faculty meetings had taken place discussing the need to have original scholarship reviewed but that this process has long been in place as a source for improving the standards of quality and citation rate and in no way is associated with the FSB. In addition, even at MSU, the vanguard of Russian academic institutions, the practice of First Department vetting seems to be selectively engaged, where certain departments are required to submit scholarship while other departments are not. It is not readily clear, to the *Times*, *Nature*, or the faculty of MSU, what decision-making process is involved to determine which departments receive scrutiny. And as one might expect in this situation, wherever there is confusion or ambiguity, there is suspicion and dread. Given the history of Soviet censorship and contemporary worries about academic freedom, it is not entirely shocking that academic and media groups in Russia would profess concern about the insidiousness of the overall process. But I cannot help but see some less sinister possibilities that explain this situation.

Anyone affiliated with university administration, *any* university administration, is well acquainted with what can only be called an interminable and seemingly illogical bureaucracy that often eludes the principles of rationality and sanity. The idea that a huge institution like Moscow State University might make decisions that are not standardized or universal, that do not apply to all departments across the board, and even perhaps that seem contradictory and inexplicable to its faculty is an idea so commonplace all over the academic globe that it is almost not worth mentioning. The essence of academic bureaucracy often seems to be about good intentions badly performed. The inconsistency of First Department application across Russian universities could and likely is easily explained by this frustrating intellectual reality all scholars face, regardless of a country's specific history with censorship. But even this is minor compared to the larger issue not being properly discussed in the *Times* article: standard procedures of oversight on scholarship that deals with sensitive topics and materials.

The *Nature* journal understandably focuses on the hard sciences, but the sensitivity issue applies to all academics, even students, who produce material that engages national security interests. The idealistic utopia that some academics proclaim should be the standard for intellectual engagement has always been a myth: there is no country and no university where professors and advanced students can simply write whatever they want and go talk to whomever they want whenever they want, especially at institutions that either have a connection to government or have persons under their employ or guidance who are also affiliated with government agencies. This is not about Russia slowly creeping into some weird form of Soviet revanchism. This is about all countries. For example, my own program has had issues with this challenge as it concerns the analytical commentary endeavor *The Caspian Project*. Given that I run an international security and intelligence studies program in the United States, it is not outrageous to learn that some of my students are already employed or were formerly employed by the US government or American military. Every single student in my program that has had this affiliation and wanted to contribute to *The Caspian Project* has had to submit their work ahead of time to vetting services either in the US government or the military to simply ascertain that no classified information was accessed in order to write the pieces and no secret information was revealed in the pieces themselves. In America, some have derisively referred to this as a "post-Snowden reflex," implying the United States intelligence community still stings from the embarrassment of the theft and release of thousands of classified documents by Edward Snowden. While there may be a small bit of truth to that, the reality is this process has always existed in America and will exist in any other country that considers itself important on the global stage and as having significant national security secrets to maintain (i.e., every single country on earth, quite frankly). Articles like the one in *Nature* or the commentary provided by the *Moscow Times* fails to understand or recognize just how easy it is to unknowingly violate national security laws in a given country. Consideration of this aspect is sorely needed within this debate and is what I provide here.

Academics who do not have familiarity with or exposure to working with the government often have a Hollywood take on national security and what it means for information to be top secret and classified. The old American Supreme Court adage in the 1970s about pornography ("What is porn? I'll know it when I see it") does not apply here, though most academics unwisely think it does. Unfortunately, the process of classification and top secret designation is not intuitive, logical, or easily grasped. An academic can easily be working on materials or topics that seem far removed from issues of national security, and yet the conclusions and originality devised from said sources end up pushing the work incredibly close if not beyond the standards under which the government works and is beholden to. This is why preemptive vetting is a much safer process for the academic: failing to get that formal approval exposes the scholar in question to the accusations seen in the *Times* article. It is not a question of how many times the material has been discussed in public or whether or not it has been published previously. The *Times* uses these questions to illustrate that vetting is inherently unjust, intimating that the questions do not establish any real clarity or explicit rules: some scholarship that is presented openly then causes problems after the fact for the scholars as they come under greater scrutiny for their work. In my world here in the United States, political publications are an area where it is most assuredly not better to "ask forgiveness rather than seek permission." Too many academics working in important areas of national security, whether directly or indirectly, cannot be so cavalier: put simply, asking forgiveness does not usually go over so well when dealing with a country's intelligence community. I know for a fact that is the case for America. There is no reason it would be any different for the Russian Federation. The fact that information can go unnoticed at first just means it is a failure of bureaucracy, which is why academics in every country are usually charged with the responsibility of putting their information through the vetting process themselves. Host governments as good as admit that they do not believe in the efficacy of their own bureaucratic institutions. And rightly so.

This is what leads us to the final important point about academics in general: while on the whole wonderfully engaged and purely intentioned when tackling new scholarship, our naiveté as a group can get a bit overwhelming. When tackling scholarship that clearly cannot touch national security interests in any way, this trait can be endearing if also eccentric. When researching issues that do matter to national security, this trait makes us dangerous to ourselves. In such a way, the existence of a First Department at a university (an organ that does not exist in American universities and thus makes the still-required vetting process more labyrinthine and unknowable for scholars and students alike) can potentially speed up what no doubt will always be an excruciating example of bureaucracy run amok. But dealing with an inefficient, illogical, and sometimes inexplicable bureaucratic organ ahead of time is far superior to dealing with the unemotional, ruthless, and cutting professionalism of your country's law enforcement. This reality should be considered when we read articles like the one in the *Times*. Are Russia's First Departments an example of censorship rearing its ugly head back into the world of the academy or a saving grace helping academics avoid their own worst habits? Bureaucracy can indeed often be dumb. But that doesn't always automatically mean it is also a demon.

Interview with Rethinking Russia, International Analytical Think Tank

I Personally Feel There Is Ample Evidence to Show That There Have Been Many Opportunities Missed by the US to Establish New Connections and Interaction with Russia

OCTOBER 18, 2016

Rethinking Russia continues interviews on the topic of relations between Russia and the West. This time Rethinking Russia spoke with Matthew Crosston, Miller Endowed Chair for Industrial and International Security, professor of political science, director, the International Security and Intelligence Studies Program, Bellevue University, USA.

Rethinking Russia: What are some of the reasons you would give for the political tensions between Russia and the state you reside in?

Matthew Crosston: The simple reality is that there is a "Cold War residue" that mentally still plagues too many decision-makers within both the Russian Federation and the United States. I personally feel there is ample evidence to show that there have been many opportunities missed by the US to establish new connections and interaction with Russia, but that mental residue proved too strong on the authorities in power. Keep in mind this is not me being overly idealistic or utopian: those new relations might not have ended up friendly, but they would have been based upon more modern factors that truly left behind legacies of past empires and history. This would have been progress, in my opinion, even if adversarial or skeptical relations continued between the two countries.

RR: What groups of state and non-state actors would you say benefit from tense relations between the USA and Russia, cultivated both in the political elite and the general population? Why do they benefit from this tension?

MC: Given what I said above, it is clear that the intelligence communities, defense industries, and military-industrial complexes of both countries benefit from a failure of the US and Russia to reconstitute their relationship and cultivate new understanding. This is not to say they want actual war between the two. Indeed, simply remaining tense and adversarial keeps the relevance, profitability, and primacy of these organizations quite high. In addition to this, in America certainly, an entire sub-industry has been developed and maintained around this continued animosity, based on literally dozens of think tanks and intellectual analytical centers. In a media age of complete and constant saturation, conflict sells much more than peace. How we overcome that as a society, quite frankly, remains a mystery.

RR: What groups of state and non-state actors propagate this tension in the political sphere? In society as a whole? Would you say that these groups cooperate to propagate tension with Russia?

MC: I've answered this to a degree above, but it is important to add that the political party system in the United States as a whole,

Democrat and Republican, is at the moment de facto accepting the status quo. That is, new members of Congress come in basically understanding that Russia and the United States are rivals, will always remain rivals, and any maneuver performed by Russia is one aimed at propagating misunderstanding and tension. In some ways it can be argued that it is a self-fulfilling prophecy, where we create the very atmosphere we publicly declare to be lamentable. Ironically, however, I do not believe in coordinated and purposeful "cooperation" to maintain this animosity, if that implies a conspiracy-like effort to keep the two countries apart. Alas, reality is almost worse: it means the acceptance of animosity between the two countries is seen almost as an organic process, innate to current politics, and immune to change.

RR: Would you say people in the USA are generally weary of Russia? Why? Where do you think this weariness originates from? Do you think this weariness renders people's choice of the media they read/watch selective? Do you think a negative opinion of Russia amongst people has an impact on your state's decision-making?

MC: In this case you cannot really get around the totality of information inundation that happens within the United States, as it concerns "maintaining a single narrative." What I mean by that is if a relatively unaware and uninformed public only gets a single argumentation, a single line of reasoning, regarding another state's perspectives, attitude, and purpose, and that argument is resoundingly negative, then "Russia-fatigue" becomes a fait accompli—a foregone conclusion. As a specialist who often focuses his work on Russian-American relations, it can be quite disturbing how often we find "strong" opinions here in America about Russia, but then follow-up questions reveal that strong opinion to be founded upon very skewed or extremely limited and partial information. There is a challenge in the intellectual community, I believe in both countries, to produce louder voices, with more compelling arguments, about the need for change and attitudinal innovation. At this point, those voices, unfortunately, are rare and largely quiet.

RR: Has the perception of Russia by the politicians in the USA changed since 1991? What about popular opinion? If yes, why has this opinion changed on both levels?

MC: An entire generation has passed since the dissolution of the Soviet Union. I was a college student, spending an entire year abroad in a formerly closed city of Tambov in 1991, completely by myself in order to intensify the immersion experience, becoming the first American ever to study in that city. When I think back to those days, at all of the hope, the presumptive positivity about what the future would hold for Russian-American relations, it is difficult to not shake my head in disappointment today. Mutual decisions made on both sides entrenched old thinking so that whenever one country misstepped, the responding counter-reaction was amplified in a negative way. It seems now that it would be fair to say our hope was misplaced because neither side was truly ready to change its thinking fundamentally. Thus, we were rather naïve and perhaps ignorant. What is the famous quote about insanity? To do the same thing over and over again but expect a different result. That is what best explains relations between the United States and Russian Federation since 1991. Our thinking, on both sides, continued in the same light, over and over and over, while the authorities kept publicly expecting the dawning of a new day. Perception changes, especially when it comes to states that are long-time rivals and adversaries, with a dutiful attempt to alter thinking even when political action is fairly limited. There has to be a first step with an acceptance of doubt and skepticism but within an atmosphere of hopeful progress. For the most part, the major thinkers on these relations since 1991 have never sincerely tried to change their own thinking while demanding major political action and change. This goes a long way in explaining why we have only seen distrust and cynicism increase in the new millennium.

RR: Do you think cooperation between the USA and Russia is desirable? Is it viable? What forms should this cooperation take? Do you see any impediments to cooperation? Which ones? What groups of state and non-state actors would you say benefit from a cooperation relations between your state and Russia?

MC: I have long been in the very small academic camp of contrarians that believes cooperation between the United States and Russia is not only desirable and viable, but deeply necessary across a number of important global security issues. The problem with the current state of affairs is that we look at this relationship process in a binomial way: it is either 1, signifying perfect cooperation, or 0, signifying total absence of any connectivity whatsoever. This is unhelpful. Indeed, it also ignores the complicated and multilayered reality that is global affairs. The United States and Russia have too many common security and political interests across the global stage to think they should not be striving to achieve new levels of interaction that ultimately lead to sustained cooperation. It is not contradictory to "get along" on some issues while being stridently "opposed" to each other on other issues. This is simply the nature of international relations. It always has been. It always will be. And yet, for some reason, there has always been a reluctance to let American-Russian relations follow this same structure. It is incredibly frustrating to an expert who thinks the benefits of even partial cooperation far outweigh any supposed risks of engagement. Overall, we need to stop waiting for total success if it means we are not allowing for the existence of small progress. It seems logical, given the great historical weight holding Russian-American relations back, groaning under the weight of negative legacy, that we need to move forward only by political and diplomatic "baby steps." In time, looking back, we will cover the same amount of ground as when we all stood around in 2016 waiting for some giant irrational leap of instantaneous progress.

RR: Do they benefit from cooperation in different spheres or only in particular ones? Which ones?

MC: First and foremost, the singular most pressing security issue of our time, the fight against radicalism and terrorist extremism, is and always has been an obvious point of collaboration and camaraderie between the United States and Russian Federation. The fact of the matter is that the two countries above all others most interested in and most passionate about the elimination or constraining of radical Islamist terrorism are the United States and Russian Federation. And yet, despite this inarguable point of connection, the two have been incredibly limited on this issue. Perhaps on an even more important long-term peacebuilding front, greater collaboration and synchronicity in terms of economic engagement could have far-reaching effects on central and Eastern Europe and the greater Caspian region. For example, if Russia and the United States (or its closer diplomatic geographical cousin, the EU) had better understanding and better "trust cache" between each other, then would the events of Eastern Ukraine and Crimea even have come about? Ukrainian activism notwithstanding, it is quite possible the very need for Maidan would have been severely undermined. Pushing better and more cooperative economic interdependence will not just help Russian-American relations in specific but will release so much tension that presently exists across many smaller regions in general.

Interview by Nora Kalinskij

ИНТЕРВЬЮ

Соединенными Штатами было упущено множество возможностей установить новые связи с Россией

Rethinking Russia продолжает серию интервью об отношениях России и Запада. На этот раз мы провели беседу с Мэтью Кросстоном, заведующим кафедрой промышленной и международной безопасности, профессором политологии, директором программы по изучению международной безопасности и разведывательной деятельности Университета Белвью, США.

Rethinking Russia: Могли бы Вы выделить несколько причин политических противоречий между Россией и США?

Мэтью Кросстон: Реальная причина предельно проста: до сих пор существует осадок холодной войны, который поглощает лиц, принимающих решения, в России и США. По моему мнению, есть множество очевидных доказательств того, что Соединенными Штатами было упущено множество возможностей установить новые связи с Россией, однако этот осадок не позволил Вашингтону это сделать. Не думайте, что я идеализирую эти потенциальные новые отношения или рассуждаю об утопии: возможно, они и не закончились бы крепкой дружбой, но, по крайней мере, они основывались бы на более современных предпосылках. На мой взгляд, это стало бы прогрессом, даже если бы отношения между двумя странами остались конфронтационными и скептическими.

RR: Какие группы государственных и негосударственных акторов, на Ваш взгляд, получают выгоду от напряженных отношений России и США на уровне политических элит и на уровне населения? Почему?

MK: Исходя из того, о чем я уже говорил, можно сделать вывод, что спецслужбы, оборонная промышленность и военно-промышленные комплексы обеих стран извлекают выгоду из того, что России и США не удается восстановить отношения и добиться взаимопонимания. Это не означает, что они хотят, чтобы между двумя государствами началась война. Просто напряженности и враждебности достаточно для того, чтобы востребованность, прибыльность и важность этих акторов были достаточно высокими. Кроме того, в Америке на почве сохраняющейся враждебности с Россией сформировалась целая отрасль, которую образовали десятки мозговых и аналитических центров. В эру медиа война продается гораздо лучше, чем мир. Как мы, как общество, с этим живем, откровенно говоря, остается для меня загадкой.

RR: Какие группы государственных и негосударственных акторов способствуют усугублению этой напряженности в политической сфере и в обществе в целом? Считаете ли Вы, что эти группы акторов сотрудничают с целью усугубления напряженности?

MK: Частично я уже ответил на этот вопрос ранее, но важно добавить, что партии США, Демократы и Республиканцы, сейчас фактически принимают статус-кво. Таким образом, новые члены Конгресса полагают, что Россия и США являются врагами, всегда останутся ими, и любой маневр, предпринимаемый Россией, направлен на усиление недопонимания и напряженности. Можно сказать, что это отчасти самореализующееся пророчество: мы сами создаем атмосферу, которую потом публично называем крайне неблагоприятной. В то же время я не верю в то, что специально координируются некие действия, нацеленные на усугубление напряженности в отношениях России и США, если в этом заложены некие элементы заговора. Как это ни прискорбно, реальность еще хуже: для нее характерно полное принятие вражды между двумя государствами как вполне органичного процесса, являющегося неотъемлемой частью текущей политической повестки и неподдающегося изменениям.

RR: Относятся ли граждане США с недоверием к России? Почему? Каковы, по Вашему мнению, истоки этого недоверия? Считаете ли Вы, что это недоверие влияет на выбор американскими гражданами того, из каких СМИ получать информацию? Считаете ли Вы, что негативное отношение американцев к России влияет на процесс принятия политических решений в стране?

MK: Просто невозможно не утонуть в потоке информации, который обрушивается в Соединенных Штатах, если речь идет о поддержании единой картины. Я имею в виду, что, если не слишком хорошо информированная и просвещенная публика сталкивается только с одной линией аргументации относительно перспектив, намерений и целей другого государства, и она негативная, то негативное отношение к России становится данностью. Поскольку я специализируюсь на российско-американских отношениях, я крайне часто сталкиваюсь с множеством мнений о России, в правдивости которых авторы не сомневаются ни на секунду, и которые, как выясняется впоследствии, основываются на искаженной или весьма ограниченной информации. Предполагаю, что сейчас в обеих странах эксперты пытаются «перекричать» такие мнения, приводя более убедительные аргументы о необходимости перемен и изменений в восприятии друг друга. В данный момент, к сожалению, их голоса являются достаточно редкими и недостаточно громкими.

RR: Изменилось ли мнение американских политиков о России с 1991 г.? А мнение населения? Если да, то каковы причины этих изменений?

MK: После распада СССР сменилось уже целое поколение. Когда я учился в колледже, я провел весь 1991 г. в городе Тамбове для полного погружения в среду и был первым американским студентом, учившимся в этом городе. Когда я вспоминаю то время, надежду на то, что будущее развития российско-американских отношений будет позитивным, сложно сдержать нынешнее разочарование. Решения, принимаемые обеими сторонами настолько укоренили старое мышление, что когда бы одна страна не оступалась, ответные действия второй только усиливают негативный эффект. Сейчас кажется, что наши надежды не сбылись по причине того, что ни одна из сторон не была на самом деле готова фундаментально изменить свое мировоззрение. Мы были весьма наивными и, возможно, невежественными. Как говорят о безумии? Безумие – это повторять одно и то же действие снова и снова, но надеяться на иной результат. Именно этим и характеризуются отношения России и США с 1991 г. Мировоззрение обеих сторон оставалось прежним, а власти ожидали, что начнётся новый день. Восприятие меняется, особенно в случае государств, на протяжении долгого времени являющихся соперниками, когда предпринимается попытка изменить мировоззрение даже при ограниченности пространства для политических действий. Необходим первый шаг, принимающий сомнения и скептицизм, но совершаемый в атмосфере надежды на прогресс. Зачастую с 1991 г. наиболее известные эксперты по российско-американским отношениям требовали масштабных политических действий и перемен, ни разу при этом не пытавшись изменить свое собственное мировоззрение. Можно долго объяснять, почему в новом тысячелетии мы наблюдаем только недоверие и цинизм.

RR: Считаете ли Вы сотрудничество России и США желательным? Жизнеспособно ли оно? Какие формы должно принимать это сотрудничество? Видите ли Вы какие-либо препятствия на пути выстраивания сотрудничества? Если да, то какие? Какие группы государственных и негосударственных акторов, на Ваш взгляд, получат выгоду от сотрудничества России и США?

МК: Я уже давно являюсь одной из «белых ворон», которые считают, что сотрудничество России и США не только желательно и жизнеспособно, а просто крайне необходимо в вопросах обеспечения глобальной безопасности. На данный момент наша проблема заключается в том, что мы смотрим на эти отношения как на биномные: 1 означает идеальное сотрудничество, 0 означает полное отсутствие каких-либо связей. Это едва ли способствует налаживанию отношений. И, конечно, такая тактика не учитывает сложность и многогранность международных отношений. У Соединенных Штатов и России слишком много общих интересов, политических и в сфере безопасности, чтобы не стремиться к достижению новых уровней взаимодействия, которые в конечном счете приведут к устойчивому сотрудничеству. Вполне возможно находить точки соприкосновения в некоторых вопросах, будучи оппонентами в других. Это природа международных отношений. Она всегда такой была и такой и останется. Но почему-то всегда существовало некое сопротивление тому, чтобы российско-американские отношения развивались по этому же принципу. И это сильно разочаровывает эксперта, который полагает, что выгода от сотрудничества, по крайней мере, в каких-то сферах существенно перевешивает предполагаемые риски. Нам необходимо перестать ждать абсолютного успеха и начать допускать небольшой, постепенный прогресс. Это было бы логично с учетом исторического контекста, который не дает развиваться отношениям двух государств, и негативного наследия, от которого мы должны избавиться, предпринимая маленькие политические и дипломатические шаги.

RR: Выгодно ли этим акторам сотрудничество двух стран во всех сферах или только в каких-то конкретных?

MK: Прежде всего, наиболее актуальная проблема обеспечения безопасности в наши дни, борьба против радикализма и экстремизма, есть и всегда будет наиболее очевидной сферой для сотрудничества и товарищеских отношений России и США. Суть дела заключается в том, что двумя странами, наиболее заинтересованными в искоренении или ограничении исламистского терроризма, являются Соединенные Штаты и Россия. Но, несмотря на эту очевидную общность взглядов, два государства принимали и принимают крайне мало совместных действий. Возможно, еще большее значение в долгосрочной перспективе будет иметь развитие сотрудничества в экономической сфере, которое будет иметь далеко идущие последствия для Центральной и Восточной Европы и Каспийского региона. Например, если бы у России и США (или их близкого геополитического друга – ЕС) было больше понимания и доверия, случились ли бы вообще события, произошедшие на востоке Украине и в Крыму? Вопреки активности украинских граждан, вполне возможно, что просто не было бы потребности в Майдане. Большая экономическая взаимозависимость не только благоприятно сказалась бы на отношениях России и США, но и существенно снизила бы напряженность во многих других регионах мира.

БЕСЕДОВАЛА НОРА КАЛИНСКИ

America's Lost Generation

Russian Expertise within Generation X

MAY 15, 2015

2015 is starting to look and sound and feel an awful lot like 1965. If you find yourself sitting at home wondering how fifty years could go by with so much historical change and global shifting and yet still end up basically back at the starting point of a quasi–Cold War between the United States and Russia, then please allow me to offer one slightly unique explanation as to how this has all come to pass: it's my fault.

Well, all right, it's not exactly my personal fault, for I am a member of what is known in the United States as generation X. I am also a recognized expert on Russia. And unfortunately, the combination of those two things (a generation X Russian expert) is about as rare a sighting as a unicorn surfing the Loch Ness monster off the shores of Ibiza. The reason for this might be somewhat surprising to our readers and is most certainly not openly discussed in our various academic, professional, and diplomatic conferences. There is not a dearth of generation X Russian experts because somehow we all magically just forgot there was a place called Russia starting in the early 1990s. No, there is a giant numerical gap because we forgot the wonderfully inexplicable uniqueness of Russia, despite over one thousand years of political intrigue and historical evidence. We forgot that Russia will never be irrelevant.

The celebration in the West of the dissolution of the Soviet Union and the eternal victory of democracy over all other political systems was quietly and unassumingly accompanied by an almost unconscious de-emphasis in prestigious American graduate schools. Russia was pushed aside because, after all, it had lost the Cold War—surely its destiny was to become a quasi-democracy, a political also-ran, and an economic swamp that would be basically unimportant on the global stage. Russia did face a demographic crisis in the first half of the 1990s, actually watching its overall population shrink instead of grow, and the academic and governmental communities in the United States shook their collective heads and felt justified in thinking that if democracy was not in fact the end of history, it was at least the end of needing to focus on Russia. And so by 1997, when many generation Xers were naturally advancing through their advanced doctoral degrees and various PhD programs, selecting dissertation committees, and deciding on deep and complex theses, they were subtly but decisively given a strong piece of advice: leave Russia alone.

Now, keep in mind this was well-intentioned advice. By 1997, Russia seemed to most in the West as, at best, a place to perhaps investigate the problems of crime and corruption or flawed democratic transition. That is how the West viewed Russia from a high-level academic perspective, from the level of elite graduate schools training generation X, mentoring this next generation of experts to take the mantle and lead American-Russian relations into the twenty-first century. The ultimately not-so-subtle hint was simple yet powerful: if you truly want a job in academia and want to be able to do "important" work, Russia is just sooooo yesterday. If you want to be on the cutting edge, look to the Middle East. Hop on the Islamist bandwagon; that is where the *real* action (and job demand) is going to be! Of course, the seismic event on September

11, 2001, just a short three years later, seemed to scream to the now-advanced PhD generation X students that their mentors were prophets and had to be obeyed! And thus the United States lost an entire generation of Russian scholarship.

Barely any new thinkers or innovative minds have emerged from generation X when it comes to studying and understanding the Russian Federation. When one examines and codes the media sources and academic work that news organizations reach out to for quotes and expert opinions about Russia today, one is hard pressed to find a quote from anyone under forty-five or anything not sickeningly dependent on a Soviet assumption for explaining behavior. Please keep in mind I am not trying to be particularly ageist in my argumentation. The problem is not so much how old a person is but rather under what system of educational rigor and mentorship a person has likely been trained given their particular year of birth. Is it merely coincidence that almost every single Russian foreign-policy maneuver today is characterized more often than not as some sort of revanchist attempt to resurrect (symbolically or literally) the power and glory of the Soviet Union? Is it merely odd happenstance that Putin is evaluated only in terms of Soviet dictatorship and not even from the perspective of Machiavellian realpolitik? Go back and look for yourselves. Read as many sources of information you can find. Whether it be the missile-defense shield in Poland and the Czech Republic, or Iran, or Syria, or the bombings near the Sochi Olympics, or finally Maidan and Eastern Ukraine, the analyses one sees could have basically been cut from the *New York Times* in 1964 and just had the key words altered. No imagination, no innovation, nothing new whatsoever. We have become dullards.

Even worse, within the think tanks, graduate schools, and academic associations in the United States that pride themselves on specializing in Russia, there are professional consequences for standing against the orthodoxy. Sometimes, it seems, academic freedom can be restricted so that there is only a particular kind of freedom. As scholars and academics, we are meant to be above such petulance and pettiness. But we are not. Not always. Perhaps worse still, Russia's stubborn unwillingness to remain in that little irrelevant black box created by American academia the past fifteen to twenty years means that there is now a new generation of PhD students emerging once again intrigued, concerned, and fascinated by Russia. This new generation, the millennials, will be entering PhD programs within the next five to ten years. But the majority of the programs they enter and with which they feed their renewed Russian interests will *still* be run by the baby boomers, a generation that cut its teeth under the Cold War and still believes it as the only political vision available for Russia.

PART VI

REGIONAL POLITICS AND GEOSTRATEGY

Sons of Orthodoxy

EU Austerity and a Russian-Greek Orthodox Alliance

BRIAN HUGHES JUNE 30, 2015

The bitter fight that has been raging between the European Union and Greece has now extended for five long months. With the referendum on July 6, it may all be mercifully put to an end. With strong indications that the public will resoundingly reject another bailout and the crippling austerity that comes with it, Greece will finally be free of the hated institutions that, as they repeatedly claimed, paralyzed their economy. However, the path that leads to a once again stable and prosperous economy is likely not to be found quickly. When the vote finally arrives, Greece will most likely revert to the drachma and default, whereupon the economy will enter yet another depression. As of now, the European Union appears to be washing its hands of Greece. Fascinatingly, Russia may be the only country that has the immense means and political savvy to navigate this breakup to the benefit of Greece and to its own global positioning interests and national security priorities beyond the Caspian.

This was never a two-sided fight. Greece and the European Union stared down each other, forgetting that Russia was patiently waiting on the periphery. The European Union adamantly stated that austerity would eventually work, while Greece weighed in with equal vehemence against the "indecency" that such economic measures were forcing on the Greek people. So much focus has been on the rhetoric and horribly complex political posturing inside of the twenty-eight-country European Union that the world has quietly missed the fact that Russia could emerge the only real winner, leaving the European Union to struggle with the consequences of being rejected by a fallen EU member that chose an alternative path.

Russia and Western European powers are in the midst of a tumultuous diplomatic relationship at the moment, and it's difficult to argue that Russia isn't coming away with the upper hand. Vladimir Putin has shrugged off sanctions, recession, and drastic inflation, all while increasing personal popularity and national territory. He likewise outflanked the more-hawkish Western voices in Syria by utilizing Russian soft power, coordinating a chemical weapons disarmament. With a meager 18 percent debt-to-GDP ratio, Russia has the financial depth and flexibility to do as it pleases. Lending a helping hand to Greece would be a simple first step to begin prying Greece away from the European Union and into a welcoming Russian sphere of influence.

Greece has recently been torn between Russia, an "Orthodox brother nation," and its EU counterparts. The Greek economy was exploding with prosperity before the global recession of 2007–2008, and this newfound wealth was largely facilitated by its close relationship to the European Union and inclusion in the euro currency. On the other hand, Greece has historical, cultural, and religious connections with Russia. In addition, tourism and diaspora between the two countries is quite high. With six years of economic downturn and multiple recessions following the initial depression, Greek positive sentiment toward the European Union has plummeted to roughly 25 percent. Meanwhile, two-thirds of Greeks have a favorable view of Russia, an opposite perspective from much of the European Union.

Russia's relationship with the current Greek political hierarchy began on strong footing, as Prime Minister Alexis Tsipras attempted to block sanctions against Russia just days into office. After sanctions were imposed with the United States' urging, Greece reportedly told Russia that they were able to reduce their intensity. This may be the strongest leverage that Greece can offer Russia: while still a member of the European Union, even without its currency, Greece can use its vote to sway sanctions. While it is a difficult task for Greece to diametrically oppose the wishes of stronger Western powers, one dissenting vote to new sanctions significantly weakens impending ones. Previously, the European Union warned of isolationism if Greece bowed to Russia with respect to sanctions and warned Greece not to challenge the EU position. In the wake of default this threat will prove hollow, while isolation from the European Union may drive Greece further to the side of Russia. The Greek government would be walking a dangerous tightrope between Russia and the EU, but with few options for an immediately stable economic future they may gamble.

In addition to challenging sanctions, Greece has also fought against the position held by the European Union in regard to Russian natural gas. EU members are attempting to move away from reliance on Russian gas and the Gazprom Empire. In April, Greece signed on for inclusion in the Turkish Stream gas line project (although that project has yet to begin). Many anticipated that this was a ploy to bluff Europe into accepting easier loan terms, but deciphering what was political brinksmanship and genuine agreements may prove difficult: Russia is going to accept the contract either way. The European Union is stuck between offering Greece the demanded debt write-down and further bailouts or gambling with the standard line of austerity and possible "moral hazard." This was certainly a fight the creditors never wanted to face, with the political implications singularly negative and no positive outcomes readily imaginable. The EU outcome that would have subdued Russian influence would have been to keep the status quo. When it became clear that the Syriza party had no interest in doing so, the European Union could only keep pressing Greece until it broke. Unfortunately, the break may occur but may consequently create a new alliance the European Union never anticipated: an Orthodox alliance that renders EU influence in the Adriatic severely compromised.

Greece has until July 20 to decide whether to accept bailout funds or simply fall out of the euro. The latter move will show the rest of the European Union that membership is not a strictly one-way road and any prospective members may be hesitant in accepting membership. Highlighting the weakness of European partnerships and rigidity of monetary control would represent a large prize to Russia, always interested in embarrassing Western powers when it has opportunity to do so, given what it considers to be like behavior from the United States and the European Union.

Make no mistake: the European Union is giving every opportunity to Russia to advance in the economic vacuum that will be left behind as default sweeps through the markets of Greece. For six months it has let the confidence in the euro, and the European Union itself be shaken through vicious back-and-forth political rhetoric. While the concessions that Greece demanded were far more than the European Union felt allowable, Greeks understandably balked at even more austerity. With Russia actively participating in Greece's alternative plans, the European Union needs to be legitimately concerned about watching Russia slowly pull Greece away from Western Europe and more toward its Orthodox brother and the more East-leaning shift it is trying to create in the Caspian and beyond to China. If Greece rebounds as a result of Russian influence, it will give pause to other newer and potential EU members facing similarly severe austerity measures. The European Union can still salvage this situation, but it will take drastic compromise since Greek voters appear resolved to accept a Euro exit. With severe austerity, the question simply becomes, "how can a state effectively govern when it has little decisions over its budget?" Greece seems to be saying it cannot and therefore is seeking alternative answers to this European economic stick. It proclaims to want economic dignity back. And Russia just might be the country holding the dignity carrot.

Russian Victim?

Repositioning Strategies and Regional Dreams of Dominance

JEANETTE HARPER JULY 21, 2015

As a new wave of non-Western countries strive to elevate their profiles and expand their global influence, Russia is taking steps to help secure its future as their leader. The status-obsessed country has expressed its desire to integrate the former Soviet republics in central Asia and the Caucasus into a new Moscow-centric coalition called the Eurasian Union. This alliance would help promote Russia to a greater position of authority in the areas of politics, energy, economic governance, and international security.

However, Russia has some major hurdles ahead. In the year since Russian president Vladimir Putin announced the official annexation of Crimea to the Russian Federation, the country has experienced a serious downturn in terms of Western affection. While the move did, for the most part, improve Putin's image in the eyes of the Russian people—who had begun to doubt the president's ability to foster economic growth and prosperity—it clearly demonstrated the potential to lead to a complete breakdown of relations with its old rival, the United States. The United States, whose sanctions have forced Russia's economy to turn inwards, views Russia's actions as aggressive and challenging.

These US-imposed sanctions—retribution for what it considers Russia's stealth invasion of Ukraine—are concerning to the countries of central Asia and the Caucasus because Russia has expanded its control over their key industries (like energy, transport, and telecoms) and has helped keep them afloat economically during difficult times with generous economic cooperation and postponements of debt. Russia still has strong economic, security, and cultural ties with the former Soviet republics, which have significant ethnic Russian populations, host Russian military bases, and get most of their news and entertainment from Russian media providers, but the sanctions can seriously threaten the future of these relationships.

As much as Russia longs to draw these countries into an even tighter embrace, they appear to be seriously rethinking this new reunion with Russia. Many are concerned with Russia's growing role and its flailing economy, which was already slowing before the Ukraine crisis. These nations can't help but be wary of the implications of a new union with Russia so relatively soon after the dissolution of the Soviet Union (in geopolitical terms, a single generation is not a long time.) Unfortunately, the reality is that as Russia continues to divorce itself from the West it will likely call on its former Soviet neighbors to choose their alliances. This at a time when the countries of central Asia and the Caucasus would most prefer maintaining multiple alliances with as many countries that want to cooperate with them.

Since their bequeathed post-Soviet independence, the "stan" countries have been wedged between the two superpowers of Russia and China and have been in close proximity to the instability of Iran and Afghanistan. Making the best of this geographical arrangement, they have learned how to keep the region relatively stable by balancing the interests of the superior regional powers and considering the interests of the United

States. Even though they are not particularly happy with the events within Ukraine, their desire to keep a delicate balance in the region (friends to all, neutral most often) is most likely the justification for not isolating Russia or publically criticizing Putin's Ukrainian strategies.

And then there is the issue of Iran and its recent nuclear deal with the P5+1 countries. The Caucasus countries of Azerbaijan, Georgia, Armenia, and the Central Asian "stans" may see the lifting of Iran's sanctions as an opportunity for them to move away from Russian dependence. Iran is no longer off limits as a trade partner, and a southern route through it would effectively change the dynamics of trade in the region, giving the smaller countries of the region more leverage at the bargaining table. This would make it at least plausibly easier to resist Russia's growing sphere of influence.

At the same time, Russia, who played an essential role in securing Iran's deal, has every intention of benefiting from it by securing lucrative contracts for itself in Iran's key sectors such as energy and shipping. Also, it will most likely use the prestige and status of being Iran's main ally to improve its global position, if not necessarily its international image. Iran stands to benefit from the relationship as well. Under sanctions, Iran's underdeveloped sectors suffered, and now they are free to build up. This means they will need foreign investment—a role Russia is only too happy to fill. The Kremlin has expressed its desire to peacefully cooperate with Iran in the development of Iran's civilian nuclear energy program.

But for many, this does not bode well. Eventually, the issue of Iran's arms industry will come up again. In five years when the embargo is lifted per the deal, there will be fierce competition among countries that would sell arms to Iran. With Russia becoming increasingly at odds with the West, its emphatic support of and alliance with Iran—whose nuclear deal does not do much to improve its relationship with the United States per se—is highly suspicious and, in my opinion, goes beyond just helping it recover economically. Because Iran has been clear about its intention to uphold its anti-American policies and has plans to continue providing its support to its allies in the region—who also have negative feelings toward the West—this union should be looked upon with at least some concern and apprehension.

With Russia recently joining the Asian Infrastructure Investment Bank and taking action to integrate the Eurasian Economic Union with the Silk Road Economic Belt, there is no doubt that Russia is positioning itself to reemerge as the dominant figure in the non-Western world, a figure that desperately desires to have the same kind of influence the United States has over its Western allies. But if this is what Russia really wants, it will have to change the way it relates to its smaller neighbors. Instead of projecting the image that it wants to "collect them," perhaps it should instead redirect its diplomatic energy to soothe them as real partners, equal and engaged.

While international relations have never been Russia's strong suit in the West—take its revoked G8 membership status as evidence—this doesn't mean it isn't capable. For example, it could start by improving its image by ceasing to present itself as a victim. It could, instead, start to take responsibility for its own misfortunes. It could stop referring to the breakup of the Soviet Union as a tragedy and can instead treat it as an opportunity to reinvent itself to become a vital part of the international community. The last thing the international community wants to see is Russia head down the road to total economic collapse, but if the country continues to violate international norms, it will only further isolate itself—maybe even to the point of another Cold War with the West.

For Members Only

The Consequences of the Caspian Summit's Foreign Military Ban

MEGAN MUNOZ JULY 30, 2015

Last September brought with it major changes to the hotly contested Caspian Sea region. These changes were revealed at the IV Caspian Summit held on September 29 in Astrakhan, Russia. Of the greatest significance was the unanimous vote by the "Caspian 5" (Russia, Iran, Azerbaijan, Turkmenistan, and Kazakhstan) to no longer allow foreign military presence in the Caspian region and that all issues that were to arise would be solved between the littoral states only. The political declaration, according to an announcement by Vladimir Putin and signed by all five presidents "sets out a fundamental principle for guaranteeing stability and security, namely, that only the Caspian littoral states have the right to have their armed forces present on the Caspian."

Iran's President Hassan Rouhani echoed this sentiment, stating, "There is consensus among all the Caspian Sea littoral states that they are capable of maintaining the security of the Caspian Sea and military forces of no foreign country must enter the sea." The five further agreed to expand cooperation on the Caspian Sea in terms of meteorology, natural disasters, and environmental protection. The declaration also revealed clear formulations on the delimitation of the seabed, with each country having exclusive sovereign rights to a fifteen-mile area. This puts to rest an issue that had been contested since the breakup of the Soviet Union and the emergence of the new independent states. Apart from being a unique body of water in terms of its biological and ecological resources, the Caspian Sea comes with a massive amount of oil and gas reserves, an estimated eighteen billion tons with proved reserves of four billion tons. These numbers put the Caspian Sea directly behind the Persian Gulf in terms of the world's largest oil and gas reserves.

This declaration also outlined many other projects in the works for this region—a major one being the joint construction of a railroad that would encircle the Caspian Sea, connecting key Caspian ports and cutting transportation time in half. The five states also signed an emergency prevention and response agreement that called for joint efforts in responding to emergencies in the region. Additionally, plans were revealed for a joint emergency response exercise to take place in 2016 that will test the capabilities and partnerships between the nations and develop procedures of notifying and coordinating rescue units.

Disguised underneath these projects, exercises, cooperation, and initiatives is a very real threat to the United States and NATO. Russia and Iran have long felt threatened by the possibility of a foreign military presence in the Caspian Sea, and Moscow was determined to find a way to ensure it would not lose any more influence in the global energy sector (this in light of Europe slowly but surely diversifying away from Russian gas after the Ukrainian crisis began). The best way to do this was to bring these nations into the fold of Kremlin interests, while making them feel their own interests were also being served. By strengthening relations in their own backyard, Russia has been able to increase influence and gain back power in the region. Shutting NATO out of the region also significantly increases Kazakhstan, Azerbaijan, and Turkmenistan's dependence on Moscow in many different aspects. Another added bonus is that with a clear alliance made up of Iran, Russia, Turkmenistan, and Azerbaijan, Ukraine (absent any "outsider presence") would be comparatively easy to control.

The effects of this agreement have already resulted in major changes to relations between Caspian nations and the United States. For years Azerbaijan has welcomed American-Azeri relations by stepping up logistical support for NATO operations in Afghanistan and even serving in Afghanistan as part of the ISAF, but relations have clearly cooled between the two nations. There were also serious talks between Kazakhstan and the United States about building a base on the border in Aktau that would cater to the needs of the United States and NATO troops, but since the signing of this declaration the project has been halted. Finally, the geopolitical shift in the region has resulted in the closing of the north route for NATO military equipment being sent to Afghanistan. Prior to this Caspian Summit agreement the United States had played an active role in helping Azerbaijan, Turkmenistan, and Kazakhstan bolster their military defenses and develop their own navies. The maintaining of close relations in this region was of great political and strategic importance to the United States, not only due to its vast oil and gas riches (originally outside of Russia's control) but its strategic location that connects it with many regions of Western interest.

Other ways that Russia has benefited from this deal include: the creation of a rapid-response force unfurling along the Caspian Sea coast as a means to extend influence over the Nagorno-Karabakh enclave and its troops in the Armenian Gyumri base; jumpstarting cooperation with Giorgi Margvelashvili, the new Georgian prime minister; maintaining the ability to block Georgian and Azerbaijan pipelines; improving relations with Turkmenistan; and beginning plans for building a pipeline with Turkey (named the Turkish Stream) out to Europe, which will compete with the Trans-Anatolia Gas Pipeline project (sponsored not coincidentally by the United States, the European Union, and Azerbaijan).

The United States has another reason to worry about being blocked from the region—Chechnya. In Azerbaijan, jihadists from the Jamaat (Community) Group are already operating and maintaining connections with Chechen Islamists, the Caucasus Emirate, and Syria's Islamic State: the attack on Eurovision in 2012 and the murder of several Shiite clerics all carry their hallmarks. This insurgency is threatening to turn the region into one of the most ungovernable locations in the world where neither aggressive use of military/intelligence force (counterterrorism operations courtesy of Russia) nor engaged economic assistance will be able to help the situation. With the United States unable to join together with forces in the region this threat will not just remain present but will likely only continue to grow.

Arguably, the signing of this agreement to ban foreign militaries has been the biggest game-changer to take place in the Caspian over the last twenty years. Restricting the West's involvement in the region not only decreases energy development and security in the oil and gas-rich Caspian sea basin, but also wounds in several other respects: it reduces the ability to deter adversaries in the region against attacks; it weakens what were growing US alliances; it allows Moscow to project its power over the other Caspian nations with little interference; it cuts off access to ports for deployments to the Middle East; it does not allow for responses to humanitarian crises in the region; and it does not allow for the United States to project its own power and reach as easily as it once did. All of these make the United States and NATO much weaker than before the Summit began. Round one in this heavyweight prize fight has clearly gone to the Russian bear.

Dethroning the Dollar Dictatorship

ANDY DEAHN & MATTHEW CROSSTON SEPTEMBER 26, 2015

Russian President Vladimir Putin has loudly projected that his nation and the other Caspian nations will leave the dollar behind. Mr. Putin has exclaimed that the United States runs a "dollar dictatorship" when it comes to global market oil prices and affirms that his nation's currency will not become a victim subjected to its rule.

In order to combat this "dictatorship," attempts have been made to enhance relations with China in order to integrate both the ruble and the yuan into the global market more dominantly. His belief is that in doing so he will weaken the dollar while strengthening both national currencies. However, Mr. Putin is potentially committing a mistake, as he is generally associating a strong currency with national strength and views the decline in the ruble's value as an offense against Russia's prowess. His statements now are clearly political, meant to project an aura of strength that disregards the economic realities facing the Kremlin. Rather than take meaningful counteractions that create positive momentum and strong economic stimuli, Putin sometimes seems more focused on capitalizing on his celebrity status to "tweak the American eagle" as it were. Putin's projection that Russia will leave the dollar behind can be interpreted as an attempt to manufacture a sense of Russian exceptionalism that will counter what Russia perceives as constant American exceptionalism on the global stage—which Putin considers an insult. However, these geopolitical playground battles do not outweigh the realities of the world economy and how Russia needs to create serious policies to deal with sanctions and weak oil prices.

While China is Russia's largest trading partner and has become the world's largest consumer of fossil fuels—a vital aspect to Russian economic health—the Chinese financial crisis that occurred in August 2015 has weakened the yuan, consequently placing increased pressure on the Russian economy as well. The Chinese economic meltdown and the resultant devaluation of the yuan held global implications. From Wall Street to Venezuela to Saudi Arabia, economic downturns were observed. On Wall Street the drop in the stock market created panic among brokers and investors, and in Saudi Arabia and Venezuela a drop in oil prices impacted their economies rather severely, given both have bet some of their financial futures on China's continual thirst for commodity imports. Russia, however, which exports approximately 14 percent of its annual oil production to China, has a lot more to lose from the Chinese economic decline. This is because oil and natural gas are at the heart of the Russian economy. These commodities account for over 75 percent of export revenues and over 50 percent of government budgetary resources. The Russian ruble, which is directly linked to global oil prices, has been steadily decreasing in value throughout the last twelve months. The ruble's devaluation can be seen in the correlating data between the market price for oil and the value of the ruble compared to the US dollar. The market price for oil dropped from $104 USD per barrel to around $50 USD per barrel from September 2014 to September 2015. At the same time the value of the ruble, which in the beginning of September 2014 was 36 RUB to 1 USD, had slipped by September 2015 to 68 RUB to 1 USD—a steep devaluation rate not seen since the 1997 global financial recession.

In addition to having the value of its currency decline, for every dollar that global oil prices drop Russia loses an estimated $2 billion a year in revenues. When combined with other harmful realities like Western sanctions, Russia's relative dependence upon a singular commodity market, failure to modernize its energy sector while oil prices were high, and its lavish spending all make it clear that pontifications about a dollar dictatorship should not be Russia's focus. Indeed, there is something of a flawed logic behind the entire premise: why does President Putin believe he can leave the dollar behind by tying the punished ruble with the declining Chinese yuan? In the near-term at least, this strategy is destined to fail.

One regional influence Russia is also somewhat disregarding (or making too many positive assumptions about) in this endeavor and that will potentially become of greater geopolitical importance is the Islamic Republic of Iran, now that the new nuclear accord has been struck and many sanctions lifted. By hedging their bets too heavily on China and disregarding up-to-the-minute regional economic shifts, Russia is possibly inflicting its own monetary wounds while uselessly shifting blame onto the United States for its economic woes. The lifting of Iranian sanctions means that Russia could face a newly invigorated, oil-producing, heavyweight regional competitor, one that could reshape the power balance in the Caspian Sea region and may not necessarily be willing to be as close an ally to Russia as Russia assumes it will be.

A more economically and politically independent Iran, and its ability to influence regional power shifts, would allow for the other Caspian states to modernize and diversify their economies. This would mean that Turkmenistan and Azerbaijan may finally be able to break free of the Russian influence that has basically engulfed them since the Soviet era by building the Trans-Caspian pipeline. Likewise, Kazakhstan, a nation whose economy is also built upon the same commodity market as Russia, may finally be able to lessen the havoc that the Russian currency decline is playing within its own borders. Right now there are few analysts seriously considering these potentialities, both here in the West and within Russia. This is an error. Russia clearly thinks the new nuclear accord will lead only to improved ties and deeper economic prosperity for both itself and Iran. But there is ample historical evidence to consider that an emboldened and newly stabilized Iran simply might not need Russia as much as Russia needs it. This future reality could signal a dramatic change in the Russian-Iranian relationship, and not in Russia's favor. The longer Moscow assumes this is a geostrategic impossibility and that its only concern is battling the dollar dictatorship, the more danger the Kremlin creates for itself.

We already know that a devalued yuan is further assisting oil prices to drop on a global scale, placing great strain on the Russian economy as well as on some bordering Caspian states. Historically, when the Kremlin feels threatened, it shifts blame to other scapegoats rather than seriously tackling its problems. The current sharp slowdown of Chinese economic growth has already impacted multiple Russian economic sectors, including energy, metallurgy, timber, and agriculture. The future alliance with Iran is not an automatic guarantee. Western sanctions still grind along. The Caspian littorals may see opportunities to loosen Russia's economic grip over their local economic standings. Clearly, plenty of real problems exist. So it would behoove Russia to stop spending time on economic fantasies of dethroning the dollar dictatorship. That seems to be the least of its real problems.

Why the Bear Is Back in Vietnam

RAKESH KRISHNAN SIMHA JUNE 11, 2015

Russian-Vietnamese ties that seemed to be cooling after the end of the Cold War are warming up all over again. More than twenty years after Moscow abandoned its largest foreign base, Russian military aircraft are once again welcome visitors at Cam Ranh Bay. The renewed Russian presence in Vietnam has predictably set the alarm bells ringing in the Pentagon, with the Commander of the US Army in the Pacific confirming that Russian strategic bombers circling the massive American military base in Guam are being refueled at Cam Ranh Bay.

On March 11, Washington wrote to Hanoi, requesting that the Vietnamese authorities not assist Russian bomber flights in the Asia-Pacific. The Vietnamese reaction was to remain publicly silent. According to Phuong Nguyen of the Washington-based Center for Strategic & International Studies, "From the perspective of many Vietnamese officials who fought against the United States during the war, Moscow helped train generations of Vietnamese leaders and supported Hanoi during its decades of international isolation." Nguyen adds: "Few things are more vital to Vietnam than an independent foreign policy. Given Vietnam's complex history, its leaders do not want their country to be caught between major powers again. Anything that resembles US interference in Vietnam's dealings with Russia could unnecessarily aggravate this fear."

Although the Vietnamese consider the United States an increasingly important partner in Southeast Asia, it's Russia that tops the pecking order. As per an agreement inked in November 2014, Russian warships visiting the deep-water port of Cam Ranh only have to give prior notice to the Vietnamese authorities before steaming in, whereas all other foreign navies are limited to just one annual ship visit to Vietnamese ports. Located at the gateway to the Indian and Pacific Oceans, Vietnam is of critical importance to Russia. Permanent basing of air and naval assets in Vietnam helps the Russian Pacific Fleet solve its problem of having to pass through the narrow straits of the Sea of Japan to gain access to the Pacific.

To be sure, the current Russian presence is minimal compared with the firepower of the 1980s, when Moscow's Pacific Fleet consisted of an incredible 826 ships, including 133 submarines, 190 naval bomber jets, and 150 antisubmarine aircraft. Even back then, Moscow's buildup was hardly aggressive. According to Alvin H. Bernstein of the US Naval War College, it was "unlikely to have a specific, aggressive, regional intent since that would be quite out of character for a power" that has revealed itself as "cautious and non-confrontational." Three decades on, Moscow under President Vladimir Putin is once again seeking to enhance its role as both an Asian and global power, and as Bernstein noted, the country wants to be "prepared for all contingencies and opportunities". This is also part of Russia's Look East policy. In fact, much before US President Barack Obama announced its pivot to Asia, Russia was already pivoting east, making inroads into once pro-American countries such as Indonesia and Malaysia. However, it is in Vietnam where Russian diplomacy is in overdrive. But first, let's do a quick review.

Vietnam is a small country with a military that punches way above its weight. For those with short memories, the Southeast Asian country handed out resounding defeats to France and the

United States in back-to-back wars. Stupendous bravery, clever battle tactics, and a never-say-die spirit were decisive in winning those wars, but a key factor was that the Vietnamese had powerful friends. During the Vietnam War, Russia played a critical role in Vietnam's defense, supplying a massive quantity of weapons. Over the course of the twenty-one-year war, Russian assistance was worth $2 million a day. In return, Vietnam offered Russia free use of the Cam Ranh Bay base. As part of this agreement, the Russians stationed MiG-23 fighters, Tu-16 tankers, Tu-95 long range bombers, and Tu-142 maritime reconnaissance aircraft at the base. Cam Ranh became Moscow's largest naval base for forward deployment outside Europe. Some twenty ships were berthed daily at the base, along with six nuclear-attack submarines. The base played a pivotal role in helping Russia in its Cold War faceoff against American-led forces in Asia and the Pacific. For instance, when the US Seventh Fleet sailed up the Bay of Bengal to put pressure on India during the 1971 India-Pakistan War, the Russian Pacific Fleet was quickly able to dispatch nuclear-armed submarines and warships to defend India.

Despite Cam Ranh Bay's importance to Moscow geopolitically and its value as an intelligence-gathering post, the Russian presence practically evaporated after the disintegration of the Soviet Union. Military bases on the scale of Cam Ranh Bay cost an insane amount of money to operate, and Russia no longer had cash to burn. In 2001, even the listening station was abandoned.

Although the Russian military presence declined, strong ties continued to bind Russia and Vietnam. In the backdrop of Vietnam's high-decibel spat with China for control of the oil-rich Spratly Islands, Hanoi went on a high-octane hardware hunt. Vietnam's legendary air force acquired twenty-four Su-30 combat jets from Russia and by the end of 2015 it will operate thirty-six Sukhois, becoming the third largest operator of this advanced, supermaneuverable aircraft.

However, it is the Vietnam People's Army Navy (VPAN) that is really beefing up. In 2009, Vietnam signed a $3.2 billion deal with Russia that includes six Kilo class submarines and the construction of a submarine facility at Cam Ranh Bay. Another big-ticket acquisition was that of 50 Klub supersonic cruise missiles for its Kilos, making Vietnam the first Southeast Asian nation to arm its submarine fleet with a land-attack missile. Weighing two tons, the Klub has a two-hundred-kilogram warhead. The antiship version has a range of three hundred kilometers, but speeds up to three thousand kilometers an hour during its last minute or so of flight. According to Strategy Page, the land-attack version does away with the high speed final approach feature, and that makes possible a larger four-hundred-kilogram warhead. Russian-built submarines armed with the potent Klubs are expected to play a critical role in any conflict in the South China Sea. According to one analyst, the land-attack cruise missiles mark a "massive shift," advancing Vietnam's naval capabilities. "They've given themselves a much more powerful deterrent that complicates China's strategic calculations." It is believed Chinese warships have no effective defense against missile like Klub, which is why China has gone apoplectic about Russia selling them to Vietnam. While the Kilos are being built, Russia and India are currently in charge of training Vietnamese officers who will work in the submarines.

In addition to its submarine armaments, in 2011 the VPAN acquired two Gepard-class guided missile stealth frigates from Russia at a cost of $300 million, with the Gepard fleet set to increase to six by 2017. These versatile ships are equipped for surface attacks, anti-submarine warfare and air defense. The VPAN's other acquisitions include four Svetlyak-class fast patrol boats with anti-ship missiles; twelve frigates and corvettes of Russian origin; and two Molniya-class missile fast attack ships built with Russian assistance, with four more expected by 2016.

Vietnam has also acquired advanced radars; 40 Yakhont and 400 Kh-35 Uran anti-ship missiles; Kh-59MK anti-ship cruise missiles; R-73 (AA-11 Archer) short-range air-to-air missiles; 200 SA-19 Grison surface-to-air missiles; two batteries of the legendary S-300 surface-to-air systems; VERA passive radio locators; and two batteries of the K-300P Bastion coastal defense missiles.

According to a research paper by Portugal-based academics Phuc Thi Tran, Alena Vysotskaya G. Vieira, and Laura C. Ferreira-Pereira, "The acquisition of military capabilities is critical, not only purely for the sake of defense and strategic calculations, but also for the important function it plays in the safeguarding of both economic interests and the security of oil field explorations in the South China Sea. This latter aspect is particularly critical given the role that Russia has been playing herein. Indeed, the lion's share of these exploitation projects has being undertaken by Vietnam jointly with Russia."

While defense gets more traction in the media, it is energy that's the single biggest area of cooperation between Moscow and Hanoi. The Russia-Vietnam joint venture Vietsovpetro has generated big dividends for both countries. The company has produced more than 185 million tons of crude oil and more than 21 billion cubic meters of gas from oilfields in the South China Sea. Nearly 80 percent of

Vietnamese oil and gas comes from Vietsovpetro, and the income corresponds to around 25 per cent of GDP.

Russia has also made considerable investments in Vietnam's heavy and light industries, transportation, post, aquatic culture and fishing. These projects have led to other spinoffs—impressed by the profits generated by Russian corporations, a slew of other companies such as Mobil, BP, and TOTAL have ramped up investments in Vietnam. Vietnam's strategic hedging toward Russia is closely connected to its economic cooperation in oil exploration, which brings significant economic benefits to both sides. Strong defense ties between the two countries has enabled Vietnam to acquire modern military equipment, providing the country with the ability to advance joint explorations of oil and gas, despite growing Chinese opposition toward these projects. At the same time, Russia is returning to reclaim its great power legacy. Cooperation with Vietnam offers Moscow a myriad of opportunities to secure political and economic influence with various emerging powers in the heart of the planet's most dynamic region.

Challenging Russia's Arctic

America's Uneven Policy

GREGORY ROUDYBUSH OCTOBER 26, 2015

The policy of the United States concerning climate change in the Arctic has been and is one that is ever-changing. Since 2009 there have been adaptations to the policy in order to face the concerns of today while anticipating the challenges of tomorrow. However, if the current policy does not continue to change in an effective manner to meet the evolution of Arctic challenges, the United States will be further behind the curve. This will have an impact on both allies and adversaries that are active in the region, most especially the Russian Federation.

The current policy of the United States concerning the Arctic region was originally developed in 2009 under the Bush Administration as National Security Presidential Directive (NSPD) no. 66 and Homeland Security Presidential Directive (HSPD) no. 25. This policy discusses topics and issues that concern international governance of the Arctic, territorial claims, international scientific cooperation, maritime transportation, economic and energy issues, environmental protection, and conservation of resources. It takes into account that due to climate change there are new issues that must be addressed concerning the United States' interests. This policy has been so useful that Obama only added to the policy rather than replace it.

In May of 2013, the National Strategy for Arctic Region was released with the implementation plan following in January of 2014.

Much like the original policy, it focuses on climate change and the challenges that come with it. It discusses maintaining freedom of the seas for maritime transportation, working within international institutions such as the Arctic Council to address issues between states, and working to protect the environment and conserve resources in the region. The unwritten portion is how much of this is meant to countermand Russian initiatives in the region.

The NSPD 66/HSPD 25 has been effective in stating how the United States plans on approaching the Arctic region for energy development. Anders Rasmussen stated in "A Place Apart: A Peaceful Arctic No More," "that the US Geological Survey indicates that the region contains approximately 13 percent of the world's undiscovered oil and 30 percent of the world's undiscovered gas deposits, as well as vast quantities of mineral resources including rare earth elements, iron ore, and nickel." Being able to exploit these resources would be beneficial to the United States, yet it has been slow to approve permits for companies to explore parts of the Arctic. Thus, while the policy does address energy issues, it may be ineffective in providing greater energy independence, especially given how aggressive Russia wants to be and has been in recent years in the Arctic region.

NSPD 66/HSPD 25 and the National Strategy for Arctic Region both address economic issues and advancing American security interests. Currently, though, the United States does not have a modern fleet of Arctic ice breakers, while Russia has the largest number of Arctic-capable ships. The United States' lack of a modern fleet of Arctic ice breakers means that it cannot advance its security interests and address economic issues that relate to maritime traffic. When this is coupled with not belonging to a significant international convention (UNCLOS), the United States will have a hard time protecting and promoting its interests in the region and countering a Russian Federation that has assertively declared the Arctic region a major focus of its own national security portfolio.

The current policy has also been ineffective in getting the United States Congress to agree to the United Nations Convention on the Law of the Sea (UNCLOS). As Dobransky points out, the NSPD 66/HSPD 25 came up short largely due to the United States still not being a member of UNCLOS. This becomes a serious issue if another state makes territorial claims that are accepted by following UNCLOS procedures. The United States would be unable to contest these claims or have its counterclaims recognized by the international community. This could have large detrimental ramifications in the future as other Arctic states make more claims in the region.

The United States might have better success with other means of international cooperation. Its policy puts an emphasis on international cooperation and working within existing international bodies. This allows the United States to work out conflicts of interests with other states through the use of diplomacy. As Richard Weitz stated in "Russia Tensions Threaten U.S. Arctic Council Agenda," the United States is working with other countries to challenge Russia's broad territorial claims in the Arctic, which include the Northern Sea Route. The Arctic Council consists of eight states with many other states in observer status. With so many states displaying interest in the Arctic region, it is important for the United States to emphasize and practice more international cooperation, whether it is a part of UNCLOS or not.

The current policy of the United States on the changing conditions in the Arctic region has had mixed results up to this point.

The policy addresses many of the current issues that are present in the Arctic while anticipating the ever-changing future of the region. However, there is no substantive progress to challenge the clear elephant in the room: Russia. There is no state today acting more assertively and proactively than Russia in regard to the Arctic. American policy was clearly developed to answer this reality, and yet the details of said policy are markedly poor answering that challenge specifically. Just as Russia took steps recently at the IV Caspian Summit to ensure its military dominance over the Caspian Sea, it seems quite intent on ensuring an economic and political dominance over its other great sea body to the north. This likely means the immediate future of the Arctic is going be decidedly more bold bear than bald eagle.

New Grounds for War

How the Power of Siberia Pipeline Impacts the Arctic

ALEXANDER S. MARTIN MARCH 24, 2016

The Power of Siberia Pipeline, a joint Russian and Chinese venture in which Russia has agreed to provide $400 billion of natural gas (LNG) to China over the course of thirty years, presents a complex vector of potential conflict. Arctic ice melt, energy resource shortage, and increasing geopolitical tensions are all implied. The complex nature of these issues and the uncertainty regarding their eventual manifestation places the pipeline in the realm of emergent conflict.

The Arctic nations, in particular the five littoral Arctic Ocean states—the United States, Canada, Russia, Norway, and Denmark—are most at risk. China is also a key player, due to both its role as recipient of Russian LNG and its Arctic ambitions. These states are all members of the Arctic Council, the principal body involved in international Arctic governance. While many observers consider Arctic diplomacy via the Arctic Council a success, and point to the generally cooperative nature of international Arctic interaction, this hides the geopolitical divide that exists at the core of the Arctic Council. Most of the five littoral Arctic states belong to Western international and supranational organizations like NATO or the European Union (EU). However, the growing interdependence of Russia and China, and both states' geostrategic expansionist ambitions, will likely complicate future efforts to prevent Arctic tensions and conflict.

PRODUCTIVE POLICY

Arctic diplomacy via the Arctic Council has a long history of cooperative conflict resolution. The most notable instance of successful Arctic diplomacy is the landmark 2010 resolution of a Russian and Norwegian Barents Sea border dispute after decades of negotiation. This is largely a result of the unique application of the rule of international law in the Arctic. The predominant legal framework governing Arctic activities is the 1982 Convention on the Law of the Sea (UNCLOS), which establishes freedom-of-navigation rights, sets territorial boundaries, sets exclusive economic zones (EEZs) and rules for extending continental shelf rights, and has created several conflict-resolution mechanisms. This has provided the Arctic states with a solid and widely accepted legal framework within which to conduct Arctic activities and provided effective mechanisms to address disputes.

The five littoral states reaffirmed their commitment to peaceful and cooperative action within the framework of UNCLOS in the Arctic with the 2008 Ilulissat Declaration. The declaration commits its signatories to address sovereignty and jurisdiction issues through the "extensive legal framework" that governs Arctic activity. Signatories also promised to strengthen cooperation multilaterally, through existing organizations such as the Arctic Council and Barents Euro-Arctic Council. This emphasis on cooperation is reflected in the five littoral states' Arctic strategy documents, which share a number of basic goals and principles. These include: a peaceful, safe, and secure Arctic; sustainable economic and social development; environmental protection; addressing the rights and needs of indigenous Arctic peoples; and the maintenance of sovereignty. Another particularly promising development is the signing of the Agreement on Cooperation on Aeronautical and Maritime Search and Rescue in the Arctic. This treaty, signed in 2011 by Canada, Denmark, Finland, Iceland, Norway, Russia, Sweden, and the United States, encompasses previous agreements like the Tromsø Declaration and commits its signatories to expanded cooperation and information sharing in Arctic search-and-rescue missions. The Arctic Council has historically had a reputation for keeping its dealings separate from other international controversies, and has developed an air of isolation from political turbulence.

This analysis demonstrates that Arctic states have taken great pains to maintain the cooperative, peaceful nature of national and international activity in the Arctic. In particular, the dogged adherence to international law has provided a unique way to manage disputes. In addition, the Arctic Council has proven a valuable forum in which member states can address concerns, pursue cooperation, and effectively manage increased access to the Arctic. Its ability to compartmentalize Arctic policy from other international disputes has proven mostly resilient. This history of Arctic cooperation is what makes the impact of Russia's strategies concurrent to the Power of Siberia Pipeline most intriguing.

COUNTERPRODUCTIVE POLICIES

The insulation from international tumult the Arctic cooperation has enjoyed thus far may be eroding. Russia's annexation of Crimea, linked to the Power of Siberia Pipeline by precipitating the international sanctions which served as a catalyst to signing the deal, has become an important enough threat to influence Arctic policy. In protest of Russia's supposed revanchism, the Canadian chair of the Arctic Council refused to attend an Arctic Council meeting in

Moscow. The Canadian government saw this action as building on other penalties, like sanctions and travel bans, it had already imposed on Russia. While well-intentioned, Canada's policy of including the Arctic in its attempts to isolate Russia may have unintended consequences, particularly in light of Russia's ongoing military expansion there.

Russia has been increasing its military capacity in the Arctic for several years now. On December 1, 2015, Russia's Arctic Command Headquarters became operational, one of the most visible signs of Russia's "plan to form a combined arms group and construct a unified network of military facilities in the country's Arctic territories, by hosting troops, advanced warships, and aircraft to strengthen the protection of its northern borders." This can be seen as a fulfillment of Russia's 2009 Russian Arctic Strategy until 2020. This strategy emphasized the national security dimensions of Russia's Arctic policies, with a discussion of the need to militarily protect Russian interests. In addition, Russian President Vladimir Putin has explicitly stated that any Russian military buildup in the Arctic is a result of US submarines already present in the Arctic. This has begun to trouble Russia's Arctic neighbors and is rightfully seen as "a direct challenge to the longstanding consensus that the Arctic should be kept free of military rivalry."

Such challenges amid Western fears of Russian expansionism and heightened tensions do not bode well for future efforts to mitigate or avoid crisis in the Arctic. Recent backtracking notwithstanding, Canada's decision to link Arctic cooperation with its wider foreign policy has set a precedent in which other states may choose to prioritize contentious foreign policy over the previously pristine Arctic cooperation. Likewise, Russia's military buildup violates one of the fundamental tenets of Arctic engagement: that of keeping it free from military competition. In light of these developments, the potential for conflict over the Power of Siberia Pipeline, arising from the geopolitics of climate change, energy scarcity, and divergent strategic positions, should become much more likely.

The Power of Siberia Pipeline poses the potential for conflict due to the unique forces shaping its place in world affairs. As such, careful and effective policy is necessary to avoid such an undesirable outcome. International cooperation in the Arctic provides the most appropriate policy issue to explore these potentialities. Arctic policy has a reputation for cooperation even in the face of political adversity. For the majority of its existence the Arctic Council, along with related Arctic bodies, have served as valuable arenas for engagement and conflict resolution. However, recent developments give cause for concern that the Arctic may prove as contentious and competitive as global stages. In total, while Arctic policy offers much in the way of useful means to arbitrate disputes and manage conflicts, there is growing evidence that it will succumb to the tendency toward competition and conflict. Thus, the melting ice may one day reveal new grounds for war.

The Mighty Have Fallen

American Space Dependency on Russia

NENAD DRCA MAY 27, 2016

The space program that gave the United States much-deserved global recognition is looking very different today. Somewhat embarrassingly, the United States relies on the Atlas V rocket, powered by a Russian rocket engine, to transport crucial space satellite technology.

It is concerning to the United States to heavily depend on Russia, at the moment still under sanctions for interfering in Ukrainian unrest. Thus it seems imperative that this situation needs to change for the long-term benefit of the American space program. In order to be ready for future conflicts, which may include space, US armed forces need to rely on space technology such as GPS, communication satellites, and intelligence-gathering equipment.

The United States must maintain uninterrupted and independent access to space due to twenty-first-century national security interests. By heavily depending on Russia, Washington is supporting the defense industry of a state that carries, to put it mildly, deep skepticism toward American power. It is unwise policy to depend on Russia for vital space missions and even worse policy when this dependence might help Russia takes steps against US national security interests. Russian Deputy Prime Minister Dmitry Rogozin has described American fees for the space transport as "free money" that is invested directly into Moscow's missile development program. NASA spokesman Mr. Allard Beutel stated recently that his agency still has a transport contract with Russia until June 2020.

This idea of American space dependence on Russia is receiving increasing criticism in Washington. Recently Senator John McCain said: "today Russia holds many of our most precious national security satellites at risk before they ever get off the ground." His concerns were not unfounded because in 2014 Rogozin, in light of impending sanctions, openly threatened to prohibit the export of Russian rockets that facilitate deployment of the American satellite program. If that happened the United States would have no means of deploying its essential satellite technology into space. What is more disconcerting in light of these facts is the new federal budget proposed to cut NASA's Fiscal Year 2017 funds even further. In perspective, NASA's budget is dangerously small when compared to regular expenditures. Former NASA administrator Mike Griffin stated that Americans spend more annually on pizza (27 billion USD) than on space. Due to such changes NASA's mission today is much weaker than several decades ago. The United States, first to send men to the moon in 1969, now struggles in the twenty-first century to reach beyond low-earth orbit without expensive Russian assistance. How the mighty have fallen indeed.

While proposed budget cuts to NASA have been causing bitter debates in Congress, the reality is that the empirical results of any good change will take years to become visible. In 2011, policymakers decided to eliminate NASA's Constellation program: $9 billion dollars of diligent labor to construct a new Orion spacecraft and Aries rocket canceled. Some of the main objectives of the program were the completion of a new International Space Station and a return to the Moon by 2020, with a subsequent manned trip to Mars. The Constellation program was meant to reinvigorate American space supremacy. No other nation, including Russia, China, India, and Japan, was meant to be able to successfully compete or outmaneuver such an advanced program. Now those countries do not even need to bother.

In 2015, Russia deployed seventeen unmanned satellites into orbit, further expanding its capacity for remote sensing systems and intelligence collection. In addition, both Russia and China are developing provocative new space technologies such as anti-satellite weapons. That would allow Russia and China to deny access to any adversary during conflict. The intense reliance of modern warfare on satellite access is impossible to underestimate. The possibility of having Russia and China interrupting and disabling vital communications and navigation space equipment should therefore be very concerning to the United States. The threat is so serious that US policymakers have authorized an additional $5 billion dollars to be used on defensive and offensive capabilities to overcome deficiencies in the American military space program.

Russia is developing its own array of military equipment that could track, approach, inspect, and possibly sabotage foreign satellites in orbit. While China has publicly announced its space endeavors are nothing more than peaceful science experiments, Russian officials have remained silent. Ironically, both Russia and China have been promoting for years a treaty on the prevention of the placement of weapons in outer space and the threat or use of force against outer space objects. Interestingly, Washington opposes this treaty, which was submitted to the United Nations by Russia and China, believing Russia and China are being disingenuous. In other words, the United States feels both Moscow and Beijing will work on space militarization while letting the treaty automatically counter any potential rival entrants. The fear is that Russia and China want to use the treaty only to curb a resurgence of American space capabilities. Regardless of whether or not these suspicions are true, the problem with any space treaty will be the difficulty in achieving real compliance and oversight verification.

China's vice foreign minister Cheng Guoping has stated on several occasions that Beijing intends to increase its cooperation with Russia on several space projects. In the meantime, Russia is planning to build its own space station by the year 2024. The Chinese government is also planning to construct its own orbiting space station by the year 2020. In 1998, when the International Space Station launched, it was the most expensive project ever built at approximately $150 billion. The United States generously gave more than $100 billion toward its construction. Today, only Russian rockets equipped with a Russian docking system can bring necessary ISS supplies. Realistically, the United States is approaching a critical moment when space dependency on Russia will have to end. Perhaps the arrival of successful private companies such as Space X will fill the void left by diminished NASA support. By allowing private industry to compete and provide necessary services, the need for Russia might diminish.

Frankly, American policymakers have been too slow to act on minimizing the negative consequences of their budget cuts in crucial space areas. Allowing Russia or China to militarize space while also making America addicted to Russian space services can only lead to vulnerability in critical military areas. Placing Russia or China in the leadership position for space would cause great concern among many nations and even negatively impact global economic security. Many civilian and scientific organizations have their satellites in low-Earth orbit. It is fair to assume that as of today most of them prefer a leading American presence over Russian or Chinese. But that preference right now is not matched by any empirical reality.

Corruption and mismanagement in the Russian space programs might help even the playing field: it was reported that over $1 billion cannot be accounted for in the Russian space program. Even at its best, the Russian space program budget is only slightly bigger than NASA's smallest budget. The United States still has the leading technology assets. They are simply being hindered by poor policy choices. Both Russia and China depend on media propaganda to maintain their image of power and strength in space. The United States space program does not need more media coverage but better policy to move forward. But so far, that policy wisdom has yet to emerge. As a consequence, the future of space remains crowded, confused, and potentially conflict-ridden.

Interview with Rethinking Russia, International Analytical Think Tank

Walk the Line: Russia as Chair of the United Nations Security Council

MATTHEW CROSSTON OCTOBER 23, 2016

Miller Endowed Chair for Industrial and International Security, Professor of Political Science, Director, the International Security and Intelligence Studies Program, Bellevue University, USA.

October 1 began what could be one of the more interesting Chairships of the United Nations Security Council, with Russia taking over and being charged with a rather delicate balancing act: between conducting the numerous affairs expected to be covered by any standard Chair of the UNSC and deftly handling the "special" relationship with the United States that has recently become woefully deficient. Even more intriguing, some of the most vivid recent examples of that degrading relationship have been exhibited within the UNSC itself.

On the general business front, Russia will see issues dominating the Middle East and Africa at the top of the schedule:

- Developments in Syria.
- Settlements and their legality in the Israeli-Palestinian conflict.
- Implementation of resolution 1559 in Lebanon.
- Ongoing hostilities in Yemen.
- Problems within South Sudan.

- Activities of MINUSCA in the Central African Republic.
- Various political challenges occurring within the Democratic Republic of Congo.
- Activities of MINUSMA in Mali.
- Activities of UNAMID in Sudan (Darfur).
- Returning functionality of MINURSO in Western Sahara.

There will also be important and fascinating discussions during the first month with Russia as Chair that will consider women, peace, and security as well as a private briefing conducted by the International Court of Justice. Perhaps more directly relevant to Russia will be the debates it has put on the docket pushing UN cooperation with regional and subregional organizations. More specifically, the Collective Security Treaty Organization, the Shanghai Cooperation Organization, and the Commonwealth of Independent States will all receive what has been in the past rare attention at the highest UN level. It will be intriguing to see if Russia chairing the Security Council can enable greater impact and focus on these organizations that have in the past been quite important to Russian interests.

All of this regular business, however, pales in comparison to the intrigue and drama that will undoubtedly emerge when it comes to Russia interacting with the Permanent American Envoy to the UN, Samantha Power. She has always held relatively adversarial positions toward Russia and recently made major headlines when she accused Russia of engaging in disinformation campaigns in Syria and called Moscow actions within the country "barbaric."

Russia, never one to back down from a challenge, whether physical or verbal, responded rather forcefully through the personage of

Maria Zakharova, the official spokesperson for the Russian Ministry of Foreign Affairs. Some of the highlights of her comments were rich in both imagery and dismissiveness:

- When Samantha Power says something, then one wants to cry out in fear for the future of the world, considering this future is subject to these kinds of minds.
- The US special UN representative, not finding any other argument, compared Russia and Syria's actions to being barbaric. I understand that she did this for the sake of imagery and in the absence of any facts. But even so, one has to know something about the history of the world:
    1. If we consider things in a historical context, then both the Celtic and Slavic tribes belonged to the barbarians. Therefore, Samantha Power is wrong to not identify with them.
    2. If we talk about historical parallels, then Samantha Power is not right for a second time, because a barbarian is he who does not belong to an empire. Let's take into account that there is only one empire today and it is not Russia.
    3. From the point of view of imagery, Samantha Power is not right again, because there is nothing more barbaric that the world has seen in recent history than Washington's deeds in Iraq and Libya.
- There are two reasons why the Americans are turning the Security Council into "Samantha Barbara":
    1. The first is that Washington cannot fulfill the obligations it took upon itself in separating terrorists from

"moderates".

2. The second is that Washington needs to divert attention away from the investigation of its strikes on Deir ez-Zor.

- Samantha . . . the more you talk, the less work there is for "Kremlin propaganda."[1]

Aside from the fact that this retort is gloriously forthright, given how banal and uninteresting most diplomatic discourse tends to be, it rips open the continuing divide between the United States and Russia and how likely this chasm is going to be more exposed and possibly widened by Russia chairing the UNSC.

At the heart of the current version of American-Russian animosity are the "competing interventions" in Syria. In its simplest form, America wants to intervene and replace Assad while Russia wants to intervene and keep Assad in place. The funny thing is that both countries actually agree on the fact that Assad is basically a horrible human being. For America, replacing tyrants in the Middle East has become something of a fun pet project (hello Hussein, hello Khaddafi, hello Mubarak, hello Saleh), and Assad fits this model quite well. For Russia, the horror of Islamic State[2] encroachment (which took over pieces of Syrian territory directly because of the state paralysis that occurred due to American support for rebel opposition groups) is emblematic of what is guaranteed to happen when you meddle in Arab autocracies and seek to replace them with

1 J. Arnoldski, trans., "Zakharova: When Samantha Power Opens Her Mouth, No 'Kremlin Propaganda' Is Needed," Fort Russ News, September 27, 2016, http://www.fort-russ.com/2016/09/zakharova-when-samantha-power-opens-her.html.

2 Terrorist organization ISIS is prohibited in Russia.

. . . to be determined. Indeed, it has always been the amorphous and ambiguous nature of rebel opposition to Assad that posed the biggest security threat and concern to the region according to Russian intelligence analysis.

Consequently, America has been deemed too cavalier with its diplomatic equivalent of "anyone but Assad," and Russia has been the one to forcefully reply back, "Be careful what you wish for." It was Russia more than any other country that made the global community finally ask questions about the actual composition of Syrian opposition groups: not just the fact that they suffered from horrific internal dissension but that there were far too many radical Islamists mixed in liberally with so-called moderate Arabs. Because of the torturous hell that was the Chechen conflict, Russia has always been quick to prefer authoritarian stability over democratic instability when it comes to areas infected by such radicalism. This is especially so in the Middle East, which Russia considers close enough to be a near backyard and too close to its own southern flank.

And so here we sit with Russia as the new Chair of the Security Council. Ideally, this should lead to continuous engagement and new opportunities to establish dialogue and cooperative interaction. Alas, idealism no longer seems to operate anywhere within the diplomatic space devoted to Russian-American relations. The attitudes are poor. The professionalism is low. The animosity is high. The United Nations Security Council, that august body where only the most dangerous threats are considered, might be taking a cue from Ms. Zakharava sooner rather than later: disappointingly, it might indeed resemble "Samantha Barbara" as opposed to something more serious.

Золотая середина

Россия как председатель Совета Безопасности ООН

МЭТЬЮ КРОССТОН

Заведующий кафедрой промышленной и международной безопасности, профессор политологии, директор программы по изучению международной безопасности и разведывательной деятельности Университета Белвью, США

1 октября началось, пожалуй, одно из самых интересных председательств в Совете Безопасности Организации Объединенных Наций – его возглавила Россия. Теперь она будет вынуждена находить компромисс между разрешением множества вопросов, которые стандартно находятся в ведении председателя Совбеза, и решением собственных «особых» вопросов, таких как отношения с Соединенными Штатами, которые в последнее время находятся в удручающем состоянии. Еще большую интригу создает то, что некоторые из наиболее наглядных примеров ухудшения этих отношений были продемонстрированы непосредственно в самом Совете Безопасности.

Основные будущие направления деятельности России как председателя Совбеза будут связаны преимущественно с Ближним Востоком и Африкой:

- развитие событий в Сирии;

- варианты решения палестино-израильского конфликта и их легитимность;
- реализация резолюции 1559 по Ливану;
- непрекращающиеся военные действия в Йемене;
- проблемы Южного Судана;
- деятельность Многопрофильной комплексной миссии ООН по стабилизации в Центральноафриканской Республике;
- политические изменения в Демократической Республике Конго;
- деятельность Многопрофильной комплексной миссии ООН по стабилизации в Цен
- тральноафриканской Республике в Мали;
- деятельность Смешанной операции Африканского союза в Судане (Дарфур);
- восстановление функциональности Миссии ООН по проведению референдума в Западной Сахаре.

В первые месяцы председательства России также состоятся важные содержательные дискуссии о правах женщин, мире и безопасности, а также Международным Судом будет проведена частная встреча. Вероятно, более непосредственно близкими для России станут инициированные ей дебаты о сотрудничестве ООН с региональными организациями. В частности, Организация договора о коллективной безопасности (ОДКБ), Шанхайская организация сотрудничества (ШОС) и Содружество независимых государств (СНГ), которым ранее уделялось мало внимания, теперь будут в центре внимания на высшем уровне. Будет интересно наблюдать, сможет ли

Россия добиться большей влиятельности этих организаций и большего внимания к ним, принимая во внимания тот факт, что они были крайне важны для российских интересов.

Однако все эти вопросы общего характера меркнут на фоне интриги и драмы, которые разворачиваются, когда речь заходит о том, как Россия будет взаимодействовать с постоянным представителем США при ООН Самантой Пауэр. Она всегда достаточно враждебно относилась к России, а совсем недавно вызвала сенсацию, обвинив Москву в дезинформировании о происходящем в Сирии и назвав ее действия в стране «варварством».

Россия, не привыкшая пасовать перед трудностями, реальными или вербальными, решительно ответила на это устами Марии Захаровой, официального представителя МИД России. Некоторые ее выражения отличались образностью и саркастичностью:

- «Когда Саманта Пауэр что-то говорит, то хочется плакать от страха за будущее мира – оно в руках, которые подчиняются именно таким головам»;
- «Постпред США при ООН, не найдя никакой иной аргументации, сравнила действия России в Сирии с варварскими. Я понимаю, что она сделала это для образности и в связи с отсутствием каких-либо фактов. Но даже если так. Ведь нужно же хоть сколько-нибудь знать мировую историю:
  1. Если рассуждать в историческом контексте, к варварам принадлежали и кельтские, и славянские племена. Поэтому Саманта Пауэр не права, не причислив себя к ним.

2. Если говорить об исторических параллелях, то Саманта Пауэр не права второй раз, потому что варвар — это тот, кто не принадлежит империи. Хотя . . . Учитывая, что империя сегодня лишь одна, и это не Россия . . .
3. С точки зрения образности Саманта Пауэр не права третий раз, потому что ничего более варварского, чем Ирак и Ливия в исполнении Вашингтона мир в новейшей истории не видел».

- «Причин этой «Саманты Барбары», в которую американцы превращают Совбез, две:
  1. Вашингтон не может выполнить взятые на себя обязательства по отделению террористов и «умеренных».
  2. Вашингтону нужно отвлечь внимание от расследования своих ударов по Дейр-эз-Зору».
- «Саманта . . . Чем больше Вы говорите, тем меньше работы у «кремлевской пропаганды».

Кроме того, что этот ответ победоносно прямой (особенно с учетом того, каким банальным и неинтересным обычно является дипломатический дискурс), он «вспарывает» тот разрыв, который существует между Соединенными Штатами и Россией. И, вероятно, он станет еще более очевидным и, возможно, даже усугубится в период председательства России в Совете Безопасности.

Ключевым фактором нынешних противоречий в российско-американских отношениях является «соперничество интервенций» в Сирию. Говоря простым языком, Америка хочет осуществить интервенцию и свергнуть Асада, а Россия – осуществить интервенцию и оставить его у власти. Забавно то, что обе стороны, по сути, согласны с тем, что Асад ужасный человек. Для Америки смещение ближневосточных тиранов стало чем-то вроде увлекательного хобби (привет, Хусейн, Каддафи, Мубарак, Салех), и Асад очень хорошо вписывается в существующую модель. Для России ужасы вторжения «Исламского государства»[1] (которое захватило часть сирийских территорий именно по причине парализованности государства, наступившей из-за поддержки Соединенными Штатами оппозиции) являются наглядным примером того, что гарантировано случится в случае вмешательства в жизнь арабских автократий и попыток заменить их . . . (подлежит определению чем). Согласно данным анализа российских спецслужб, именно аморфность и неопределенность позиций оппозиции Асада создали серьезную угрозу безопасности страны и региона.

Таким образом, США слишком беспечны в своей политике «кто угодно, только не Асад», и только Россия решительно отвечает им политикой «будьте осторожны в своих желаниях». Именно Россия заставила мировое сообщество задуматься о том, из кого на самом деле состоит сирийская оппозиция, задуматься о том, что проблема не только в разногласиях в ее рядах, но в том, что в составе оппозиционных группировок радикальные исламисты перемешались с так называемыми «умеренными арабами». Будучи наученной кромешным адом Чеченского конфликта, Россия предпочитает авторитарную

1 Деятельность террористической организации «Исламское государство»

стабильность демократической нестабильности, когда речь заходит о регионах, где присутствуют подобные формы радикализма. Это как раз случай Ближнего Востока, который Россия считает достаточно близким для того, чтобы быть сферой ее стратегических интересов, и в то же время слишком близким к ее собственным южным рубежам.

Теперь Россия возглавила Совет Безопасности ООН. В идеале ее председательство должно привести к появлению новых возможностей для ведения диалога, сотрудничества и взаимодействия. Увы, уже не существует идеалистических представлений о российско-американских отношениях. Отношения государств в плохом состоянии. Профессионализм на низком уровне. Противоречия высоки. Совет Безопасности, эта величественная организация, обращающаяся только к самым серьезным угрозам, могла бы последовать совету госпожи Захаровой: к сожалению, это может показаться «Самантой Барбарой» в сравнении с чем-либо более важным.

Russian Arctic Development Hampered by Moscow's Strategic Engagements

ELENA PAVLOVA & VICTOR CHAUVET MAY 21, 2014

On April 22, a meeting of the Russian Security Council for Arctic state policy took place in Moscow. Russia decided to push for the development of its Arctic areas in the next few years, referring to the creation of new transport infrastructures, the implementation of large-scale mining programs, and the strengthening of its military presence. In a separate announcement, Russian president Vladimir Putin declared that a new state agency should be created to implement Russia's policy in the Arctic and thereby improve the quality of governance and decision-making in the area. The Russian president made the point that the Arctic remained in Russia's "special sphere of influence," a region where all aspects of Russian national security—from political-military, economic, and technological aspects—are concerned.

Indeed, oil and gas reserves in the Russian Arctic could exceed 1.6 trillion tons of oil equivalent, and the continental shelf could contain about a quarter of all shelf stocks of hydro-carbonic raw materials in the world. Parallel to their production of minerals and the reconstruction of infrastructures, Russia plans the development of Arctic transit corridors—including the Northern Sea Route. Thanks to changes in the Arctic climate more favorable to commercial navigation, cargo transit on the Northern Sea Route has increased twofold since 2010. As a result, this route has become increasingly attractive, especially since the transit from the Japanese port of

Yokohama to Rotterdam is almost twice as short as the traditional international route through the Suez Canal.

In order to protect the country's interests and regional borders, Russia will build a unified network of naval facilities on its Arctic territories in order to host advanced warships and submarines. The army is also planning to form a new strategic military command in the Arctic. Russia has also announced plans to reopen airfields and ports on the New Siberian Islands and the Franz Josef Land archipelago. Remember: Russia has been seeking to reinforce its military presence in the Arctic for some time now, and these changes had already been mentioned back in 2009 in the Basic Concept of State Policy in the Arctic.

In the context of existing and potentially new sanctions against Russia over the Ukrainian crisis, the tilt of Russia toward Asian markets seems inevitable. Furthermore, considering the interest of certain Asian countries in the Arctic (and especially concerning the Northern Sea Route), has become a new vector of Russia's Asian foreign policy, designed to integrate Russian and Asian economies through a regional integration process in the Russian Oriental bloc. China, once again, is the cornerstone of Moscow's strategy, and Beijing is particularly interested in standing in the Arctic race in terms of economic outlets and potential growth drivers.

However, the Ukrainian crisis is affecting Russia's Arctic strategy within the Arctic Council. Canada, holder of the rotating presidency of the Arctic Council until May 2015, already refused to take part in the meeting of the working group of the Council in Moscow in mid-April, and announced on April 17 that Canada is sending six new CF-18 aircrafts in Lask in Poland as part of NATO's redeployment to the east. Inuk-ethnic Canadian environment minister and current Canadian representative in the Arctic Council Leona Aglukkaq justified the country's boycott of the Arctic Council as being due to the "illegal occupation of Ukraine by Russia in Crimea and elsewhere".

This is the first time that an Arctic Council meeting has been boycotted by one of the member states, so this event remains historic in Arctic cooperation. The international community, considering the latest in Ukraine over Crimea and the country's east, feels threatened by Moscow's potential appeal to use force and coercion to get what it wants in the Arctic. The question is there: if Moscow does not respect states inviolability on the continent, why would it respect Arctic governance? Moscow's strategic commitments on both sides of its tremendous territory are interconnected and affect one another. As Prime Minister Harper is seeking to introduce a security dimension in the Arctic Council, Moscow will probably take actions to match its North and West strategies. Whether or not these actions will respect international law is a completely different story.

Mongolia and the New Russian Oil Diplomacy

SAMANTHA BRLETICH MARCH 4, 2016

Russia signed an inter-governmental agreement in January 2016 that would resettle Mongolia's debt, totaled $172 million, and 97 percent of Mongolia's total debt. The debt forgiveness signals Moscow is moving closer to Ulan Bataar as it slowly loses grip on other former Soviet Union republics economically. Mongolia presents an increased market opportunity for Russia and its petrol products. The use of financial instruments and debts to bring countries closer to Russia and to gain political concessions are a mainstay in Russia's diplomatic toolkit.

The crashing oil market impacted Russia's economy by shrinking Russia's GDP and the regional economy, causing many former Soviet republics to rethink their economic policies and alliances. Countries heavily interconnected with Russia, politically and economically, suffered because of the crash of the commodities market and Western sanctions on Russia. Remittances dropped among the central Asian states, affecting their GDP. The slowed Russian economy has forced Kazakhstan and Kyrgyzstan—two of Russia's closest allies out of the former Soviet Union—to seek economic opportunities elsewhere.

Kazakhstan's currency, the tenge, plunged 100 percent in the last five months and the exchange rate was 352.08 tenge to one US dollar on 18 February. According to a February 23 Reuters report, Kazakhstan's economy will grow only 0.5 percent, as opposed to the originally forecasted 2.1 percent. Kazakhstan will also cut its oil output to 74 million tons. Kazakhstan is now looking to Middle Eastern investors such as the United Arab Emirates. Kazakhstan seeks to diversify its economic partners and expand its bilateral economic partnerships, becoming a bridge between Europe and Eurasia.

The economic squeeze in Kazakhstan prompted discussion of raising rent rates for Russia, who leases four of Kazakhstan's military and space sites, including the Sary Shagan and Emba missile testing grounds. Russia pays $24 million for all four sites, which is not enough according to Kazakhstan MPs. Russia is also currently leasing Baikonur Cosmodrome from Kazakhstan for $115 million a year until 2050.

Meanwhile, Kyrgyzstan has also cancelled plans for a hydroelectric power plant (HPP) as the two companies responsible for the project, Inter RAO and RusHydro, were unable to finance the completion of the Kambar-Ata-1 HPP. Vladimir Putin signed the agreement to construct the HPP in 2012 and costs were projected at $3 billion. RusHydro was to build four smaller hydropower plants (HPP) costing $727 million. Kyrgyz authorities are trying to find a way to avoid paying Russia a $40 million debt for a HPP in the Upper Naryn region.

Results for Kyrgyzstan in the Eurasian Economic Union (EEU) are mixed. Kyrgyzstan joined the EEU because of a large population of migrant workers in Russia, to strengthen bilateral ties, and gain access to traditional and regional markets. Kyrgyzstan's inclusion in the EEU did indeed generate more migrant workers; about 544,000 Kyrgyz work in Russia today, according to Minister of Economy Kylychbek Dzhakypov. For the migrant workers, remittances dropped 28.3 percent by the end of 2015. By comparison, Tajikistan's and Uzbekistan's remittances dropped by half.

In light of Russia's economic losses elsewhere, it is strategically sound for Russia to strengthen ties with Mongolia, even though internally, the resettlement of the debt favors Mongolia's government. Mongolia's prime minister survived a no-confidence vote in January 2016, facilitated by Mongolia's poor economic performance. Mongolia's economy grew only 2.3 percent in 2015, the slowest growth rate in seven years since the 2009 global economic downturn. A drop in commodity prices, dwindling foreign investment, and a slowdown in Chinese trade also contributed. One indicator of increased foreign direct investment is the end of negotiations over the Gatsuurt gold mine deposit permitting mining operations and the end of the dispute over Tavan Tolgoi. Debt forgiveness may be way to lure Mongolia to import more energy from Russia. In 2011, Mongolia imported 90 percent of its petrol products from Russia. As of 2013, Mongolia imported $1.03 billion worth of refined petroleum products, accounting for 67 percent of all imports from Russia. In 2014 imported 91 percent of its petroleum products from Russia, including gasoline, jet fuel, and diesel. However, by 2015, trade volume between Russia and Mongolia had decreased by 2.8 percent.

Mongolia's energy dependence makes it vulnerable to supply shocks and Russian politics. Russia terminated gas supply during strained relations and spikes in anti-Russia sentiment during the Ukraine affair, and during April 2011, Russia cut its diesel supply to Mongolia because of shortages in its domestic supply, which drove up costs of mining operations and logistics.

Energy dependence affects mining operations and infrastructure, which Mongolia lacks. Improved infrastructure in the country would mainly be used to export mining goods. Thus, due to concerns of sovereignty and control, Mongolia has implemented a "Third Neighbor Policy." Many fear that Chinese and Russian construction projects would make movement of Mongolia's mining tonnage more dependent on the two countries. Another argument is that "such [railway] links would make Mongolia a natural resource backyard for China and even facilitate a Chinese demographic influx" into Mongolia. Mongolia, to avoid energy dependence, needs to expand the "Third Neighbor Policy." Mongolia should use its status as a democracy to obtain increased cooperation and funding from the European Union and other Asian nations such as Japan and South Korea. Mongolia's other neighbors are all democracies. Mongolia also needs to diversify its economy from only exporting mineral resources. If it does not, Russia will most likely take advantage of opportunities to advance the Mongolia-Russia bilateral relationship and to enhance Russia's position in the region. The question is whether Russia's maneuvers will bring Mongolia closer to it or ultimately push Mongolia away?

"Pivot to the East" and Russia's Southeast Asia Gambit

TONY RINNA JANUARY 22, 2016

Throughout 2015, the Russian Federation engaged in a variety of initiatives in a region that often falls outside of the conventional analysis of Russia's foreign policy—Southeast Asia. After a period of relative neglect, dating back to the late Soviet era in some cases, Russia has once again emerged as an external actor in this region. Of course, Russia has been somewhat active in Vietnam lately and has made some inroads with that country, such as the reopening of Cam Ranh to Russian naval vessels. Yet in addition to a revival of Russia-Vietnam ties, there are a few other states in the region that have generally been closer to either China or the United States with which Russia has begun to deepen relations. In particular, China's longtime partners Cambodia and Myanmar have increased their bilateral cooperation with Russia, while even steadfast US ally Thailand has begun to develop a friendlier connection with Russia.

It is too soon to state that Russia has emerged as a major player in Southeast Asia, nor is there substantive evidence that Russia will actually attain this status in the region long-term. Nevertheless, Russian overtures to several Southeast Asian states give a clear indication that Russia's "Pivot to the East" policy extends far beyond its relationship with China. In fact, the very fear that Russia's Asian policy orientation may be limited to or even subordinate to China is likely one of the biggest reasons why Moscow has begun to extend its hand of friendship to various countries in the region.

One country with which Russia has not had strong ties but has recently reached out to is Cambodia. Dmitri Medvedev, Russia's prime minister, visited Cambodia in November 2015, where he and his Cambodian counterpart Hun Sen reached a number of agreements. The various measures implemented included agreements on foreign investment as well as a memorandum of understanding and cooperation on money laundering. It was the first time since 1987 that Moscow had conducted an official-level visit to the country. Since that time, China has been Cambodia's most important major partner, especially under the leadership of Hun Sen.

Similarly with Cambodia, Myanmar has generally been under greater Chinese influence. Moscow's relationship with the secretive government in Yangon, while growing, especially in terms of small-scale military cooperation, has also been rather limited. In the late summer of 2014, however, the Russian government signed an agreement with Myanmar to increase the volume of trade between the two countries from $117million to $500 million, although trade figures indicate that Russia had not been able to significantly boost its exports to Myanmar going into 2015. Nevertheless, the two countries pledged at the end of 2015 to continue fortifying their bilateral relationship.

Yet another unlikely potential partner for Russia is the traditional US ally of Thailand. When Prime Minister Medvedev paid an official visit to that country in 2015, the Thai military government was in a slightly strained relationship with its allies in Washington. For Bangkok, the visit from the Russian prime minister offered a sense of legitimacy, especially in light of criticism from the United Nations. Furthermore, the governments in Bangkok and Moscow, as well as the Russian and Thai business communities, have hoped for deeper development in economic cooperation. This includes an increase in Russian arms sales to Thailand as well as the possibility of conducting trade using the Russian ruble and Thai baht. Of course, such Russian overtures toward the Thai kingdom do not necessarily pose any strategic challenges to the United States and its relationship with its longtime ally.

With Russia experiencing some degree of economic and political isolation for its foreign policy adventures over the past two years, Russia has found itself in a favorable position to develop closer ties with other isolated countries. This may explain in particular Russia's developing ties with Myanmar, as well as Russian overtures to the current Thai government, which has drawn some scorn from Washington. Conventional thinking about Russia's recent overtures to various states in Southeast Asia seems to be that Russia is attempting to demonstrate to the United States that it is a global power with far-reaching interests. While there is certainly merit to the position that Russia's foreign policy activities in Southeast Asia have been taken primarily with the United States in mind, one must also consider the Chinese aspect of Russia's growing role in Southeast Asia.

In fact, there is a high likelihood that Russia is seeking not so much to undermine the United States in Southeast Asia but rather attempting to hedge against the rising power of China. With the United States' deep strategic presence in Southeast Asia firmly established, it makes little sense that Russia would sincerely attempt to undercut the United States in the region, especially when Russia has so little influence or even historic legacy in Southeast Asia to begin with. Rather, an increased Russian economic and, in limited terms, security presence in Southeast Asia provides an outlet whereby Russia can show that it is an Asian power independent of its relations with China. Furthermore, a stronger Russian presence in Southeast Asia allows for Russia to establish itself as a competitor in what has otherwise, in some respects, been part of a Chinese sphere of influence. This is especially true given the fact that many Russian policy elites perceive that China has been encroaching on Russia's traditional sphere of influence in central Asia.

Russia's influence in Southeast Asia will likely remain dwarfed by that of China and the United States for the time being. Yet slowly and quietly, Russia is emerging as a player in the region once again. Its ability to increase and project influence in Southeast Asia, an area not traditionally part of its sphere of influence, may in fact be a metric by which to gauge the success of Russia's "Pivot to the East" and its future aspirations to be a complete and total global power.

Russia and Nigeria Deepen Cooperation

KESTER KENN KLOMEGAH JUNE 3, 2017

Russia and Nigeria have taken steps to deepen their economic and political ties after foreign minister of the Federal Republic of Nigeria, Geoffrey Onyeama, held diplomatic talks with his counterpart Sergei Lavrov during an official working visit to Moscow on May 29–31. Lavrov held talks with Onyeama and his delegation on May 30. The foreign ministers discussed issues pertaining to the steady development of bilateral ties in political, trade, economic, and humanitarian areas. They concentrated on prospects of cooperation in the nuclear industry, hydrocarbon processing, infrastructure projects, and exports of Russian industrial products to Nigeria. The ministers further held an in-depth exchange of views on international and regional issues, focusing on countering terrorism and extremism; settling crises in Africa, primarily in the Sahara and the Sahel; and fighting pirates in the Gulf of Guinea.

After the closed meeting, Lavrov told a media conference that the meeting noted a strong potential for cooperation in areas such as hydrocarbon production and processing, nuclear power industry and agriculture, and further expressed mutual interest in continued military-technical and military cooperation and training civilian specialists and law enforcement officers for Nigeria at Russian universities. "Certainly, the complicated problems that persist on the African continent require coordinated actions of the Africans themselves, with the support of the international community,"

Lavrov said. Russia consistently demands that Africans first find the "keys" to African problems, and that the international community should provide moral, political, and material support to these efforts. Russia, for instance, has advocated for the fastest possible elimination of instability on the continent, primarily in the Sahara-Sahel zone, South Sudan, Mali, and the Central African Republic.

The Russian Foreign Affairs minister, however, noted Nigeria's considerable contribution to peacekeeping efforts in all of these regions and added that Russia would be ready to contribute to common efforts to strengthen regional stability through the appropriate channels at the UN Security Council, through its bilateral relations with African countries, including training peacekeepers and equipping peacekeeping contingents in African countries. Russia and Nigeria plan to step up an uncompromising fight against international terrorism that threatens national security in both countries and, objectively, the security of all countries. With regard to Nigeria, this of course refers to the heightened activity of the Boko Haram terrorist organization that was associated with the organization sometimes called ISIS. "We will continue to support the Nigerian government's efforts to fight this evil. Of course, the well-known initiative of President Vladimir Putin on establishing a wide-ranging anti-terrorist front based on international law and without attempts to artificially bar someone from taking part in it remains relevant," Lavrov stressed in his comments.

Dr. Maurice Okoli, chairman and CEO of Markol Group, which is based in Moscow but with business links to Nigeria, China, and Britain, explained that the visit of Nigerian Foreign Minister Geofrey Onyeoma and his business delegation to Russia came at the right time when Nigeria as a country is facing numerous challenges:

"Russia and Nigeria have enjoyed a very good political and economic relationship that has lasted for many years, and this visit will definitely lift that relationship to another level. We are also looking forward that the visit will touch political and economic issues for the mutual benefits for both countries. It is our hope that this visit will help to boast cooperation between Nigeria and Russia especially in the area of fighting Boko Haram insurgency thereby improving security and stability in Nigeria and the region in general."

Dr Okoli added: "Russia as a country has experienced Islamic insurgency in the past and having a great wealth of experience in handling such issues, I have no doubt that Russian government advice and support will be of an immense value in dealing with the problem of the Boko Haram insurgency in Nigeria and West Africa sub-region." There is high optimism among business elites for raising Russian-Nigerian economic cooperation. Russia plans to help Nigeria explore for oil and gas. Nigeria has expressed interest in Russia, helping it build nuclear power plants, petroleum pipelines, railways, and other domestic infrastructure. Both Russia and Nigeria have a wealth of minerals—and some could be the basis of additional commerce between the two nations. Nigeria's natural resources include gold, bauxite, zinc, tantalum, iron ore, and coal. Nigeria and Russia are both "large economies" and "rich in natural resources," Goodie Ibru, head of the Chamber of Commerce of Lagos, Nigeria's largest city, said at one of the bilateral economic conferences held previously, adding that "although Nigeria is smaller in terms of technology and infrastructure development, there's a lot for both countries to benefit from."

The federal government of the Republic of Nigeria has, indeed, expressed its support for any genuine Russian investment. And also quite recently, Ibrahim Usman Gafai, charge d'affaires and minister plenipotentiary at the embassy of the Federal Republic of Nigeria in Moscow, told the Ghana News Agency (GNA) in an interview that economic relations between both countries have steadily developed during the past few years with a number of leading Russian companies establishing their presence in Nigeria. Tellingly, Russian investment in Nigeria covers such areas as energy, iron and steel, and hydrocarbon. Over the years, diplomatic relationships have also witnessed the establishment of a Russia-Nigeria Business Council (RNBC), which oversees economic activities between the two countries. So far, the two countries have held three meetings of the Joint Commission, the platform for the two countries to sit down and draw up agreements and the Memorandum of Understanding (MoU) on how to conduct businesses and investment in each other's countries. However, the last such meeting was held as far back as 2009.

Russia's trade figures with Nigeria and many African countries are hard to find. Interestingly, Russia and Nigeria's two-way trade was a modest $350 million in 2013. Authorities in both countries have repeatedly said that it should be many times larger, given that Russia is the biggest market in the former Soviet Union and Nigeria the biggest market in Africa. "Unfortunately, trade volume between Nigeria and Russia has been comparatively low and highly skewed in favor of Russia. There has been an attempt to balance the current trend through boosting economic relations between the two friendly nations" Ibrahim Gafai acknowledged in the GNA interview. On the other hand, Russian businesses are encouraged to participate in various annual trade fairs organized by different chambers of commerce in Nigeria. In addition, Moscow's Nigerian Embassy will continue to call on the two countries to create an investment forum to showcase their potentialities in each other's territories. The major challenge facing investors from both sides of the divide is dearth of information on each other's business environment. This has, over the years, created a condition of uncertainty and misgivings among prospective investors. As part of the initiatives to contribute to revamping the Nigerian economy, Nigerians under the auspices of Nigerians in Diaspora Organization in Europe (NIDOE), the Russian chapter, in collaboration with Russia-Nigeria Business Council, Institute of African Studies, and Russian ministries and agencies have adopted corporate strategies in identifying and wooing potential Russian businesses and industry directors to invest in Federal Republic of Nigeria.

Within the context of strengthening these relations, it is also necessary to foster cooperation with support from the Intergovernmental Russian-Nigerian Mixed Commission for Economic, Scientific, and Technical Cooperation, and also to step up direct contacts between members of the Russian and Nigerian business communities as suggested by the Ministry of Foreign Affairs of the Russian Federation. Ultimately, we are witnessing an extremely diverse and multi-pronged effort between the countries to intensify and deepen bilateral relations. At the moment those efforts have not truly borne fruit in terms of data-quantifiable results. But both countries remain optimistic about just how much these initiatives can benefit their future national security, economic, and political interests.

Neopopulism and the Gray Cardinal

Volodin to Head the CSTO Parliamentary Assembly

NOVEMBER 26, 2016

Vyacheslav Volodin was elected as head of the Collective Security Treaty Organization's Parliamentary Assembly during the ninth plenary session in Saint Petersburg on November 24. Thus concludes a relatively fast and interesting transition personally for the influential Volodin, who in just three months has gone from the first deputy chief of President Putin's staff in the Kremlin, to being elected to the Russian Duma from his native Saratov, to quickly becoming that body's speaker, officially putting him fourth in line in terms of Russian political power, behind the president, prime minister, and speaker of the Federation Council, the upper chamber of the national parliament.

This is, of course, only a technical accounting of how power formally flows within the Russian system, in that some would say Volodin had more influence already than the prime minister and Federation Council speaker while in the Kremlin. His former position within the presidential staff basically oversaw everything from home elections to debates in parliament, NGOS, and political institutions. He was the chief strategist for Putin's presidential campaign in 2012 (which was a very important position indeed, on the heels of the Bolotnaya protests of 2011) and was in charge of the 2016 parliamentary election, which saw the ruling United Russia party win 343 of 450 Duma seats, constituting a supermajority. This is what has earned Volodin the nickname, considered a compliment or a criticism depending on what group you speak with, "The Gray Cardinal."

Volodin's transitions have been so smooth that they clearly come with the affirmation of the Kremlin. Indeed, the CSTO PA vote for his election today was unanimous. The CSTO, honestly an organization that is not new but is still little known in the West, is a military alliance comprised of Russia, Armenia, Belarus, Kazakhstan, Kyrgyzstan, and Tajikistan. It was first formed back in 1992, shortly after the collapse of the Soviet Union, with the aim to facilitate cooperation and strengthen regional security at a time when those two issues in specific were under great doubt and concern. The CSTO Parliamentary Assembly includes seventy-nine lawmakers from the member states and has three permanent committees that consider broad-based dilemmas that cover political, legal, economic, and social problems innate to the post-Soviet space and beyond. It also in part addresses issues of international cooperation and security.

Volodin himself has said it is very important for politicians to keep in touch with "ordinary citizens" of the state. Some consider this yet another extension of the neopopulism that seems to be advancing in many other countries around the globe. Many Russians see the recent election of President-Elect Trump in America as the most vivid and surprising example of this trend. But in all honesty, it is not entirely incorrect to say that President Putin himself spearheaded this trend as far back as 2011, within Russia at least, when he created the All-Russia People's Front as prime minister. At the time labeled officially by Kremlin spokespersons as a "supraparty" not beholden to or accountable to any party bureaucracy, it was roundly criticized by Western analysts as something akin to a naked power grab by the soon-to-be-once-more president. Given the tensions between

Russia and the West (that were already in evidence back in 2011), it is easy to see why such an interpretation would be promulgated. But it was something of a mischaracterization that now seems to be only more powerfully borne out by these international trends happening across so many elections. In 2011, as prime minister under President Medvedev, it seems that Putin correctly calculated and, in a way, embraced the intense dissatisfaction with the party of power. Public opinion polls and accurate regional election exit polling strongly indicated what some considered a catastrophic loss of confidence and support from regular people to those in power. The political disconnect was becoming more severe and palpable.

Thus, the creation of the All-Russia People's Front was not so much a power grab as a power reorientation by Putin before he recaptured the presidency: an attempt not so much to breathe new life into his own political career but rather to establish a channel and communication avenue directly to the electorate that was not formally connected to any specific party and therefore, arguably, not yet cynically stained by Russian political bureaucracy. This helps explains Putin's continued physical commitment to the organization and why he makes so many personal appearances when the People's Front meets, which just happened again recently when Putin fielded questions from a large audience of roughly six hundred people. It is of course ironic that Putin found it necessary to create and then support an organization that is, ostensibly, somewhat nullifying the political relevance of his own parliamentary party. But it was also a very astute strategy that read the populist tea leaves, as it were: he effectively succeeded in separating himself in the eyes of the public from the parliamentary party in power that had come to be seen as at least partially inept and corrupt.

All of this took place with Volodin not just in the Kremlin at the right hand of Putin but likely himself having a significant role in the development of this strategy. His move now to the Duma Speakership and head of the CSTO PA should be seen as an attempt to engineer a much more difficult task: to reinvigorate the party of power so as to stem the tide of popular cynicism and the feeling of bureaucratic rot. That will be no easy task. As President-Elect Donald Trump just learned when he had to formally disavow a meeting of so-called alt-right voters that had met in Washington and proceeded to salute Trump in absentia with Sieg Heil–type calls of glory uncomfortably reminiscent of Nazism, appealing to populist sentiment is easy. Staying ahead of it and not allowing it to run amok out of your control is far more challenging. But if Volodin is even somewhat successful in achieving a positive rebranding of United Russia as a party in the Duma, then Russia might at this early stage already be seeing how the Gray Cardinal is being groomed to return to the Kremlin in 2024.

This appeared, in an edited form, in Rethinking Russia in December 2016.

PART VII

CYBER, SPIES, AND INTELLIGENCE

The Industrial Spy Game

FSB as Russian Economic Developer

JARED S. EASTON AUGUST 13, 2015

Since the fall of the Soviet Union, the Russian Federation (RF) has sought to reclaim its former glory and regain recognition as a great power. Throughout this progression the national science base has been of high importance to the RF's economic development. This has been demonstrated through policy documents like the RF's National Security Strategy from 2009. The focus of this analysis is to examine the role of RF intelligence-gathering activities for the purpose of domestic modernization.

The National Security Strategy of the Russian Federation up to 2020 identified five key high-technology sectors: energy, information technology (IT), telecommunications, biomedicine, and nuclear technology (RF, 2009). Nanotechnology was also highlighted as an important investment and growth area. In 2010, the RF announced plans that scientific and technological centers would focus on the development and domestic commercialization of modern technologies, motivated in part by the success of America's Silicon Valley (Medvedev, 2010). There are many ways a nation can bolster a science and technology (S&T) foundation, not just through domestic industry, and each nation tends to use multiple options. A critical way that is not often discussed in mainstream media sources is to procure foreign knowledge and equipment through espionage activities. Russia engages this path aggressively with the likes of the Federal Security Service (FSB).

There is little doubt that the FSB has been active in S&T intelligence collection, concentrating on foreign nations for domestic modernization and improving Russia's competitiveness in the global economy. The modern era of intelligence-collection capabilities sees the American intelligence community as dominant. Before the modern era (pre-2001), the RF operated one of the world's largest S&T information-gathering apparatus, which worked almost as a substitute for legitimate industrial domestic research & development (Almquist, 1990). For the RF, intelligence support to the scientific community and its own domestic industrial complex was the standard, not the exception, and in 2010 Russia confirmed that it made no secret of its motivations to gather S&T intelligence for the benefit of its national security interests defined broadly.

The RF intelligence complex, including the FSB, has been obliged by federal law "to assist the country's economic development and its scientific and technical progress and to ensure the military-technical security of the Russian Federation." This activity is in line with Article 8 of the Federal Law on the FSB. The collection of S&T intelligence and "industrial espionage practices established a template for Soviet and later Russian [FSB] intelligence gathering that remains in use to this day; as long as US technology maintains its preeminent global position, such espionage will likely continue" (Sibley, 2004). This was validated in 2010 by the American Office of the Director of National Intelligence (ODNI), which stated that the RF "continues to strengthen its intelligence capabilities and directs them against US interests worldwide. Moscow's intelligence effort includes espionage, technology acquisition and covert action efforts" (Blair, 2010). Jonathan Evans, the head of the domestic British Security Service (MI5), noted in 2007 that "the scope of the Russian intelligence gathering was equal to the Soviet effort during the Cold War . . . [and] that Russian intelligence services were particularly interested in British science and technology (Brogan, 2007).

The RF, and specifically the FSB, has extensively leveraged operational cover from diplomatic missions abroad and the posting of illegal agents in their target countries to approach foreign researchers and entrepreneurs. They would often establish a career in one or several third countries, allowing agents to use academic research institutions or commercial companies as platforms for espionage activities (Kouzminov, 2006). But it has also been observed that the triumphs of human intelligence (HUMINT) operations during the former Soviet era are unlikely to be achieved in the present day RF. In the modern era the primary method for collecting S&T intelligence is through cyber espionage. In 2008, the United States noted that more than 1 trillion USD worth of data was lost to cyber espionage (Ackerman, 2009). This fact is further confirmed with the knowledge that the RF is developing advanced offensive cyber capabilities (McAfee, 2009). In addition to cyber espionage, scientific and technological intelligence can be exploited through signals intelligence. This is another area where the RF intelligence services have leveraged the previous Soviet foundation with modern advancements in current technologies.

In conclusion, while the FSB has advanced significantly in S&T intelligence collection since the former Soviet period, "the FSB's increased influence may prove to be counter-productive in terms of economic modernization and industrial restructuring. Despite its self-confidence, the FSB is scarcely prepared to manage all the industrial complexes with international standing" (Gomart, 2008). This last point is crucial, as it implies that the gains made covertly through the intelligence community could in fact have an unintended detrimental effect on economic progress and industrial modernization happening more organically with native companies across Russia. This is not the desired effect, of course, but a consequence of the classical dilemma in modern market economies that try to figure out how much governmental intervention is positive before it hits a tipping point and becomes a net negative impact on development. This is not even considering the likely more severe stress this reliance on covert activity has on the entrepreneurial spirit and risk-taking that is crucial for any developing economy in the twenty-first century. The Russian Federation operates no differently than the US intelligence community agencies in that it pursues its own national security interests and aims to improve its domestic standing on the global stage. The issue it should consider, however, is whether or not some old-school spy thinking might be a less effective long-term strategy, even if it does produce more immediate results.

All Eyes on Me

The Emergence of a Russian Surveillance State

JONATHAN HARTNER AUGUST 17, 2015

Before analyzing the activities and assessing the ethics of any intelligence organization, it is first necessary to remember that intelligence organizations are secretive by nature and it's impossible to assess their methods in full given most countries' secrecy laws. This is especially the case with Russia's Federal Security Service (FSB). Much like its predecessor, the KGB, its activities continue to be troublesome for diplomats, journalists, and citizens alike. The Russian government uses propaganda, deception, and manipulation to a much higher degree and with great effectiveness. The Russian surveillance state, largely powered by the FSB and driven by the threat of terrorism, is resurgent and becoming ever more intrusive.

One example of Russia's use of deception and propaganda, according to David Frum on The Atlantic website on April 18, 2014, even went so far as to include the notorious former NSA contractor Edward Snowden in a propaganda stunt (Q & A forum) with Russian President Vladimir Putin. During the session, which was televised on Russian television, Edward Snowden challenged Putin on government surveillance in Russia. To this, Putin simply stated: "We don't have a mass system for such interception and according to our law it cannot exist." This is typical of the deception that the government uses and this statement was widely regarded by experts and watchdog agencies as false.

It would also be foolish to assert that the American intelligence establishment does not continue to engage in covert operations involving ethically questionable methods given the information available. However, it has found itself at the heart of major controversies concerning its collection methods just in the last decade which have forced greater transparency and greater debate, both internally and externally. An analysis of the outcome of the controversy over the NSA's collection of bulk data, for example, sparked a greater discussion on the legality of the NSA's collection programs and took place both within Congress and the public media. The constitutional legality of these covert programs caused a lot of problems for the government in the courts. The president, the director of National Intelligence, and other senior officials were made to answer for the programs before the Supreme Court and Congress (Mornin, 2014).

This level of transparency cannot and likely will never be found in Russia. Political and legal discourse between academia, the justice system, and the general public is certainly lacking as well. The evidence is clear: as noted in the Atlantic article cited previously regarding Putin's interaction with Edward Snowden: "Russian journalists will not 'revisit' (as he puts it) the truthfulness of Putin's answers. Russian journalists who do that end up dead, in at least 56 cases since 1992. Anna Politkovskaya, the journalist who pressed Putin hardest, was shot dead in her own apartment building in 2006, after years of repeated arrests, threats, and in one case, attempted poisoning." (The Atlantic, April 2014) Detailed statistics provided by the Committee to Protect Journalists (CPJ) do indeed support these claims (Akhmednabiyev, Beketov & Gekkiyev).

It wouldn't be completely inaccurate to think of Russia as an American surveillance state on PEDs (performance-enhancing drugs). It's asserted that "over the last two years, the Kremlin has transformed Russia into a surveillance state—at a level that would have made the Soviet KGB (Committee for State Security) envious" (Borogan and Soldatov, 2013). The 2014 Winter Olympic Games in Sochi demonstrated Russia's resurgent surveillance state. The System of Operative-Investigative Measures (SORM) was Russia's strategy to legally analyze all electronic traffic and it was used to its maximum extent at the Games. The U.S. Department of State issued travel warnings to Americans traveling to Sochi to watch the Games, giving advice such as "sanitizing" electronic devices, restraining from using local wireless internet, and considering the use of burn phones and destroying materials when leaving the country. Joshua Kopstein noted in "Sochi's Other Legacy" that drones, soldiers, surveillance blimps, thousands of cameras, and high-tech scanning devices were also used (*New Yorker*, February 2014).

Naturally, this surveillance state extends far beyond Sochi. According to Soldatov and Borogan, the Russian government has tightened its grip on the country in the name of national security and safety. Seven investigative and security agencies have been granted permission to legally intercept everything from phone calls to e-mails, with the FSB establishing the procedures. What's more, these agencies are only required to show warrants (once obtained) to their superiors in the FSB; the parties being investigated have no right to see the warrant, unlike in the United States. The FSB itself has control centers directly connected to computer servers and their usage of SORM systems has increased. These surveillance methods are not restricted to Russian citizens, either.

British Journalist Luke Harding claimed in 2014 that he was constantly followed around Moscow when he lived there, his flat was repeatedly broken into by FSB agents (who purposely left clues to let him know who it was), and that Russian agents made it clear that they were eavesdropping once by cutting phone service after he made jokes about President Putin. The author was finally kicked out of Moscow in 2011 after living there for four years. Aside from this, it is clear that other states, such as the British government, know that the FSB targets foreign diplomats using the same techniques.

The FSB and the Russian surveillance state, driven by the Putin administration's Soviet-style political maneuvers, has seen a resurgence particularly in the last decade. This is a divergent path from that of the American intelligence community, which, while it may be no less controversial in it activities around the globe, is certainly more beholden to domestic laws and the system of checks and balances hallmarked in American democracy, thereby rendering it open to debate and criticism.

China and Russia

Cyber Cousins but Not Cyber Brothers

AUGUST 26, 2015

There seems to be a strong divergence in perception behind China's desire to command cyberspace offensively. On the one hand, there is the assumption that this is a natural manifestation of its growing desire to achieve global superpower status. On the other hand, there is the counterargument that emphasizes China's own perception of being unable to operate effectively against the United States in a conventional military confrontation.[1] Indeed, many Chinese writings suggest cyberwarfare is considered an obvious asymmetric instrument for balancing overwhelming US power.[2] This latter argument is more compelling based on the stark military realities:

- In overall spending, the United States puts between five and ten times as much money into the military per year as does China.
- Chinese forces are only now beginning to be brought up to speed. Just one-quarter of its naval surface fleet is considered modern in electronics, engines, and weaponry.
- In certain categories of weaponry, the Chinese do not compete. For instance, the US Navy has eleven nuclear-powered aircraft-carrier battle groups. The Chinese Navy is only now

1 Magnus Hjortdal, "China's Use of Cyber Warfare: Espionage Meets Strategic Deterrence," *Journal of Strategic Security* 4, no. 2 (2011): 1–24.

2 Ibid.

moving toward the complete construction of its very first carrier.

- In terms of military effectiveness—i.e., logistics, training, readiness—the difference between Chinese and American standards is not a gap but a chasm. The Chinese military took days to reach survivors after the devastating Sichuan earthquake in May of 2008 because it had so few helicopters and emergency vehicles.[3]

Given this state of military affairs, a Chinese perception of insecurity is not surprising. Even more logical is the Chinese resolve to evolve its asymmetric cyber capabilities: such attacks are usually inexpensive and exceedingly difficult to properly attribute, meaning the victim is unlikely to know who was directly responsible for initiating the attack. It is even more complex for states, where cyberattacks can be launched from inside of neutral or allied countries.[4] Given an authoritarian state's capacity for paranoia, it is illogical for China to not develop its offensive cyber capabilities. In this case the weakness—conventional military strength—is quite real. To that end, the People's Republic of China has endeavored to create its own set of lopsided military advantages in the cyber domain:

- The Pentagon's annual assessment of Chinese military strength determined in 2009 that the People's Liberation Army had

3 James Fallows, "Cyber Warriors," *Atlantic* 305, no. 2 (March 2010).

4 Gunter Ollman, "Asymmetrical Warfare: Challenges and Strategies for Countering Botnets," in *Proceedings of ICIW2010: The 5th International Conference on Information Warfare & Security* (Reading, UK: Academic Conferences International, 2010), 509–14.

established information warfare units to develop viruses to attack enemy computer systems and networks.

- The PLA has created a number of uniformed cyberwarfare units, including the Technology Reconnaissance Department and the Electronic Countermeasures and Radar Department. These cyber units are engaged on a daily basis in the development and deployment of a range of offensive cyber and information weapons.
- China is believed to be engaged in lacing the United States' network-dependent infrastructure with malicious code known as "logic bombs."[5]

The official newspaper of the PRC, the *Liberation Army Daily*, confirmed China's insecurity about potential confrontation with the United States in June 2011. In it, the Chinese government proclaimed that "the US military is hastening to seize the commanding military heights on the Internet. . . . Their actions remind us that to protect the nation's Internet security we must accelerate Internet defense development and accelerate steps to make a strong Internet Army."[6] Clearly, the Chinese have sought to maximize their technological capacity in response to kinetic realities. This is not to say the United States is therefore guaranteed to be in an inferior position (information about American virtual capabilities at the moment remains largely classified), but

5 George Patterson Manson, "Cyberwar: The United States and China Prepare for the Next Generation of Conflict," *Comparative Strategy* 30 (April–June 2011): 122–33.

6 Don Reisinger, "Chinese Military Warns of US Cyber Threat," CNET.com, June 16, 2011, http://news.cnet.com/830 1-1 3506_3-20071 553-17/chinese-miiütary-warns-of-u.s-cyberwar-threat.

the overt investment, recruitment, and development of Chinese virtual capabilities presents opportunities that the United States should also be willing to entertain.

How does all of this compare and contrast with the Russian approach to the cyber domain? Anyone studying cyber conflict over the last five years is well aware of Russia's apparent willingness to engage in cyber offensives. The 2007 incident in which the Estonian government was attacked and the 2008 war with Georgia are universally considered examples of Russia using cyber technology as the tip of their military spear. While it is true that Russia actively encourages what has come to be known as "hacktivism" and lauds "patriotic nationalist" cyber vigilantism as part of one's "civic duty," there are still distinct differences with China.

Much of Russia's cyber activity, when not in an open conflict, seems to be of the criminal variety and not necessarily tied directly into the state. Indeed, Russia seems to utilize organized crime groups as a cyber conduit when necessary and then backs away, allowing said groups continued commercial domination. Russia, therefore, almost acts as a rentier state with criminal groups: cyberweapons are the "natural resource," and the Russian government is the number-one consumer. This produces a different structure, style, and governance model when compared to China.

PARSING CYBER ROGUES

	CHINA	RUSSIA
PURPOSE	Protectionist	Predator
PSYCHOLOGY	Long Term / Rational	Short Term / Cynical
STYLE	Strategic	Anarchic
GOVERNANCE MODEL	State Centric	Crimino-Bureaucratic

PURPOSE

China's purpose in developing its cyber capability seems motivated by protectionist instincts, based largely on the perception that it is not able to defend itself against the United States in a straight conventional military conflict. Russia's purpose seems utterly predatory. This is no doubt influenced by the fact that most of the power-dominating cyber capability in the Russian Federation is organized and controlled by criminal groups, sometimes independently and sometimes in conjunction with governmental oversight.

PSYCHOLOGY

The operational mind-set of China seems to be both long term and rational. It develops its strategies based on future strategic objectives and its position within the global community. Most if not all of China's goals in the cyber domain can be clearly understood if rational self-interest is taken into consideration. Russia's cyber mind-set is dominated by short-term thinking, largely motivated by the pursuit of massive profit and wielding inequitable political power. When analyzing just how much of Russian cyber activity is in fact controlled by the desire for wealth, it is hard to not have an overall impression akin to state cynicism.

STYLE

The atmospheric style in which Chinese cyber activity takes place is strategic. The state strives to control the cyber environment and maintain influence over all groups in the interest of the state. The Russian cyber atmosphere unfortunately resembles nothing if not anarchy. The state engages criminal groups whereby the relationship's authority structure is blurred if not nonexistent. As a result, there is little confidence that the government of Russia exclusively controls its cyber environment.

GOVERNANCE MODEL

It is clear that China's cyber governance model is state centric. This may not be most ideal for democracy, but it shows how China does not allow competing authorities or shadow power structures to interfere with its own national interests. Russia's cyber governance model is crimino-bureaucratic. It is not so much that the state is completely absent from the cyber domain in Russia: it is rather the ambiguity of power and authority that defines the cyber domain. Russia may enjoy claiming the allegiance of its patriotic nationalist hackers, but it does not in fact tightly control its own cybernetizens, at least not in comparison to China.

While both Russia and China are not afraid to use offensive cyberweapons, there are dramatic structural, motivational, strategic, and philosophical differences. Russia seems to embody a criminal-governmental fusion that has permeated the entire state apparatus. The cyber domain there is used for temporary forays to achieve state objectives and then returns to more permanent criminal projects. As such, the domain is not truly state controlled, is relatively anarchic, and cannot establish any deterring equilibrium. China, on the other hand, may be the first state to truly embrace the importance of tech war: it has realistically assessed its own kinetic shortcomings and looked to cyber for compensation. In short, it has fused Sun Tzu with Machiavelli: better to quietly overcome an adversary's plans than to try to loudly overcome his armies.

This analysis paints Russia in a relatively stark strategic light. While these differences do not give rise to a trusted alliance with China, the manner in which China approaches its cyber domain presents interesting new ideas about how the United States or the West should approach the global cyber commons. Russia has room to improve still on the cyber front if its interests are in greater cooperation internationally with the world's other great powers. If it prefers its current lone wolf approach, then it is doubtful the cyber commons will ever see any organized or honored regime of rules and proper behavior.

A Perfect Cyber Storm

Russia and China Teaming Together

LAURA GARRIDO AUGUST 29, 2015

United States intelligence agencies have listed cyber-attacks as the top threat to American national security, ahead of terrorism. These threats are increasing in sophistication, scale, frequency, and severity of impact. Also, the range of actors, attack methods, targeted systems, and victims are expanding. In February 2015, James Clapper, the director of National Intelligence in the United States, announced that the estimation of the Russian cyber threat had been elevated, pushing Russia to the number one spot on the list of countries which pose the greatest danger to the United States.

Since the collapse of the Soviet Union, Russia has faced political, military, and economic challenges which it worried could mean that its national interests could be ignored by other powers. In order to protect their interests defensively, and free up their offensive capabilities for deployment elsewhere, Russia and China signed an agreement in April 2015 vowing not to attack each other, while also agreeing to share intelligence and software and cooperate in law enforcement and investigations. This is a direct challenge to the United States because not only are Russia and China working together to get ahead in the energy race but this agreement meant they were now trying to combine their capacities in the digital world.

China and Russia, by far, have the most sophisticated cyber capabilities in the world. The offensive cyber capabilities of each individual country was a threat already to the United States, but if they now work together in earnest, the United States could be facing an unprecedented cyber danger. According to senior military officials, Russia's Ministry of Defense is establishing its own cyber command that will be responsible for conducting offensive cyber activities such as propaganda operations and inserting malware into enemy command and control systems. A specialized branch for computer network operations is also being established by Russia's armed forces. Computer security studies claim that unspecified Russian cyber actors are developing ways to access industrial control systems remotely. Industrial control systems manage critical infrastructures such as electrical power grids, urban mass-transit systems, air-traffic control, and oil and gas distribution networks. As Blank notes, "These unspecified Russian actors have successfully compromised the product supply chains of three ICS vendors so that customers download exploitative malware directly from the vendors' websites along with routine software updates" (2017).

Russia was one of the first nations to move assertively into the cyber sphere. In 1998, long before most nations even began thinking about cyber-security, the Kremlin-backed "Directorate K," a government agency, began operations to monitor and defend against hackers and spammers. However, in recent years Directorate K has taken on a more offensive role in the digital sphere. Russia has been cyber-probing the United States for many years. In 1999, it was discovered that the Moonlight Maze virus had been stealing information from the Department of Defense, Department of Energy, NASA, and military contractors for two years.

In early 2015, Russian hackers were able to access an unclassified server belonging to the United States Department of State. Through this they were able to penetrate sensitive areas of the

White House computer system and access information such as the real-time, nonpublic details of President Barack Obama's schedule. The FBI, Secret Service, and other United States intelligence agencies were all involved in investigating the breach and said that it was the most sophisticated attack ever launched against an American governmental system. The breach was pinpointed to hackers working for the Russian government based on "telltale codes and other markers," even though the intrusion was routed through computers all around the globe. The attack was believed to have begun with a phishing e-mail launched using a State Department e-mail account that the hackers had previously stolen.

China has also recently increased the amount of time, manpower, resources and money spent on cyberespionage. China's People's Liberation Army (PLA) includes a special bureau within its intelligence community specifically managed for cyber espionage. The PLA, according to recent intelligence reports, is not only capable of advanced surveillance and collection but also possesses malware that could take down foreign electricity and water grids. However, it seems that China so far has only been motivated to commit financial and economic espionage, rather than any outright physical infrastructure attacks. Nevertheless, the United States has been getting compromised by China for many years. Rubenstein says that "it is estimated that in the last few years, Chinese hackers have attempted attacks on two thousand companies, universities, and government agencies in the United States" (2014). In 2003, China launched Titan Rain against United States military and government agencies. Titan Rain targeted US defense networks in an attempt to obtain confidential national security information. While no information was reported as stolen, it was considered to be one of the largest attacks in cyber espionage history. Titan Rain is particularly unnerving because the attack was meant to be completed in as little as twenty minutes and was able to target high-profile agencies such as NASA, the US Army Information Systems Engineering Command, the Defense Information Systems Agency, the Naval Ocean Systems Center, and the US Army Space and Strategic Defense Installation simultaneously in one day.

These cyber threats from Russia and China were always a major concern for the United States because they undermined American economic competitiveness and at least tried to compromise national security interests. As of now, a "cyber Armageddon" may not be a high risk but low- to moderate-level attacks over time could pose serious financial and security risks to the United States. Especially if this supposed cyber alliance ever truly takes root and begins to create new innovative cyber strategies for attacks. In the United States alone, the value of the information that is compromised due to international hacking is somewhere between 25 billion to 100 billion dollars annually. With Russia's tactics of using cyber-attacks to block any and all communications from within a nation-state and China's habit of economic and financial cyber-attacks, the two countries combining could be a perfect storm of political and economic havoc that may not yet have the United States' proper attention and deterrence capacity.

THE FSB AND SIGINT

Absolute Power at Home and Abroad

BRUCE ADRIANCE AUGUST 29, 2015

The Russian Federal Security Service (FSB) should easily be considered one of the most influential and powerful intelligence organizations in the world today. Its primary functions and roles include: law enforcement, counterintelligence, domestic surveillance, and internal intelligence functions at the national level. These roles mirror many of the functions assigned to the Federal Bureau of Investigation in the United States (FBI). However, while many of these functions would put the FSB squarely in the realm of law enforcement instead of security or intelligence, the FSB also has mission responsibilities that organizations such as the FBI do not. The most significant being the mission of signals exploitation (SIGINT). This article focuses on the SIGINT capability of the FSB and its threat to US political, economic, and diplomatic policies as well as the threat in the new environment of cyberespionage.

Initially an internally focused organization, the FSB threat profile changed in 2003 when, under Presidential Edict No. 314, the missions and authorities of the Federal Agency for Government Communications and Information (FAPSI) were transferred to the FSB. This meant the FSB would now have both the resources and authorities for SIGINT collection against its adversaries and information assurance for all Russian government information systems. This transition established the FSB as a much larger player in the intelligence exploitation community and a larger threat to US interests. Most Western intelligence services separate the responsibilities and missions of SIGINT to a single intelligence organization, like the National Security Agency (NSA) in the United States, which has only that authority. Other intelligence services handle matters such as counterintelligence and military-related intelligence. This is not the case with the FSB, which after Presidential Edict No. 314 controls elements of all major aspects and disciplines of intelligence, essentially giving it both unfettered access to collected intelligence as well as the ability to potentially restrict other Russian organizations from accessing the collected data. What exists is a single intelligence service with the capabilities to conduct human intelligence, counter-intelligence, law enforcement, border security, countersurveillance, and signals collections. This represents a significant amount of authority and global reach that cannot be compared to any one intelligence service within the United States or most other modern developed states. With the transition of SIGINT responsibilities, increased authority on border security, and cryptographic responsibilities to the FSB, the comparison of it to the US intelligence community also transitioned. Its domestic protection roles still most closely align with the FBI, but its SIGINT responsibilities mirror that of the National Security Agency (NSA), while the border security functions are more akin to the US Customs and Border Patrol (CBP) or even Immigration and Customs Enforcement (ICE).

On top of all of this, the FSB has become increasingly connected to all issues cyber as well. The world continues to become more interconnected. The internet has become an integral part of our daily lives and, for some, even a necessity. It supports everything from e-commerce to sensitive governmental correspondence. So when a country's intelligence service inserts itself into business transactions, there becomes an increased risk that sensitive data could be siphoned off and used to support both commercial and national intelligence interests at home and abroad. Even though the Russian IT registration requirement is only for private companies operating within Russia, this means little in the interconnected world of the internet where data crosses many geographical boundaries between transmitter and receiver. The internet is a medium susceptible to signals collection just like any other, and when countries or intelligence services have access to all internet-based traffic that falls within their borders, then that threat is not only very real but actually amplified.

One example of this threat is the Russian SORM program. SORM, or System for Ensuring Investigated Activity, is a mechanism that permits the FSB to monitor all phone and internet traffic coming in and out of the Russian Federation. While arguments are that this program is a law enforcement and internal security tool, the FSB still remains an intelligence service with a mission set that goes beyond internal security and law enforcement. It is worth noting that until a Russian Supreme Court ruling was handed down in late 2000, the FSB was under no obligation to inform Internet Service Providers (ISPs) that agents were accessing the system. The work undertaken by the FSB to support signals exploitation is not just limited to Russian companies, therefore, but extends to international entities with a presence in the Russian Federation.

On April 11, 2011, for example, a government source told the Interfax news agency that the FSB was not proposing a ban on Gmail, Skype or Hotmail in Russia. The FSB expert speaking at this meeting only expressed concerns that a number of those servers provide services outside of the national legal framework. The inferred concern was that because these companies utilize encryption for securing the communications of users, and none of them are directly based in Russia, the FSB requirement under SORM may not be implemented properly. It is interesting that the FSB would take the time for an interview to highlight its effort to find a solution to make the functioning of these services on Russian territory comply with national laws. This statement, while perhaps innocuous on the surface, speaks to the potential level of penetration the FSB can gain into all aspects of communications, both traditional and emerging.

On June 8, 2011 Microsoft Russia made a statement with respect to the FSB and the online communications service Skype. In a statement carried by the Russian Federal Security Service–owned but supposedly editorially independent Russian news agency Ekho Moskvy, Microsoft denied claims it had provided the FSB with encryption algorithms for the internet service. It did, however, admit that the source code for the program was provided. With its charter to protect and monitor cryptographic systems for the Russian government, the FSB has access to those individuals who both create and decipher cryptographic algorithms as part of the newly transferred FAPSI functions. With these vast resources, it is not a giant leap of logic to think the FSB will be sorely tempted to conduct eavesdropping on any entity it wishes, without the support of said company, as long as a suitable connection to national security is found.

These two examples are a sample of how cyber seems to be a new focus of FSB SIGINT collection efforts. And while, for now, they focus solely on what has occurred within Russian territory, it is important to note the FSB has recognized links in over eighty countries and formal offices in at least eighteen of them. This level of global reach and interaction means its SIGINT mission can be transferred anywhere the FSB maintains a presence. As these capabilities are deployed, they provide the FSB with a larger SIGINT capability than most intelligence agencies around the world. The FSB of course formally declares that it honors all international treaties and pursues only legitimate inquiries that hold potential harm to the sovereign interests and national security of the Russian Federation. The problem, of course, is just how fungible those sovereign interests might be over time and how relevant the old adage about absolute power corrupting absolutely might become.

Brothers-in-Unethical-Arms

The American and Russian Intelligence Services

AMY HANLON NOVEMBER 10, 2016

Two of the largest foreign intelligence agencies in the world, the United States' Central Intelligence Agency (CIA) and the Russian Federation's Foreign Intelligence Service (FSB), ironically appear more similar in their organization, methods, and ethics than not. Similar to the CIA, the Russian foreign intelligence service operates under different levels of concealment from foreign governments. Both foreign intelligence services use "official cover," meaning they pose as government employees in the country's embassy which offers diplomatic immunity if the agent is caught. They also both have "nonofficial cover" agents (NOCs), where the agents "typically pose as private business employees and are subject to less scrutiny and, in many cases, are never identified as intelligence agents by the host government." This role does not provide diplomatic immunity if caught (Bender, 2015, and Finn, 2003). The questionable ethical practices of both agencies have tarnished their names in the international public eye at times. Their politicization of intelligence, financing of insurgents or rebels in other countries, and the use of torture, have sparked international condemnation from many different corners.

Both foreign intelligence services have been accused of being too political. As noted by Robert Gates in his 1992 address to the CIA, discussing recent Congressional allegations of the agency's politicization of intelligence:

> Almost all agree that [politicization of intelligence] involves deliberately distorting analysis or judgements to favor a preferred line of thinking irrespective of evidence. Most consider classic solicitation to be only that which occurs if products are forced to conform to policy maker's views. A number believe politicization also results from management pressures to define and drive certain lines of analysis and substantive viewpoints. Still others believe that changes in tone or emphasis made during the normal review of coordination process, and limited means for expressing alternative viewpoints, also constitute forms of politicization (1992).

Similarly, the international community accused Russia's foreign minister, Sergey Lavrov, of politicizing intelligence when he insisted that there were still serious grounds to believe the deadly chemical attack in Damascus was a "provocation" staged by Syrian rebels, despite evidence in the United Nations report that seemed to suggest government forces were to blame (Mackey, 2013). In an April 2015 interview with retired Lieutenant General Leonid Reshetnikov, one can see a similar example of Russian politicization as he discusses how the United States "ditched Israel" to work with Iran to "encircle Russia," overthrow President Vladimir Putin, and divide the country (Chuikov, 2015). Both foreign intelligence services have done such things either to promote their own world view or to promote a particular agenda favored by the presidential administration in power. The problem with politicization is that it distorts information and thus leads to poor analysis and ultimately leads to skewed results rather than fair, balanced, and accurate assessments. Skewed intelligence hinders policy makers and governments alike and prevents opportunities for understanding and collaboration.

Both the United States and Russia fund insurgents or rebels throughout the world. Currently, the CIA is funding the Syrian rebels against the government of President Bashar al Assad in Syria and "vetted rebels" in Saudi Arabia against the Islamic State (Mazzetti, 2014). Similarly, both the United States and the Parliamentary Assembly of the Council of Europe have accused Russia of financing terrorism with respect to militarily arming rebels in Ukraine (Office of Foreign Assets Control, 2014, and EuroNews, 2015). Arming the rebels, however, in either case, is rarely done in a vacuum: this can lead to the arms or finances falling into the hands of other unwanted extremist groups who wish harm the United States and/or Russia. In other words, the secret maneuvers often can backfire and strengthen the very opposition the CIA or FSB had hoped to defeat. As noted by President Obama, there aren't many examples of pure success where the CIA [only] provided financing and arms to an insurgency (Mazzetti, 2014).

In addition to the politicization of intelligence and the financing of rebels a third aspect where both the CIA and FSB are similar is in their use of torture to "confirm" intelligence. In October 2012, during the forty-ninth session of the UN Committee against Torture, the United Nations reported that Russia's intelligence services participated in torture, including beatings, removing finger and toenails, and sodomizing a subject with a bottle (United Nations Committee Against Torture, 2012, p. 4). Similarly, according to a previously released Senate Intelligence Committee report on the details of "harsh CIA interrogation techniques," the CIA has participated in torture including rectal feeding, sleep deprivation, insects, use of diapers, and mock executions. (*Business Insider*, 2014) Since the report's release, the Senate Intelligence Committee has removed it from their site. However, several news agencies quoted the report:

> The CIA led several detainees to believe they would never be allowed to leave CIA custody alive, the report's executive summary says. One interrogator told another detainee that he would never go to court, because we can never let the world know what I have done to you. CIA officers also threatened . . . to harm the children of a detainee . . . sexually abuse the mother of a detainee, and . . . to cut [a detainee's] mother's throat.

These methods were often found to have achieved little to no actionable intelligence. For example, in an e-mail titled "So it begins," a medical officer wrote that a detainee gave "NO useful information so far," but had vomited several times. "It's been 10 hours since he ate so this is surprising and disturbing. We plan to only feed Ensure for now," the officer said (*Business Insider*, 2014). As noted by the Senate Intelligence Committee report, torture does not usually produce actionable intelligence. Veteran and former prisoner-of-war Senator John McCain agreed: "I know from personal experience that the abuse of prisoners will produce more bad than good intelligence. I know that victims of torture will offer intentionally misleading information if they think their captors will believe it. I know they will say whatever they think their torturers want them to say if they believe it will stop their suffering" (McCain, 2014).

In conclusion, ethically speaking, both the United States and Russia's foreign intelligence services are unfavorably similar to each other as both participate in practices that hurt their international reputation for little national security gain. Arguably, none of these activities provide their government with fair, balanced, or accurate intelligence, and quite often the moral ambiguity encourages corruption and repression, let alone global condemnation. Thus, both intelligence services are similar in nature, organization, methods, and ethics—to their detriment. They are brothers-in-unethical-arms.

Cyber-Prepping the Battlefield

Does Russia Have a New Way to Wage War?

LAURA GARRIDO MARCH 25, 2016

According to the Bloomberg report, Russia may leverage vulnerabilities in critical infrastructure, including large banks, stock exchanges, power grids, and airports, as pressure points against the West. Ashmore (2009) says the future of Russian cyberwarfare is offensively poised. Mshvidobadze (2014) also claimed that analysts examining espionage malware of apparent Russia origin indicate a preparation of the battlefield for cyberwar.

Russia is developing information warfare capabilities such as computer network operations, electronic warfare, psychological operations, deception campaigns, and mathematical programming impact. Ashmore (2009) agrees that Russia is developing new information war strategies with the use of hackers that support Russian government information specialists, providing Russia with assets to use during future cyber conflicts. Heickerö (2010) also identifies the main organizations responsible for offensive and defensive cyber capabilities as the Federal Protective Service (FSO), the Federal Security Service (FSB), and the Main Intelligence Directorate (GRU). Russia's approach to information warfare and information operations differs from that of Western countries to some extent. Russia sees information as a valuable asset that has strategic value and is a key factor for the stability of the state, for the regime, and for influential actors.

According to Dr. Matthew Crosston, one of the leading experts both in cyberwar and Russian foreign policy, part of the reason why

Russia is such a major threat to the United States is not only its increasing capabilities but the reasoning and psychology behind its attacks and development of such capabilities. Russia's purpose in developing cyber capabilities seems to be predatory in nature. This predatory purpose is heavily influenced by "the fact that much of the power dominating cyber capability in the Russian Federation is organized and controlled by federal security agencies but also quasi-outsourced to criminal groups, sometimes independently and sometimes in strict conjunction with governmental oversight." Crosston also notes the cynical cyber mind-set of Russia is somewhat controlled by short-term thinking that has massive profit and political power-wielding motives.

While not all cyberattacks originating in Russia come from the state, Russia has been seen as a safe haven for cyber criminality directed against foreign interests and to some extent domestic cyber criminality. Many have pointed out that Russia has not acted resolutely enough to deal with these lawbreakers. Thus, what makes Russia especially dangerous, according to Mshvidobadze (2014), is the collusion between the Russian state and cybercriminals. Criminal operators confound attribution and hone their skills on criminal activity, which ends up being a cost-effective reserve cyber force available to the state when needed. There has also been a conjoining of criminal and governmental malware which could result in even more potent cyberweapons. All together this makes Russian cyberespionage widespread, hard to detect, difficult to attribute, and costly to counter.

Heickerö (2010) points out that Russian strategy emphasizes the importance of information warfare during the initial phase of a conflict to weaken the command and control ability of the opponent.

This was evident in the 2007 attacks against Estonia and the 2008 attacks against Georgia. Some calculate this was also extensively used during the intervention in Syria in 2015. Herzog (2011) claims that the severity of the Estonian attacks was a wake-up call to the world. It showed that potentially autonomous transnational networks, such as state-sponsored, pro-Kremlin hacktivists, could avenge their grievances by digitally targeting the critical infrastructure of technically sophisticated states. Herzog suggested that enhancing cyber security and creating new multinational strategies and institutions to counter cyber threats was essential to the sovereignty and survival of states. The biggest challenge, however, is striking a balance between Internet freedom and maintaining adequate early-warning monitoring systems.

Cordesman and Cordesman (2002) criticized the disconnect between US cyber defense and cyber offense. This was later expansively enhanced by the work of Crosston (2011; 2013; 2014). This conceptual analytic disconnect permeates US governmental efforts and the response of state and local authorities, the private sector, and nongovernmental organizations. They believe in a need for a "comprehensive annual net assessment of cyber threats that combines analysis of the threat that states present in terms of cyberwarfare with the threats that foreign, domestic, and non-state actor groups can present in terms of cyber-crime and cyber-terrorism."

Ashmore (2009) believes that the international community should work together to track and prosecute cyber criminals that operate outside the country being attacked. Also, Ashmore (2009) believes that nations should "work together to share technical data to maintain cyber defenses and keep up with the newest and ever-changing cyber-attacks" because individual hackers usually share information on new techniques that can penetrate IT defense structures. This prescription, however, requires enormous amounts of trust from both sides, which is hard to ask for even among allies. While the international community should come together to secure cyberspace, it is a completely different ballgame to ask states to share their defense techniques. Not only could this information be used to identify vulnerabilities in their defenses, if the information is stolen by hackers, it could be used against these states and in turn applied to the hackers' networks to make countermeasures impotent.

Another prescription offered by Ashmore (2009) is the creation of laws that make cybercrimes illegal with the hope that the punishments would deter potential cybercriminals. The problem with this is that there is already plenty of laws criminalizing hacking and cyberespionage, none of which have slowed the frequency of cyberattacks. Will new laws prevent the average middle-class Joe from sending vicious malware to his ex-employer out of spite? Maybe. Will new laws prevent criminal hacktivists from launching a politically motivated attack to their adversary's networks? The answer is most likely no. Just as terrorists continue to murder, maim, and rape their victims regardless of the laws that forbid such actions, those who want to hack likely will. It does not matter what laws are in place. It is this innate internal motivation of the hacker that states like the Russian Federation count on and strategically utilize. For the most part, Russia is the undisputed leader in this newly politicized world of the dark net.

FSB's Snowden War

Using the American NSA against Itself

ALEXANDER S. MARTIN MAY 24, 2016

Russia's understanding of information warfare must be understood in the context of Russian statism. Russian leaders, particularly President Vladimir Putin, view state power as essential to national health and broadly defined state power. The state attempts to maintain absolute privilege over rights, ownership, and power, and often confers these things to others as gifts or presents (Jurevicius, 2015).

Since Putin's rise to power, exclusive private ownership within the state has been weakened, and the state has increasingly used its now massive media industry as a means of influencing both the domestic population as well as foreign audiences (Kiriya and Degtereva, 2010). In terms of foreign influence, information plays a critical role in Russian political and military strategy. The Russian military divides information operations into two means of attack: information-technological means, which include attacks on national critical infrastructure and cyber-attaches; and information-perceptual means, which include propaganda, perception management, disinformation, psychological operations, and deception (Liaropoulos, 2007). Russia's exploitation of US intelligence disclosures falls within this second set of means as a form of propaganda. While the Russian state has always used propaganda as a means of ensuring Russian security, examination of this tactic is under-appreciated in the modern day (Stewart, 2014).

In relation to the West, Russian information operations, often called information warfare by Russian strategists, fill a critical strategic role in all phases of conflict. In a conflict involving kinetic operations, information warfare is used as a force multiplier "whose purpose is to guarantee the achievement of the goals of the operation" and is often seen as most effective in targeting enemy command and control structures, as well as enemy decision-making (Thomas, 1996). Tellingly, however, the Cold War notion of information warfare as a low-intensity form of conflict targeting the enemy's civilian population and its public awareness, as well as "state administrative systems, production control systems, scientific control, cultural control, and so forth" remains a key feature of Russian thinking today regarding information operations (Thomas, 1996). It is not that other nations do not accept this anymore as a part of modern warfare but rather that only Russia is so openly adamant about the properness of such techniques. In 2013, the Russian chief of the general staff wrote that modern conflict includes the "broad use of political, economic, informational, humanitarian, and other non-military measures" (Jones, 2014). Russian information warfare thinking has thus evolved beyond Soviet-era concepts into a fully modern doctrine, particularly in the more intense forms of conflict.

Critical to the effective use of Russian propaganda are its intelligence agencies, particularly the FSB. One high profile example of FSB media manipulation is the allegation that the FSB controls "troll armies," a term used to describe an estimated 200,000 FSB employees who are tasked with flooding social networks, internet forums, and media comment sections with pro-Russian content (Jurevicius, 2015). It is worth noting that this is but one aspect of the FSB's control of Russian media. While it is difficult to ascertain precisely what links exist between the FSB and Russian media corporations formally, the FSB's extensive power makes it clear that FSB-directed propaganda is likely a critical component of many Russian media operations.

In response to the expansion of US intelligence because of the Global War on Terror, Paul Todd and Jonathan Bloch wrote "just as the Cold War provided a legitimizing framework for the unprincipled and often counterproductive waging of covert warfare, so the dangers of a new era of intelligence 'blowback' are all too clear" (Todd & Bloch, 2003). Russian media propaganda against US intelligence services makes use of such allegations—of vastly expanded and illegal American power to collect information against foreign and domestic targets. While it is possible to draw from a range of incidents, the disclosures of Edward Snowden, a former NSA system administrator, have arguably been the most controversial and impactful.

Reporting on the NSA's requirement to end its collection of telephony metadata as stipulated by the USA Freedom Act, one grouping of *Russia Today* articles highlighted the conflict between privacy advocates and US lawmakers, writing "while privacy advocates described the change as only a single step with the prospect of more progress to come, lawmakers adopted a tone of finality" (*RT*, 2015). Another grouping of articles aimed at demonstrating the loophole the NSA used to continue collection against US citizens. Finally, a third implied that the vast metadata collection program did not provide the NSA with any operational or analytic value (*RT*, 2015). These article groups demonstrate not only Russia's main aim in reporting on the Snowden leaks—to undermine American image on the international stage—they are also an abstract attempt to achieve an important Russian foreign policy goal: using the expansive NSA collection effort targeted against US citizens to positively contrast with Russian maneuvers on the global stage. In the context of America always making charges against Russia for using draconian measures to limit its citizens' rights and invade their privacy, these reports are designed to highlight US hypocrisy and sow the seeds of discord and doubt among American allies about any so-called US moral supremacy.

Falling approval ratings of the US government also help determine the impact of FSB propagandizing the Snowden leaks. After Snowden leaked the disclosures, US President Barack Obama's approval ratings plummeted (CNN, 2014). Gallup poll data show now that American confidence in all three branches of the US government is declining, with the Supreme Court and Congress being at all-time lows in 2015 (McCarthy, 2014). In contrast, a recent Economist/YouGov poll found that 78 percent of Americans view President Putin as a stronger leader than President Obama (2014). A final area of impact to consider is European reactions to the leaks. As with the American public, European publics were outraged by the Snowden leaks, not only by the perceived US hypocrisy, but also by the alleged NSA collection against European diplomats and elites (Network of European Union Centers of Excellence, 2014). These disclosures have had a negative impact on US-European relations, as the EU has become increasingly reluctant to impose further economic sanctions on Russia despite US pressure (Harress, 2015). Furthermore, European leaders are showing an increased willingness to cooperate with Russia with regard to military operations and objectives in Syria (Bloomberg, 2015). While the reasons for these developments are complex and multilevel, the damage done to US-European relations has absolutely been impacted by explicit Russian intelligence efforts to refocus media perception on American image and global status.

It is important to note that this form of intelligence media propaganda is not effective in isolation. It was not Russian propaganda that caused widespread distrust of the US government. However, the FSB and Russian media conglomerates are able to effectively profit from the damning Snowden disclosures by casting the United States in a suspicious, negative light, while at the same time minimizing their own supposed flaws and political sins. More study should be devoted in future to this softer but still significant aspect of US-Russian relational conflict.

The Grand Cyber Spy Game

Russia, America, and China Stealing the World One Byte at a Time

DR. MATTHEW CROSSTON & ANONYMOUS* MAY 27, 2016

Every month another story of cybertheft linked to China or Russia emerges. Recent data breaches at Target, United Airlines, Blue Cross Blue Shield, and OPM have been linked back to Russia, while theft of key technology across major Department of Defense contractors such as Lockheed Martin and US government laboratories has been linked to China. Neither China nor Russia's government formally admit to leveraging the internet to steal secrets from other countries, but hacks have been linked directly to their intelligence services' respective buildings or individuals known to be under governmental influence. International cyber incidents in Ukraine, Georgia, and Estonia have all been apparently linked back to Russia, while the Canadian government recently set up domestic cyber-protection programs after several major corporations were hacked by Chinese intelligence. The US government struggles on how to approach these cyber intrusions. Should they be ignored so that other foreign-policy initiatives can move forward? Are these initiatives acts of war or a new method of state gamesmanship? Do these collections of vast amounts of information count as high treason, espionage, or simple economic theft? Environmental negotiations just about broke down several years ago when President Obama called out China for hacking several governmental systems during the negotiations. What does all of this signify as Russia and

China become more important strategic world partners, while still at least semimaintaining long-held intelligence and military adversarial attitudes toward the United States? Welcome to the real cyber era, where multiple players try to steal the world one byte at a time while pretending to do nothing of the sort.

The Chinese, American, and Russian intelligence services have no issue launching clandestine internet attacks to pursue what they all consider to be legitimate national security and foreign-policy objectives. Sometimes the information collected is economic, directed against or about important corporations; other times the information is military and political. In all cases the information is highly strategic. While it is true that the information the Russian and Chinese intelligence services are providing to their respective policymakers is much broader in scope than the CIA or US Department of Defense and is arguably much more domestically invasive than the FBI or DEA, both Russia and China have successfully started campaigns questioning the "purity of purpose" within American intelligence given the details of the Snowden scandal. All of which begs the questions: Should American intelligence maneuvers match Chinese and Russian cyber precedence? Is the American public aversion to cybercollection programs really just a front for a private philosophy that already rivals China and Russia? Is there something fundamentally important for states to consider in this style-versus-substance cyber spy debate?

Crucial differences in intelligence organizational culture and mission make figuring these questions out quite difficult. While the United States has been quick to leverage open-source collection for its own programs, it has supposedly been hesitant to execute the power of its cyber abilities in invasive, offensive, global scenarios (although this consideration is now being heavily debated in the classified sector, and some accuse it of already transpiring). This article will attempt to determine if Chinese and Russian intelligence services have gained a tactical advantage over the United States because of a political and bureaucratic blind spot or if the United States intelligence collection culture is different only at the superficial level and is largely the same as its rivals in terms of true cyber substance.

The first important aspect in understanding the Grand Cyber Game is to understand how the Russian, Chinese, and US intelligence communities are structured. The United States is known for the "big brothers" of its IC, the Central Intelligence Agency (CIA), the Federal Bureau of Investigation (FBI), and the National Security Agency (NSA). However, there are actually seventeen members of the US Intelligence Community. Some of these include intelligence offices for each branch of the US military, the Department of Homeland Security, the Department of Energy, the Department of State, the Department of the Treasury, the Drug Enforcement Administration, the National Reconnaissance Office (NRO), and the National Geospatial-Intelligence Agency (NGA). The first five use intelligence collection as part of a law enforcement mission, while the NSA, NRO, and NGA all harvest data and imagery collection. Traditionally, the CIA operates overseas and cultivates human sources while conducting clandestine operations. The FBI traditionally manages counterterrorism operations domestically, provides investigation support overseas when American citizens are involved, and acts under an enforcement jurisdiction to maintain the law. The NSA was established to provide cryptologic services and to protect US information systems and signals intelligence. It supports military customers, national policymakers, and counterterrorism and counterintelligence communities under the Department of Defense. However, in a post-9/11 world, these explicitly defined roles have become more blurred and opaque as global travel and transnational collections are intensely complicated by the internet.

Conversely, modern Chinese intelligence services have always had domestic and international missions intertwined. China's Ministry of Public Security (MPS) was formed in 1954 as a domestic law enforcement agency. It managed criminal investigations, security protection, public information network security, traffic control, legal affairs, counterterrorism, drug control, and other antismuggling and anticorruption duties. In 1983, the Ministry of State Security (MSS) was established as the formal intelligence and security agency of China for nonmilitary areas of interests. It has the same authority to arrest or detain people as the MPS with a nearly identical oversight mission by the courts, but it is also a separate, parallel network to the MPS. The MSS mission is to ensure "the security of the state through effective measures against enemy agents, spies, and counter-revolutionary activities designed to sabotage or overthrow China's socialist system." Similar to the CIA, the MSS gathers foreign intelligence from targets in various countries overseas while the MPS gathers information domestically to protect against domestic terrorism and political coups. Both heavily rely on cybercollection.

Russia operates with three principal intelligence services. The SVR focuses on foreign intelligence collection, but mainly with civilian affairs. It is formally responsible for intelligence and espionage activities outside the Russian Federation. The GRU is the main foreign military intelligence directorate of the General

Staff of the Armed Forces. It is Russia's largest foreign intelligence agency, deploying at least six times as many agents as the formal KGB successor, the SVR. The FSB operates in theory only across the former Soviet Republics and domestically but had its operational portfolio increased in 2003 to include the Border Guard Service and the Federal Agency of Government Communication and Information. The three intelligence services often overlap and sometimes compete against one another in the recruitment and collection of intelligence sources. Russia also established an Anti-Terrorist Center that falls under full control of the FSB. The Center's mandate was to create a database for intelligence sharing among the security services of all members of the Commonwealth of Independent States (CIS). Although the SVR has promised not to spy within CIS territories, the FSB has not. As such, it has become the de facto leading intelligence service for foreign collection activities for Russia. Interestingly, Russia has often turned a blind eye to Central Asian intelligence service activity within its borders, when Central Asian leaders are making moves against so-called political enemies (these moves are usually abductions back to Central Asia for detainment). These activities have included both the Chinese MSS and MSP. In 2001, the Shanghai Cooperation Organization (SCO) was established by China, Kazakhstan, Kyrgyzstan, Russia, Tajikistan, and Uzbekistan to work together against terrorism, separatism, and extremism. They established their own Regional Anti-Terrorist Structure (RATS), which became the mechanism of choice for carrying out abductions across national boundaries, outside of standard judicial procedures. RATS operations have been compared to the CIA's practice of extraordinary rendition and allow members to detain suspects in the six participating states outside of any rule of law. The members' operators are not subject to criminal liability, and they are immune from arrest and detention within the six states.

The reality is, on an international level, the intelligence services of all three nations operate with remarkably similar mission goals and objectives: they wish to protect the national interests of their respective states and garner advantages for said states via the acquisition of important information. While Hollywood has often focused on the political deviance and violence of intelligence missions around the world, the less exciting reality is that intelligence is more often utilized simply for political leverage. On the domestic level, the United States has long held the moral superiority card against rivals like Russia and China, largely based on the democratic system in America supposedly being more altruistic and legally minded than the so-called autocratic-type regimes in Beijing and Moscow. Snowden and other details in the past several years have started to make some at least wonder how much that moralism is built upon a foundation of sand and not stone. Finally, the stylistic aspect of intelligence public relations is significantly different between the three: the United States decidedly tries to maintain an air of secrecy and deniability over just about everything its intelligence community does or needs to do. Russia and China, while revealing no secrets, tend to be a bit more unabashed about the role and necessity intelligence plays for the furthering of state power and do not fear making public statements to that effect anywhere, anytime. For them, therefore, the only difference between the three great players in the Grand Cyber Spy Game is the costuming and marketing of their respective goals, but not the ploys, initiatives, and overall desires. When it comes to winning, it seems all three are set and determined to virtually steal, that is, "obtain" as much as possible. The Grand Cyber Spy Game demands no less.

Anonymous is currently a graduate student in international security and intelligence studies at Bellevue University and works within the US governmental system. The opinions expressed are strictly personal and do not reflect a formal endorsement of or by the United States government and/or Intelligence Community.

No Victory for Putin

The Dossier Scandal

JANUARY 20, 2017

There is no doubt whatsoever that Russia has compiled information on Trump. Russian intelligence considers it a rightful duty to compile information on persons of relevance, especially when they are conducting significant business or political relations with Russia. Trump qualified under that definition long before he even thought about running for president. Even I have been followed, during my numerous times in Russia, both openly and secretly. I have had my computer hacked and hotel phone bugged. And my affairs in Russia have come nowhere near to the financial or political relevance of President-Elect Trump.

However, there has been a breakdown in America when it comes to understanding how Russia would use such information if it indeed has a dossier of the type that many Americans suspect. Americans may love exposing things through the media with a voyeuristic passion, bringing the high down low. That's just the nature of the beast today in American Kardashian culture. But this dossier of alleged Russian intelligence on Trump has nothing to do with American celebrity culture. If it truly exists, it would have been compiled under the edict of "national security" for Russian geopolitical interests. As such, the proper Russian intelligence behavior would be to deny its existence and hold on to anything it has until a time deemed strategically best. The least efficient usage of that compromising material would be to just embarrass President-Elect

Trump publicly before he is inaugurated, TMZ "gotcha"-style. Russians simply don't work that way. Rather, keeping information secret and using it in a nonpublic but strategically effective manner for their national interests is the Russian way.

For example, the infamous WikiLeaks affair against Clinton was an example of Russians trying to smudge the character and momentum of Secretary Clinton, assuming she was indeed going to win the election. HRC positions have been decidedly anti-Russian (to the Russians, at least) over the past half-dozen years, vociferously and publicly. The email leaks were a rather limp attempt to just slow that political train down before it took office, to make her pause and understand that she should treat Russia with a judgment a bit less shrill.

"The Russian system has plenty of deficiencies, but no outsider could possibly find out what kinds of discussions are taking place in Putin's office, who is angry at who, or any of that intimate detail," said Fyodor Lukyanov, chair of the Council on Foreign and Defense Policy, which advises the Kremlin. "Putin runs a very tight ship. No leaks. No rumors confirmed. He is, famously, very professional about it." This estimation is totally true. Lukyanov is a very reliable source if you want opinions on Russia that you can consider astute and balanced: someone who is not hyperbolically pro-Kremlin but also not sheep-like and anti-Russian either. Indeed, many of the more famous Russian academics so often quoted and interviewed in the West are decidedly anti-Putin in their analyses, thereby effectively currying financial favor and scholarly status with Western think tanks and institutes.

As for the supposition that this dossier leak is a victory for Putin regardless of its truthfulness, I hold the contrarian view: if Putin's intelligence agencies do indeed have a dossier of compromising information on the president-elect, then the last thing Putin would consider a victory would be the preemptive and uncontrolled leaking of that information all over social media by an unofficial foreign agent that he did not manage. This would be a *loss*, not a victory. It would mean Putin lost control of both the process of how to use the information and the narrative of just how to release the information to particular audiences for the greatest benefit to Russia. The leak of the dossier to everyone in the world means it does not truly benefit Russian interests at all. Just leaking it and embarrassing the president-elect, with no real proof or smoking-gun evidence attached and no ulterior geostrategic purpose achieved, means this story will fade away and be replaced by some other titillating story. To a large degree this has already happened. Thus, the Russians have lost what they hoped to be tremendous strategic leverage behind the scenes and down the road. Ergo, no victory for Putin.

Americans still trying to position it as a victory are simply not astute in the ways of real geopolitics and strategy. And that applies even for the supposed Russian experts here in America who do so much advising today to media and governmental elites. The state of "Russian expertise" in America today is extremely disappointing and dull. We currently live in times that have Washington, DC, and the Slavic studies community obsessed with pushing a very narrow and very cliché orthodox narrative about the Russian Federation and its motivations. That narrative believes the only thing Kremlin officials do is sit around tables recklessly and illogically pondering ways to surpass the United States with no real calculation for national interests. Supposedly, appending that two-page summary to the formal presidential-elect briefing is confirmation of how far this relationship environment between DC and Moscow has fallen. The US intelligence community basically has felt reluctantly compelled to discuss what amounts to nothing more than a TMZ gossip report. That fact alone is what signals the immediate future of Russian-American relations will remain dark and stormy.

As for how people should consider the dossier and its creation: it was collected by a former British intelligence official hired by Republican Party operatives interested in obtaining damaging information to use against Trump in the election primaries. What that really means is that he had no access to formal governmental reconnaissance technologies or personnel. As such, you can reliably assume he simply dug deep into the rumor mills that run crazily around Moscow. The dossier is much closer to what TMZ, the famous gossip-paparazzi organization in America, produces than the CIA or MI6. It is not a true intelligence brief. The blurring of this distinction in the media has been irresponsible and laughable.

How many have actually read the dossier in full? It is utter tripe. None of it would pass muster for inclusion in a formal intelligence community briefing if it were produced by a member of the community. But none of the details in the dossier would pass a peer review for scholarly journal either. At best, it's the kind of material one finds on a deeply partisan political blog. Does this mean nothing in the dossier could be true? No, it does not. But it does mean the dossier, at best, represents a Wikipedia level of research. As I advise students about using Wikipedia for research: you can start your research using Wikipedia to learn relevant terms, actors, and events. But then you need to go deeper, far beyond Wikipedia, to understand what is verifiable and falsifiable and thus worthy of inclusion in a scholarly analysis. The dossier is Wikipedia or TMZ gossip. It is not the deeper, vetted analyses demanded by real intelligence or legitimate scholarship. This is what the American media and/or intelligence community needs to do next: transform this affair from gossip to analysis. The concern is that it does not appear that anyone, media or government, is seemingly interested in doing that deeper digging into whether this is just TMZ titillation or true debauchery that should make the American people concerned about its incoming president on a deeply moral level.

Some have scratched their heads over why US intelligence agencies appear to have legitimized the documents by supposedly including that aforementioned summary in a top-secret briefing. But the intelligence community is actually the only body in this sordid affair that can somewhat be given a pass; it faced a no-win scenario. The best analogous example is to recall the situation when Director Comey of the FBI was in preelection and facing a possible HRC indictment. Although it was underemphasized in the media, Comey himself said he reopened the investigation because he felt tremendous pressure, caught between a rock and a hard place: do not reopen when new information has come to light, and you are vulnerable to accusations of trying to engineer a particular electoral result, when the intelligence community is loath to be viewed political at all. However, reopening the case (even when you say it is just to review new material and explicitly state it is not a declaration of guilt) makes you victim to the opposite accusation: that you are still politicized and looking to engineer a particular electoral result, just a different one from the one those who would give the previous diatribe might accuse you of.

The inclusion or open discussion of the intelligence community's two-page summary on the Trump dossier is much the same dilemma: if they had not included it or mentioned it, when Buzzfeed had splashed it all over the internet already, they exposed the intelligence community to an accusation of trying to sweep something under the rug. Doing a two-page summary of the dossier with a formal declaration that it is not making a statement about its validity or reliability was an intelligence community maneuver to walk the knife's edge of a situation that had no real optimal endgame.

> "Intel and law enforcement officials agree that none of the investigations have found any conclusive or direct link between Trump and the Russian government period," the senior official said.
>
> According to the senior official, the two-page summary about the unsubstantiated material made available to the briefers was to provide context, should they need it, to draw the distinction for Trump between analyzed intelligence and unvetted "disinformation."[1]

This quote, taken from an NBC News story, is the explanation most credible and accurate in terms of how intelligence officials actually behave in such situations. The professionals I have known in the intelligence community would absolutely convey the information so that relevant actors could be aware of information likely to emerge publicly (giving them a "heads-up," as it were), but they would also emphasize whether the intelligence community takes

1 William M. Arkin, Cynthia McFadden, Alexey Eremenko, and Alexander Smith, "Trump Wasn't Told about Russian Memo During Briefing, Official Says," NBCNews.com, January 11, 2017, https://www.nbcnews.com/news/world/trump-cites-nazi-germany-rejects-dossier-alleged-russia-dealings-n705586.

the information as credible. If not credible or still unverified, then it makes sense that the dossier was presented to Trump in an informal or even just oral manner. Additionally, an almost-ignored aspect in the story is how an intelligence official tries to make people understand that there is a huge difference between "analyzed intelligence" and "unvetted disinformation." The intelligence community has tried rather valiantly to make people in America understand that until the dossier is formally declared the former, then it is decidedly the latter. It should not be blamed on the intelligence community, therefore, if most media venues and political organizations are skipping right past these clarifications and attributing meaning to the American intelligence community that it has not claimed as its own.

CONCLUSION

Calling All Iconoclasts

What this work has tried to show is how incredibly complex, unpredictable, and unorthodox Russian-American relations are today. This is an important point to make because most of the academic, media, and governmental coverage of these relations is decidedly "orthodox." What I mean by that is what has been documented throughout this work: that many of today's experts on Russia refuse to notice their own preconceived notions about it, nor do they admit to having a bias that is intensively influenced by the legacy and psychological residues left over from the original Cold War. The ultimate consequence of this is that we treat Russian-American relations in a very rigid, binomial, black-and-white categorization, with the United States of course always wearing the white hat and Russia wearing the black. This book is not a plea to reverse this: no one is trying to say Russia is an angel and America is the devil. Rather, it is a demand to allow for rationalism to enter into this contemporary discussion: not black or white but a marked shade of gray.

This matters because it would put the Russian-American engagement back on an even footing and reflect how America largely deals with every other complex foreign-policy relationship across the globe: Can anyone truly say American and Chinese interests are perfectly aligned? What about American and Saudi interests? They clearly are not, yet the United States actively engages and works with both countries on issues that have mutually reinforcing cross interests. Only Russia seems to be treated with this unhelpful and illogical black-and-white binomial. When you consider just how many mutual security interests exist between America and Russia, then you can see just how important it is to discard this orthodox Cold War predetermination and let the relationship adapt and flex and evolve according to present-day reality. Failure to do this is not just about missed opportunities: it is literally endangering the entire global community.

The effort to overcome this orthodoxy rests first and foremost with the academic community, for it is the most intense purveyor of the problem. It is not coincidence that the vast majority of the suggested reading / source list at the end of this book is full of works that are purposely structured and written to call modern Russia nothing but a mimic of the old Soviet Union. The first step in getting rid of a problem is openly recognizing it. Again, this is not to say Russia is blameless or does not operate according to its own national interests. Of course it does. As does every other country in the world, including the United States. Admitting that should not mean cooperation, engagement, and positive collaboration is impossible. It does not mean it is impossible for China, Iran, Saudi Arabia, Egypt, Poland, and the like. Why should Russia be given a special negative status when so many positive opportunities could be crafted out of this simple objective reflection of modern-day foreign affairs? The Cold War was indeed a major, history-impacting event. But not allowing Russia to move beyond it, to purposely structure analysis so that it always ends up being quasi-Soviet, means we are not just limiting Russia. We are limiting ourselves and our own American interests. That has to stop. May this work be the first step in dismantling the orthodoxy. If that happens, then we will be that much closer to realizing how much "Cold War 2.0" was really just a fake Cold War all along.

This leads us to the biggest current elephant in the room (pun intended): the issue of collusion between President Trump and the Russian Federation. There are some pieces in this work that address some of the early crucial issues, but the fact of the matter is that as of this writing, the issue is still far from over. So, my special quest at the moment is to write about it only in a way that will have long life and will not immediately become outdated, no matter what new bombshell potentially drops. That is no easy task. But there are still some basic foundational elements that I think are inarguable and should be emphasized, exactly because these are the facts being pushed aside or twisted by the anti-Russian orthodoxy.

There is something inconsistent in the way we tend to portray Russia as both a magnificent Bond villain and an incompetent rube incapable of executing any cogent strategy. We need to decide once and for all whether Russia's cyberattack on the United States was in fact a highly sophisticated cyberattack that altered the true results of a presidential election or whether it was some pretty clumsy, generic hacking that resulted in the release of fairly banal emails that might have been embarrassing for some but in no way truly altered the course of history and affected the election. It cannot be both. And if you are a student of how the media portrays and covers this story today, that is exactly what it has been and continues to be: both.

I don't believe in the value of attributing to Russia an electoral predictive capability that is apparently far superior to all the media technology and every American politics expert we have here in the United States combined. The hacking effort was not so much about securing a victory for Trump as it was about insulting, demeaning, or cautioning the expected incoming President Hillary Clinton. Historical hindsight can be a very dangerous thing, especially in presidential elections. I defy anyone to tell me on election night that they fully expected Trump to win. And if literally everyone watching the election expected a Trump loss, why would a foreign power expect differently? Russia's hacking was much more about Secretary Clinton than about President Trump. It was to act as a counterweight to the expected new president who had gone on record as not being overly friendly to Russia. So, if the hacking in and of itself was just meant to smear the anticipated President Hillary Clinton, it is inappropriate to, six months later, morph the effort into Bond supervillain nefariousness that undermined the entire structural system of American democracy. To do that is just the aforementioned orthodoxy reaching hysteria levels and bleeding into the media cage.

Until proven otherwise, I will stand on the belief (based on my lifetime of study and experience with this country) that Russia did not collude with Trump to win the 2016 presidential election. This is not founded upon any sense of moral rightness or political correctness on the part of the Russians. On the contrary, given the extensive business dealings Trump had in Russia, it is not ridiculous to surmise that Russia has long known just what type of character and person he truly is. Therefore, from the Russian perspective, it is arguable that the Kremlin would find Mr. Trump *not* a person credible or trustworthy enough with which to actually try to build a long-term, mutually beneficial colluding relationship. Gather intelligence on him? Collect compromising materials to use as they see fit? Manipulate him because he is an easier personality to influence? To all of this I can give an easy and resounding *yes*. But that also means by default that Russia's hack was not collusion.

Remember: the desire to undermine Hillary Clinton was to make the next president of the United States more mindful of how she should respect the Russian Federation. That effort was not matched by an overly sycophantic and/or fawning parallel relationship with the Republican contender. My instinct tells me that the Russians would have sought to have *both* candidates exposed to possible compromising influence. As I said before, certainly not angelic behavior, but also not collusive. This is the type of subtle and nuanced (if also admittedly amoral) discussion we need to be having about Russian-American relations.

The larger international context really cannot be forgotten in terms of this incident. Because, in the end, this affair is only going to be decided in the court of international public opinion. There will be no American court taking Russia to trial or naming Putin as a defendant. What matters is how it plays across the global stage. And on the global stage the Russian hacking incident will always be preceded by American sanctions laying waste to the Russian economy for its actions in Ukraine. As surprising as it may be, the reality is the entire world does not view the Ukraine situation (Maidan, Crimea, Eastern Ukraine) as something purely based on Russian aggression happening in a vacuum. When so many American commentators today come before a microphone to discuss how egregiously bad it was for Russia to think it could "interfere with domestic American processes," they need to know the larger context that places the same accusation at the feet of the Americans and what their sanctions did to regular Russians on an everyday economic level. It is not legitimate in the court of international public opinion for America to be livid over transgressions supposedly made against it when arguably worse transgressions were perpetrated by America against Russia two years earlier. Again, this is not to declare Russia innocent or blameless. Rather, it is to say the reality of gray-zone engagement says the sanctions cannot be ignored when bringing up hacking. So far, as of this writing, *not a single American media organization has brought these two realities together even a single time.* That is the Cold War orthodoxy to which we have enslaved ourselves. This is what must be broken.

Ultimately, this book brings together many voices for one single purpose: to open new dialogue and consider new approaches for analyzing what is still one of the most important foreign-policy dynamics in the world today. It may indeed be true that as the twenty-first century proceeds both China and India will grow to be much bigger economic players on the global stage and thus may have more important direct roles with the United States. But when it comes to security, terrorism, conflict, and war, it is doubtful any relationship will surpass the gravity and importance of Russian-American relations. What I hope to see as we move on from this work and continue the quest to break the rigid orthodoxy is a willingness to have more open dialogue, more debates, more contested viewpoints when it comes to this relationship. Allowing the white and black hats to be interchangeable according to issue and event, allowing the gray zone of engagement to finally flourish and take hold, will create new opportunities—academic, diplomatic, military, governmental—that are in fact more accurate and more objectively aligned to reality. As Putin slowly moves off his quasi-throne in the Kremlin, may the phenomenon of Putin-mongering move off with him.

SUGGESTED READINGS

Allison, Roy. "Russian 'Deniable' Intervention in Ukraine: How and Why Russia Broke the Rules." *International Affairs* 90, no. 6 (2014).

———. "Russia and Syria: Explaining Alignment with a Regime in Crisis." *International Affairs* 89, no. 4 (2013).

Antonenko, Oksana, and Igor Yurgens. "Towards a NATO–Russia Strategic Concept." *Survival* 52, no. 6 (2010).

Arkhangelskaya, Alexandra A. "Africa–Russia: New Wave?" *Global Review*, 2013.

Arkhangelskaya, Alexandra, and Vladimir Shubin. "Russia–South Africa Relations: Beyond Revival." *SAIIA Policy Briefing*, no. 75 (2013).

Aron, Leon. "The Putin Doctrine: Russia's Quest to Rebuild the Soviet State." *Foreign Affairs* 8 (2013).

Ashford, Emma. "Not-So-Smart Sanctions: The Failure of Western Restrictions Against Russia." *Foreign Affairs* 95 (2016).

Auer, Stefan. "Carl Schmitt in the Kremlin: The Ukraine Crisis and the Return of Geopolitics." *International Affairs* 91, no. 5 (2015).

Averre, Derek. "Competing Rationalities: Russia, the EU and the 'Shared Neighbourhood.'" *Europe-Asia Studies* 61, no. 10 (2009).

Babali, Tuncay. "The Role of Energy in Turkey's Relations with Russia and Iran." Paper prepared for an international workshop, "The Turkey, Russia, Iran Nexus: Economic and Energy Dimensions," Center for Strategic and International Studies, Ankara, 2012.

Bennett, Brian, and W. J. Hennigan. "Obama Orders Full Review of Russian Hacking During the 2016 Election." *Los Angeles Times*, December 9, 2016.

Birnbaum, Michael. "Russia's Anti-American Fever Goes beyond the Soviet Era's." *Washington Post*, March 8, 2015.

Bonner, E. L., III. "Cyber Power in 21st-Century Joint Warfare." *Joint Force Quarterly* 74 (2014).

Boussena, Sadek, and Catherine Locatelli. "Energy Institutional and Organisational Changes in EU and Russia: Revisiting Gas Relations." *Energy Policy* 55 (2013).

Buzan, Barry. *People, States and Fear: An Agenda for International Security Studies in the Post-Cold War Era.* Colchester: ECPR Press, 2007.

Cadier, David. "Eastern Partnership vs. Eurasian Union? The EU-Russia Competition in the Shared Neighbourhood and the Ukraine Crisis." *Global Policy* 5, no. S1 (2014).

Cameron, Fraser. "The Politics of EU-Russia Energy Relations." *Oil, Gas, and Energy Law Journal (OGEL)* 7, no. 2 (2009).

Charap, Samuel, and Jeremy Shapiro. "How to Avoid a New Cold War." *Current History* 113, no. 765 (2014).

Chatterje-Doody, P. N. "Harnessing History: Narratives, Identity and Perceptions of Russia's Post-Soviet Role." *Politics* 34, no. 2 (2014).

Cimbala, Stephen J. "Putin and Russia in Retro and Forward: The Nuclear Dimension." *Defense & Security Analysis* 33, no. 1 (2017).

Crowley, Michael, and Tyler Pager. "Trump Urges Russia to Hack Clinton's Email." *Politico*, July 27, 2016.

DelReal, Jose A. "Donald Trump on Putin: 'Nobody Has Proven That He's Killed Anyone.'" *Washington Post*, December 20, 2015.

Desai, Radhika. "The BRICS Are Building a Challenge to Western Economic Supremacy." *Guardian*, April 2, 2013.

Dimitrakopoulou, Sophia, and Andrew Liaropoulos. "Russia's National Security Strategy to 2020: A Great Power in the Making?" *Caucasian Review of International Affairs* 4, no. 1 (2010).

Djankov, Simeon. *Russia's Economy under Putin: From Crony Capitalism to State Capitalism.* Policy brief no. PB15-18. Peterson Institute for International Economics, 2015.

Dragneva, Rilka, and Kataryna Wolczuk. "Russia, EU and ECU: Co-Existence or Rivalry?" openDemocracy, September 25, 2012.

Dreger, Christian, Konstantin A. Kholodilin, Dirk Ulbricht, and Jarko Fidrmuc. "Between the Hammer and the Anvil: The Impact of Economic Sanctions and Oil Prices on Russia's Ruble." *Journal of Comparative Economics* 44, no. 2 (2016).

Ellis, J. *The Russian Orthodox Church: Triumphalism and Defensiveness.* Springer, 2016.

Fidan, Hakan, and Bülent Aras. "The Return of Russia-Africa Relations." *Bilig* 52 (Winter 2010).

Flanagan, Stephen J. "The Turkey-Russia-Iran Nexus: Eurasian Power Dynamics." *Washington Quarterly* 36, no. 1 (2013).

Forsberg, Tuomas, and Graeme Herd. "Russia and NATO: From Windows of Opportunity to Closed Doors." *Journal of Contemporary European Studies* 23, no. 1 (2015).

Freedman, Robert O. "Russia, Iran, and the Nuclear Question: The Putin Record." In *Russia: Re-Emerging Great Power*, edited by Roger E. Kanet, 195–221. Palgrave Macmillan, 2007.

Gabuev, Alexander. *A "Soft Alliance?": Russia-China Relations After the Ukraine Crisis.* European Council on Foreign Relations, 2015.

Gedmin, Jeffrey. "Beyond Crimea: What Vladimir Putin Really Wants." *World Affairs* 177, no. 2 (2014).

Gerber, Theodore P. "Beyond Putin? Nationalism and Xenophobia in Russian Public Opinion." *Washington Quarterly* 37, no. 3 (2014).

———. "Foreign Policy and the United States in Russian Public Opinion." *Problems of Post-Communism* 62, no. 2 (2015).

Giles, Keir, and William Hagestad II. "Divided by a Common Language: Cyber Definitions in Chinese, Russian and English." In *5th International Conference on Cyber Conflict*, edited by Karlis Podins, Jan Stinissen, and Markus Maybaum, 1–17. NATO CCD COE Publications, 2013.

Giles, Keir. "'Information Troops'—A Russian Cyber Command?" In *3rd International Conference on Cyber Conflict*, edited by C. Czosseck, E. Tyugu, and T. Wingfield, 1–16. NATO CCD COE Publications, 2011.

———. *The State of the NATO-Russia Reset.* Conflict Studies Research Centre, 2011.

Gilsinan, Kathy, and Krishnadev Calamur. "Did Putin Direct Russian Hacking? And Other Big Questions." *Atlantic*, January 6, 2017.

Goldman, Marshall, I. *Petrostate: Putin, Power, and the New Russia.* Oxford: Oxford University Press, 2008.

Goscilo, Helena, ed. *Putin as Celebrity and Cultural Icon.* Routledge, 2013.

Götz, Elias. "Putin, the State, and War: The Causes of Russia's Near Abroad Assertion Revisited." *International Studies Review* 19, no. 2 (2016).

Greenblatt, Alan. "Frenemies Forever: Why Putin and Obama Can't Get Along." *NPR*, September 12, 2013.

Gurvich, Evsey, and Ilya Prilepskiy. "The Impact of Financial Sanctions on the Russian Economy." *Russian Journal of Economics* 1, no. 4 (2015).

Gvosdev, Nikolas K., and Christopher Marsh. *Russian Foreign Policy: Interest, Vectors, and Sectors.* Los Angeles: CQ Press, 2013.

Hale, Henry E. "Russian Patronal Politics Beyond Putin." *Daedalus* 146, no. 2 (2017).

Haukkala, Hiski. "From Cooperative to Contested Europe? The Conflict in Ukraine as a Culmination of a Long-Term Crisis in EU–Russia Relations." *Journal of Contemporary European Studies* 23, no. 1 (2015).

Heickerö, Roland. *Emerging Cyber Threats and Russian Views on Information Warfare and Information Operations.* Stockholm: FOI, Swedish Defence Research Agency, Division of Defence Analysis, 2010.

Hemment, Julie. "*Sex, Politics, and Putin: Political Legitimacy in Russia* by Valerie Sperling." *Slavic Review* 75, no. 1 (2016).

Hill, Fiona, and Clifford G. Gaddy. *Mr. Putin: Operative in the Kremlin.* Washington, DC: Brookings Institution Press, 2015.

Hill, Fiona, and Ömer Taşpınar. "Turkey and Russia: Axis of the Excluded?" *Survival* 48, no. 1 (2006).

Hutcheson, Derek S., and Bo Petersson. "Shortcut to Legitimacy: Popularity in Putin's Russia." *Europe-Asia Studies* 68, no. 7 (2016).

Interfax. "New Arms Treaty May Be Ready by March—Experts." Corridors of Power, *Russia & CIS Military Daily*, 2010.

Jones, Erik, and Andrew Whitworth. "The Unintended Consequences of European Sanctions on Russia." *Survival* 56, no. 5 (2014).

Kamp, Karl-Heinz. "From Wales to Warsaw: NATO's Future beyond the Ukraine Crisis." *American Foreign Policy Interests* 36, no. 6 (2014).

Kandiyoti, Rafael. "New Cold War?" In *Powering Europe: Russia, Ukraine, and the Energy Squeeze*, 138–52. Palgrave Macmillan, 2015.

Kanet, Roger E., and Maxime Henri André Larivé. "NATO and Russia: A Perpetual New Beginning." *Perceptions* 17, no. 1 (2012).

Kaplan, Robert D. "Eurasia's Coming Anarchy: The Risks of Chinese and Russian Weakness." *Foreign Affairs* 95, no. 2 (2016).

Karagiannis, Emmanuel. "The Russian Interventions in South Ossetia and Crimea Compared: Military Performance, Legitimacy and Goals." *Contemporary Security Policy* 35, no. 3 (2014).

Karatgozianni, Athina. "Blame it On the Russians: Tracking the Portrayal of Russian Hackers during Cyber Conflict Incidents." *Digital Icons: Studies in Russian, Eurasian and Central European New Media* 4 (2010).

Katz, Mark N. "Russia and Iran." *Middle East Policy* 19, no. 3 (2012).

———. "Russian-Iranian Relations in the Obama Era." *Middle East Policy* 17, no. 2 (2010).

Kim, Taehwan. "Can Putin Go beyond Putinism, Or Will It Be More of the Same?" *Global Asia* 7, no. 2 (2012).

Kissinger, Henry. "To Settle the Ukraine Crisis, Start at the End." *Washington Post*, March 5, 2014.

Korppoo, Anna. "Who Is Driving Russian Climate Policy? Applying and Adjusting Veto Players Theory to a Non-Democracy." *International Environmental Agreements: Politics, Law and Economics* 16, no. 5 (2016).

Kozachenko, Ivan. "Bad News for Putin as Support for War Flags beyond Russia's 'Troll Farms.'" *Working Papers of the Communities & Culture Network+* 6 (2015).

Kotkin, Stephen. "The Resistible Rise of Vladimir Putin: Russia's Nightmare Dressed Like a Daydream." *Foreign Affairs* 94 (2015).

Kramer, David J. "The Ukraine Invasion: One Year Later." *World Affairs* 177, no. 6 (2015).

———. "Resetting US–Russian Relations: It Takes Two." *Washington Quarterly* 33, no. 1 (2010).

Kristensen, Hans M., and Robert S. Norris. "Russian Nuclear Forces, 2013." *Bulletin of the Atomic Scientists* 69, no. 3 (2013).

———. "Russian Nuclear Forces, 2015." *Bulletin of the Atomic Scientists* 71, no. 3 (2015).

———. "Russian Nuclear Forces, 2016." *Bulletin of the Atomic Scientists* 72, no. 3 (2016).

Kroenig, Matthew. "Facing Reality: Getting NATO Ready for a New Cold War." *Survival* 57, no. 1 (2015).

Kuchins, Andrew C., and Igor A. Zevelev. "Russian Foreign Policy: Continuity in Change." *Washington Quarterly* 35, no. 1 (2012): 147–61.

Kupchan, Charles A. "NATO's Final Frontier: Why Russia Should Join the Atlantic Alliance." *Foreign Affairs* 89, no. 3 (2010).

Ledeneva, Alena. "'Blat' and 'Guanxi': Informal Practices in Russia and China." *Comparative Studies in Society and History* 50, no. 1 (2008).

Legvold, Robert. "Managing the New Cold War: What Moscow and Washington Can Learn From the Last One." *Foreign Affairs* 93, no. 4 (2014).

Liaropoulos, Andrew. "The Russian Defense Reform and Its Limitations." *Caucasian Review of International Affairs* 2, no. 1 (2008).

Lichtblau, Eric, and Stephen Lee Myers. "Investigating Donald Trump: F.B.I. Sees No Clear Link to Russia." *New York Times*, October 31, 2016.

Light, Margot. "Russian-American Relations under George W. Bush and Vladimir Putin." *Irish Studies in International Affairs* 19 (2008).

Lo, Bobo. *Vladimir Putin and the Evolution of Russian Foreign Policy.* Reprint. Hoboken, NJ: John Wiley & Sons, 2008.

Lucas, Edward. *The New Cold War: Putin's Russia and the Threat to the West.* Palgrave Macmillan ed. New York: Palgrave Macmillan, 2014.

Magnuson, Stew. "Russian Cyberthief Case Illustrates Security Risks for U.S. Corporations." *National Defense*, May 1, 2010.

Malmlöf, Tomas, Bengt-Göran Bergstrand, Mikael Eriksson, Susanne Oxenstierna, and Niklas Rossbach. "Economy, Energy and Sanctions." In *A Rude Awakening: Ramifications of Russian Aggression Towards Ukraine*, edited by Niklas Granholm, Johannes Malminen, and Gudrun Persson, 71–80. FOI, 2014.

March, Luke. "The Russian Duma 'Opposition': No Drama out of Crisis?" *East European Politics* 28, no. 3 (2012).

Marten, Kimberly. "Putin's Choices: Explaining Russian Foreign Policy and Intervention in Ukraine." *Washington Quarterly* 38, no. 2 (2015).

Marten, Robert, Diane McIntyre, Claudia Travassos, Sergey Shishkin, Wang Longde, Srinath Reddy, and Jeanette Vega. "An Assessment of Progress towards Universal Health Coverage in Brazil, Russia, India, China, and South Africa (BRICS)." *Lancet* 384, no. 9960 (2014).

McDaniel, Tim. *Autocracy, Modernization, and Revolution in Russia and Iran*. 2014 ed. Princeton University Press, 1991.

McFaul, Michael, Stephen Sestanovich, and John J. Mearsheimer. "Faulty Powers: Who Started the Ukraine Crisis?" *Foreign Affairs* 93 (2014).

McHugh, Jess. "Russian Sanctions: Putin Signs Decree Ordering All Western Imported Food 'Destroyed.'" *International Business Times*, July 15, 2015.

Mearsheimer, John J. "Why the Ukraine Crisis Is the West's Fault: The Liberal Delusions That Provoked Putin." *Foreign Affairs* 93 (2014).

Medvedev, S. A. "Offense-Defense Theory Analysis of Russian Cyber Capability." PhD diss., Monterey, California, Naval Postgraduate School, 2015.

Mendelson, Sarah E., and Theodore P. Gerber. "Us and Them: Anti-American Views of the Putin Generation." *Washington Quarterly* 31, no. 2 (2008).

Milani, Abbas. "Russia and Iran: An Anti-Western Alliance?" *Current History* 106, no. 702 (2007).

Monaghan, Andrew. “The New Russian Foreign Policy Concept: Evolving Continuity.” Chatham House: Russia and Eurasia, 2013.

Mongrenier, Jean-Sylvestre. “Putin and the Sea: Fortress ‘Eurasia’ and Oceans Strategy.” *Hérodote* 4, no. 163 (2016).

Morozova, Natalia. “Geopolitics, Eurasianism and Russian Foreign Policy under Putin.” *Geopolitics* 14, no. 4 (2009).

Nelson, Rebecca M. “US Sanctions on Russia: Economic Implications.” *Current Politics and Economics of Russia, Eastern and Central Europe* 30, no. 1–2 (2015).

Newnham, Randall E. “Georgia on My Mind? Russian Sanctions and the End of the ‘Rose Revolution.’” *Journal of Eurasian Studies* 6, no. 2 (2015).

———. “Pipeline Politics: Russian Energy Sanctions and the 2010 Ukrainian Elections.” *Journal of Eurasian Studies* 4, no. 2 (2013).

Newnham, Randall. “Oil, Carrots, and Sticks: Russia’s Energy Resources as a Foreign Policy Tool.” *Journal of Eurasian Studies* 2, no. 2 (2011).

Owen, John M., IV, and William Inboden. “Putin, Ukraine, and the Question of Realism.” *Hedgehog Review* 17, no. 1 (2015).

www.iasc-culture.org/THR/THR_article_2015_Spring_OwenInboden.php.

Paganini, Pierluigi. “Crimea—The Russian Cyber Strategy to Hit Ukraine.” *InfoSec Institute*, March 11, 2014. www.resources.infosecinstitute.com/crimea-russian-strategy-hit-ukraine/#gref.

Papkova, Irina. *The Orthodox Church and Russian Politics.* Washington, DC: Woodrow Wilson Center Press, 2011.

Pavlovsky, Gleb. “Russian Politics under Putin: The System Will Outlast the Master.” *Foreign Affairs* 95 (2016).

Polyakova, Alina. "Strange Bedfellows: Putin and Europe's Far Right." *World Affairs* 177, no. 3 (2014).

Pop, Irina Ionela. "Russia, EU, NATO, and the Strengthening of the CSTO in Central Asia." *Caucasian Review of International Affairs* 3, no. 3 (2009).

Popova, Maria. "Putin-Style 'Rule of Law' and the Prospects for Change." *Daedalus* 146, no. 2 (2017).

Pursiainen, Christer. *Russian Foreign Policy and International Relations Theory.* Routledge ed. London: Routledge, 2017.

Putin, Vladimir. "A Plea for Caution from Russia." *New York Times*, September 11, 2013.

Rice, Condoleezza. "Rethinking the National Interest: American Realism for a New World." *Foreign Affairs* 87, no. 4 (2008).

Richters, Katja. *The Post-Soviet Russian Orthodox Church: Politics, Culture and Greater Russia.* New York: Routledge, 2013.

Rid, Thomas. "Cyberwar and Peace: Hacking Can Reduce Real-World Violence." *Foreign Affairs* 92, no. 6 (2013).

Robinson, Neil. "Institutional Factors and Russian Political Parties: The Changing Needs of Regime Consolidation in a Neo-Patrimonial System." *East European Politics* 28, no. 3 (2012).

Rochlitz, Michael. "At the Crossroads: Putin's Third Presidential Term and Russia's Institutions." *Political Studies Review* 13, no. 1 (2015).

Roxburgh, Angus. *The Strongman: Vladimir Putin and the Struggle for Russia.* London: IB Tauris, 2013.

Rühle, Michael. "NATO Enlargement and Russia: Discerning Fact from Fiction." *American Foreign Policy Interests* 36, no. 4 (2014).

Rumer, Eugene B., Richard Sokolsky, and Andrew S. Weiss. "Trump

and Russia: The Right Way to Manage Relations." *Foreign Affairs* 96, no. 2 (2017).
www.foreignaffairs.com/articles/russian-federation/2017-02-13/trump-and-russia.

Rutland, Peter. "An Unnecessary War: The Geopolitical Roots of the Ukraine Crisis." In *Ukraine and Russia: People, Politics, Propaganda, and Perspectives*, edited by Agnieszka Pikulicka-Wilczewska and Richard Sakwa, 122–33. Bristol: E-International Relations, 2015.

———. "The Impact of Sanctions on Russia." *Russian Analytical Digest* 157 (2014).

Sakwa, Richard. *Frontline Ukraine: Crisis in the Borderlands*. London: IB Tauris, 2015.

———. "'New Cold War' or Twenty Years' Crisis? Russia and International Politics." *International Affairs* 84, no. 2 (2008).

Saltzman, Ilai Z. "Russian Grand Strategy and the United States in the 21st Century." *Orbis* 56, no. 4 (2012).

Schmidt-Felzmann, Anke. "EU Member States' Energy Relations with Russia: Conflicting Approaches to Securing Natural Gas Supplies." *Geopolitics* 16, no. 3 (2011).

Schneider, Eberhard. "The Russian Federal Security Service under President Putin." In *Politics and the Ruling Group in Putin's Russia*, edited by S. White, 42–62. Basingstoke: Palgrave Macmillan, 2008.

Schrooten, Mechthild. "Brazil, Russia, India, China and South Africa: Strong Economic Growth—Major Challenges." *DIW Economic Bulletin* 1, no. 4 (2011).

Sergi, Bruno S. *Misinterpreting Modern Russia: Western Views of*

Putin and His Presidency. New York: Continuum International Publishing Group, 2009.

Sharov, Oleksandr. "Economy of the EU: Sanctions against Russia and Their Reverse Effect." *Journal of European Economy* 14, no. 2 (2015).

Shlapentokh, Vladimir. "The Puzzle of Russian Anti-Americanism: From 'Below' or from 'Above.'" *Europe-Asia Studies* 63, no. 5 (2011).

———. "Perceptions of Foreign Threats to the Regime: From Lenin to Putin." *Communist and Post-Communist Studies* 42, no. 3 (2009).

Simonov, V. "Anti-Russian Sanctions and the Systemic Crisis of the World Economy." *Voprosy Economiki* 2 (2015).

Simons, Greg. "Aspects of Putin's Appeal to International Publics." *Global Affairs* 1, no. 2 (2015).

Sindelar, Daisy. "The Kremlin's Troll Army." *Atlantic*, August 12, 2014.

Sinovets, Polina, and Bettina Renz. *Russia's 2014 Military Doctrine and Beyond: Threat Perceptions, Capabilities and Ambitions.* Rome: Research Division, NATO Defense College, 2015.

Slavtcheva-Petkova, Vera. "Fighting Putin and the Kremlin's Grip in Neo-Authoritarian Russia: The Experience of Liberal Journalists." *Journalism*, May 16, 2017.

www.doi.org/10.1177/1464884917708061.

Smyth, Regina. "The Putin Factor: Personalism, Protest, and Regime Stability in Russia." *Politics and Policy* 42, no. 4 (2014).

Smyth, Regina, and Irina Soboleva. "Looking beyond the Economy:

Pussy Riot and the Kremlin's Voting Coalition." *Post-Soviet Affairs* 30, no. 4 (2014).

Snyder, Timothy. "Trump's Putin Fantasy." *New York Review of Books*, April 19, 2016.

Stent, Angela. "US–Russia Relations in the Second Obama Administration." *Survival* 54, no. 6 (2012).

Stent, Angela E. "Restoration and Revolution in Putin's Foreign Policy." *Europe-Asia Studies* 60, no. 6 (2008).

Tichý, Lukáš. "Controversial Issues in the EU-Russia Energy Relations." In *Panorama of Global Security Environment 2012*, edited by Marian Majer, Róbert Ondrejcsák, and Vladimír Tarasovič, 187–202. CENAA, 2012.

Titcomb, James. "Russian Sanctions Create Burden for UK Banks." *Daily Telegraph*, July 31, 2014.

Treisman, Daniel. "Watching Putin in Moscow." *Foreign Affairs*, March 5, 2014. www.foreignaffairs.com/articles/russian-federation/2014-03-05/watching-putin-moscow.

Trenin, Dmitri. *The Ukraine Crisis and the Resumption of Great-Power Rivalry.* Moscow: Carnegie Moscow Center, 2014.

Trenin, Dmitri V., and Aleksei V. Malashenko. *Russia's Restless Frontier: The Chechnya Factor in Post-Soviet Russia.* With Anatol Lieven. Washington, DC: Carnegie Endowment for International Peace, 2004.

Uffelmann, Dirk. "Is There a Russian Cyber Empire?" In *Digital Russia: The Language, Culture and Politics of New Media Communications*, edited by Michael Gorham, Ingunn Lunde, and Martin Paulsen, 266. Abingdon: Routledge, 2014.

Veebel, Viljar, and Raul Markus. "At the Dawn of a New Era of

Sanctions: Russian-Ukrainian Crisis and Sanctions." *Orbis* 60, no. 1 (2016).

Vijayakumar, Narayanamurthy, Perumal Sridharan, and Kode Chandra Sekhara Rao. "Determinants of FDI in BRICS Countries: A Panel Analysis." *International Journal of Business Science and Applied Management* 5, no. 3 (2010). www.business-and-management.org/library/2010/5_3--1--13-Vijayakumar,Sridharan,Rao.pdf.

Walker, Edward W. "Between East and West: NATO Enlargement and the Geopolitics of the Ukraine Crisis." In *Ukraine and Russia: People, Politics, Propaganda, and Perspectives*, edited by Agnieszka Pikulicka-Wilczewska and Richard Sakwa, 134–47. Bristol: E-International Relations, 2015.

Warhola, James W., and Egemen B. Bezci. "The Return of President Putin and Russian–Turkish Relations: Where Are They Headed?" *Sage Open* 3, no. 3. http://www. journals.sagepub.com/doi/pdf/10.1177/2158244013503165.

White, Stephen, and Ian McAllister. "The Putin Phenomenon." *Journal of Communist Studies and Transition Politics* 24, no. 4 (2008).

Wolff, Andrew T. "The Future of NATO Enlargement after the Ukraine Crisis." *International Affairs* 91, no. 5 (2015).

Ziegler, Charles E. "Russian–American Relations: From Tsarism to Putin." *International Politics* 51, no. 6 (2014).

CONTRIBUTORS

BRUCE ADRIANCE

Bruce Adriance is a graduate of the master of science program in international security and intelligence studies at Bellevue University in Omaha, Nebraska, the United States.

ANIS H. BAJREKTAREVIC

Modern Diplomacy Advisory Board, Chairman

Geopolitics of Energy Editorial Member

Professor and Chairperson for Intl. Law & Global Pol. Studies

URAN BOTOBEKOV

Botobekov, doctor of political science (PhD) and expert on political Islam, is a Kyrgyz scholar, journalist, diplomat, and activist. Until 2016 he was a member of the formal governmental opposition in Kyrgyzstan.

SAMANTHA BRLETICH

Samantha M. Brletich is a researcher and writer specializing in Central Asia and governance, security, terrorism, and development issues. She possesses a master's degree in peace operations policy from George Mason University in Virginia, the United States. Her work has appeared in multiple publications focused on diplomacy and Central Asia respectively. She is currently an employee of the US Federal Government.

VICTOR CHAUVET

Partner at POLARISK Analytics, research fellow at IPSE, and author of "The Diplomatic Triangle: EU-Denmark-Greenland" (ed. L'Harmattan, Paris).

RAFAA CHEHOUDI

Graduate student majoring in international relations at the Tunis El Manar University and a member in the MENA region politics committee with the International Association for Political Science Students.

ANDY DEAHN

Andy Deahn is a 2015 graduate with a bachelor of science degree from Bellevue University's international security and intelligence studies program. He is currently employed as a Department of Defense contractor working as a member of an intelligence analysis team throughout various worldwide locations. He had previously worked as special tactics tactical air control party member in the US Air Force supporting Army Special Forces ground teams as a joint terminal attack controller.

NENAD DRCA

Nenad Drca is a former military trilingual linguist who worked across many nations over eight years. He lived and worked on three continents. This experience gave him a deep appreciation for the intelligence community. After graduating with BA in psychology he returned to work for the US Army as a DOD civilian. He received his master of science degree in international security and intelligence studies from Bellevue University.

LUIS DURANI

Luis Durani is currently employed in the oil and gas industry. He previously worked in the nuclear energy industry. He has an MA in international affairs with a focus on Chinese foreign policy and the South China Sea, an MBA, an MS in nuclear engineering, a BS in mechanical engineering, and a BA in political science. He is also the author of "Afghanistan: It's No Nebraska—How to Deal with a Tribal State" and "China and the South China Sea: The Emergence of the Huaqing Doctrine."

JARED S. EASTON

Jared S. Easton is pursuing his undergraduate degree in the international security and intelligence studies program at Bellevue University in Omaha, Nebraska, the United States.

HASAN EHTISHAM AND USMAN ALI KHAN

Hasan Ehtisham is currently an MPhil scholar in the Department of Strategic Studies at the Quaid-e-Azam University (QAU), Islamabad. He holds a master's degree in strategic studies from QAU and a bachelor's degree in economics and journalism from the University of Punjab, Lahore. His analytical research work contributes to the topics of geopolitics, terrorism, conflict resolution, military strategies, Pakistan's nuclear strategy, nonproliferation regime, arms control, and disarmament.

Usman Ali Khan is an Islamabad-based freelance writer with an MSc in defense and strategic studies from Quaid-i-Azam University.

LAURA GARRIDO

Laura Garrido finished her master's degree in the international security and intelligence studies program at Bellevue University in Omaha, Nebraska, the United States. Her primary research interests cover the post-Soviet space and the fight against radical Islamism.

AMY HANLON

Amy Hanlon finished her master's degree in the international security and intelligence studies program at Bellevue University and has been employed as a government contractor for the US State Department since 2010.

JEANETTE HARPER

Jeanette J. J. Harper graduated with her master's degree from the international security and intelligence studies program at Bellevue University in Omaha, Nebraska, the United States.

BRIAN HUGHES

Brian Hughes was a student in the international security and intelligence studies program at Bellevue University in Omaha, Nebraska, the United States, and is employed in the defense sector.

IGOR IVANOV

President of the Russian International Affairs Council (RIAC), H. E. Ivanov served as the foreign minister of Russia from 1998–2004.

KESTER KENN KLOMEGAH

Kester Kenn Klomegah is an independent researcher and writer on African affairs in the Eurasian region and former Soviet republics.

He wrote previously for African Press Agency, African Executive, and Inter Press Service. Earlier, he had worked for the *Moscow Times*, a reputable English newspaper. Klomegah taught part time at the Moscow Institute of Modern Journalism. He studied international journalism and mass communication and later spent a year at the Moscow State Institute of International Relations.

NINA LAVRENTEVA

Nina Lavrenteva finished her master's studies in the history of international relations and integration processes: cross-border cooperation at the Institute of Political Studies, the University of Strasbourg. Previously, she had finished her BA in international relations at the State University of Tyumen, Russia.

VLADISLAV LERMONTOV

Vladislav Lermontov finished his master's degree in the international security and intelligence studies program at Bellevue University in Omaha, Nebraska.

ALEXANDER S. MARTIN

Alexander S. Martin pursued his master's degree in international intelligence and security studies from Bellevue University. He earned a bachelor's degree in international intelligence and security studies, also from Bellevue University, in 2014.

MEGAN MUNOZ

Megan Munoz is currently a graduate student at Bellevue University, Bellevue, Nebraska, where she is earning a master of science degree in the international security and intelligence studies program. She works as an intelligence analyst for the state of New Jersey, previously served as an intelligence analyst in the United States Air Force for ten years, and remains a reservist.

RAHIM RAHIMOV

An independent researcher on Russia, post-Soviet space, and political Islam, Rahim holds an MA in international relations from the Hult International Business School in London, the United Kingdom, and a BA in Arab Studies from the Baku State University.

TONY RINNA

Tony Rinna is a specialist in Russian foreign policy and security affairs in East Asia. He currently resides in South Korea.

GREGORY ROUDYBUSH

Gregory Roudybush pursued his master's degree at Bellevue University's international security and intelligence studies program in Omaha, Nebraska. He served previously in the United States Marine Corps.

RAKESH KRISHNAN SIMHA

New Zealand–based journalist and foreign affairs analyst. According to him, he writes on stuff the media distorts, misses, or ignores. Rakesh started his career in 1995 with New Delhi–based *Business World* magazine and later worked in a string of positions at other leading media houses, such as *India Today*, *Hindustan Times*, *Business Standard*, and the *Financial Express*, where he was the news editor.

EVAN THOMSEN

Evan Thomsen is a graduate of the international security and intelligence studies program at Bellevue University in Omaha, Nebraska, and is currently a master's student at the world-renowned Elliott School of International Affairs at the George Washington University in Washington, DC. He has just joined with the Eastern Congo Initiative as strategic partnerships officer.

DIANNE VALDEZ

Dianne Valdez just completed her master's degree in the international security and intelligence studies program at Bellevue University in Omaha, Nebraska, the United States, and continues her interests in the geopolitics of this important region, along with political strife in Africa.

GIANCARLO ELIA VALORI

Professor Giancarlo Elia Valori is an eminent Italian economist and businessman. He holds prestigious academic distinctions and national orders. Mr. Valori has lectured on international affairs and economics at the world's leading universities, such as Peking University, the Hebrew University of Jerusalem, and the Yeshiva University in New York.

LOGAN WILDE

Logan Wilde is currently pursuing his bachelor's degree in the international security and intelligence studies program at Bellevue University. He has more than thirteen years of experience working in the intelligence community, primarily focusing on the Middle East and Central Asia regions.

"ZR"

ZR is a full-time analyst who has worked with national security issues for almost twelve years. He completed his bachelor's of science degree in the international security and intelligence studies program at Bellevue University. Upon graduation, he will continue to provide professional support to national security issues and policies.

ABOUT THE AUTHOR

Few people have careers in Russian studies longer or more distinguished than that of Dr. Matthew Crosston. His love of the post-Soviet world began twenty-five years ago while studying abroad in the previously closed military city of Tambov and continued with an undergraduate degree in Russian studies, a master's degree from SSEES–University College London, a doctoral dissertation at Brown University, scholarly collaborations with the Moscow State Institute of International Relations, and service as executive director of the East–West Fund for International Education. He has also founded the Russian Provincial Politics Summer Study Abroad Program at Clemson University and been a regular contributor to international analytic center Rethinking Russia, as well as the first American analytical blogger for the Russian International Affairs Council. Crosston's previous books include *Shadow Separatism* and *Fostering Fundamentalism*, which focuses on his unique research specialty: international security and intelligence across the post-Soviet space, with an eye to the problems of democratic consolidation and fighting radical jihadist extremism.